Steve Strevens was born in 194  e Australian bush with his parent

He left school shortly before his sixteenth birthday after failing third form 'extremely well' and joined the Navy. After ten years at sea he returned to the country and has worked as a labourer, fruit picker, truck driver, car salesman, nurseryman and florist while playing, watching and following sport.

In between work and sport he has managed to fit in a freelance writing career which has seen him published extensively in major newspapers and magazines both in this country and overseas.

He currently works in advertising and lives in country Victoria with his wife, son and failed guide dog, Taffy.

which way to the
LIZARD RACES?

which way to the
LIZARD
RACES?

A journey around Australia's *other* great sporting events

Steve Strevens

MACMILLAN
Pan Macmillan Australia

First published 1999 in Macmillan by Pan Macmillan Australia Pty Limited
St Martins Tower, 31 Market Street, Sydney

National Library of Australia
Cataloguing-in-Publication data:

Strevens, Steven.
Which way to the lizard races?: Australia's other great sporting events.

ISBN 0 7329 0994 5.

1. Sports—Australia. 2. Sports—Social aspects—Australia.
3. Australia—Description and travel.
4. Australia—Social life and customs—1990– .
I. Title.

796.0994

Typeset by Post Pre-Press Group
Printed in Australia by McPherson's Printing Group

And the backblock bard goes through it, ever seeking as he goes
For the line of least resistance to the hearts of men he knows;
Yes, he tracks their hearts in mateship, and he tracks them out
    alone—
Seeking for the power to sway them, till he finds it in his own;
Feels what they feel, loves what they love, learns to hate what they
    condemn,
Takes his pen in tears and triumph, and he writes it down for them.

Henry Lawson

CONTENTS

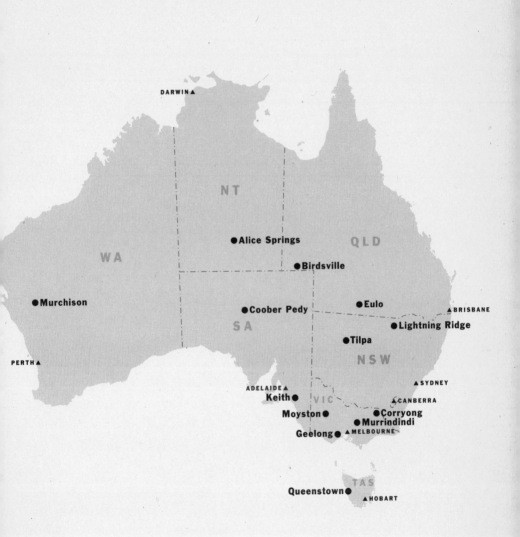

AKNOWLEDGEMENTS

This book wouldn't have been possible without the help of a lot of people—the unheralded, ordinary people who continue the best traditions of Australian sport. The people who helped me on my journeys, made me welcome and told me their tales. There are too many to mention here and indeed, some of the names have faded from memory but to all who contributed—I will always be grateful.

Special thanks to Bev Hammerton, Dee Corcoran, Sterle Welling, Justin and Julie McClure and Don McQueen, as well as Fred and Sandie Brophy and the tent boys. And to Mike Russell and Cyril Chaproniere, thanks for your interest, help and support.

The biggest thanks of all must go to Tom Gilliatt at Pan Macmillan who pointed me in the right direction with his enthusiasm and encouragement, and who was never more than a phone call away. I would also like to thank him for his choice of drinking companions.

Thanks also to Martin Flanagan, who believed in me and helped me believe in myself.

I could never have finished this project without help and support from home. Without my wife Lyn, and her thoughts, good sense and tolerance.

And, of course, thanks must go to my son and travelling companion, Zac, who has had to forego many kicks of the footy, as well as backyard Tests and One Dayers.

Finally, thanks to a special place: 'The Fort', a small weatherboard building where this all came together and where the spirits gave me comfort and inspiration.

For Lyn and Zac
The trunk of our tree that holds steady my fragile branches and faltering leaves.

And for my father

INTRODUCTION

I can't remember exactly when it happened but I know my obsession with sport started early in my life.

What I CAN remember is going to football matches with my dad, and him wrapping his battered old duffle coat around me as shelter from the cold. Inside was the feeling of warmth and the smell of complete safety.

At the change of season I would watch him play cricket on the barren grounds in the small South Australian town where we lived. His passion for sport seemed endless and it occurred to me that sport was just about the most important thing in life.

Then, as I grew up, my affliction became even worse. As a young boy I can remember Mum complaining about me running down the corridor of our typical Australian weatherboard home, practising my bowling action every time I moved from room to room. Either that or it would be taking marks using the sofa as my opponent's back. And there were sporting clubs to join, and wonderful days of being carted around in the old Holden to various matches.

At that time my school reports were all the same—'if he paid as much attention in the classroom as he did . . .' blah, blah, blah.

Didn't these people know there were more important lessons to learn?

When I left home to search the world, there were clubs of strangers, or rather, people I didn't know who were later to become friends. Families, sort of.

That's the thing about sport, isn't it? It's about community. About a place where people from all walks of life can go and feel safe that they are accepted for what they can contribute, rather than who or what they are.

And no more so than in the country—or at least that is the way it was for me. I thought that country sport was everything.

But what about other sports lovers around the country? Those who not only played the more common sports but those who invented their own. What about the people in those places far removed from the rest of the sporting world, what did they do?

I decided that there was nothing for it but to go and find out.

The journey around Australia started with a visit to my *Australian Concise Oxford Dictionary*. Here there was an entry: 'sport—a game or competitive activity, especially an outdoor one involving physical exertion that is an amusement, a diversion, fun.'

FUN!

I'm not sure, but anyone watching a television these days would probably think fun is the last thing a sportsperson should have, or want.

But believe it or not, I found people who did exactly that. In the small bush towns, as well as the real Outback, they live their lives quietly and without fuss. They go about their sport the same way. No headlines, no huge crowds.

And not all of them are like the rest of us sports nuts. They are a bit more down to earth, a bit more realistic. They don't sit around and think about thumping a backhand top spin return past Sampras, or crash tackling Campese into touch to save a grand final, or straight driving Gough into the Members' at Lord's.

No, they get on with the business at hand. Of keeping their sport and their communities together. They know that it is the binding that holds them. A common thread that runs through their lives. It gives them a sense of belonging and it's important to them. I suspect it should be important to all of us.

In the bush, where things these days are a constant struggle, you come to realise that most sport is not about the big places, the million-dollar teams, the TV rights and the corporate boxes. Rather, it is about ordinary people. The people who, in a few cases, dream of greatness, but accept that they are only a speck in sport's great Milky Way.

Out there in this wide brown land there are the people who DO have fun, who DO play sport the way the *Australian Concise Oxford Dictionary* describes. They don't do it for money, or because they want to exert an influence on the world. Mostly they do it for friendship and simple enjoyment. And if there are a few restrictions or barriers put in their way, they don't care.

These people make fun, they don't just have it.

Far away from places as grand as the MCG, Randwick Racecourse or Royal Adelaide, there are people who gather to display this country's love of the game. Whether it is obscure sports in obscure places, or the more traditional sports, they are just as passionate, and take it just as seriously, as anyone.

These are some of their stories.

CHAPTER ONE

ALL THE FUN OF THE FERRETS

I'm not sure why, but my journey started with ferrets.

I'd never heard of ferret racing.

In fact I'd never thought much about ferrets at all.

To me they were noisome creatures that weren't a lot of use for anything, apart from getting stuck down burrows while rabbiting and having to be dug out.

However, the people who kept them thought they were wonderful.

I couldn't understand what anyone saw in them.

But then I found out about Mick Veitch.

I asked the man on the Geelong Showgrounds gate for directions to the ferret races.

'Over there,' he told me, pointing in a sweeping motion as he took one hand from his foam coffee cup. I was none the wiser, but I thanked him anyway.

The pale and cool autumn sun reflected from the polished metal of the ancient fire engines, tractors and all manner of old buses and cars that were lined up as part of the vintage fair which had the ferret races as an added attraction. A few early risers wandered in between the vehicles, the older ones remembering what it was like to travel by such antiquated means, the young ones not quite believing that anyone ever did.

As well, there were noisy steam engines, an ancient organ that played the same song over and over again, and some bored-looking sheepdogs trying to round up ducks before guiding them into a pen.

Just inside the rusting fence that ran round the boundary of the dry, unused football oval, a group of farmers took turns at trying to balance their tractors on what appeared to be a trailer without any wheels—just a fulcrum. Other farmers stood around, as farmers do, arms folded, hats tipped forward to keep the sun from their eyes, and watched.

I wandered through the crowd and followed a sign that pointed around the corner of one of the pavilions. Leaning against a pole that held up the barricade at the side of the ferret racetrack was the self-proclaimed Ferret King of Australia. The Bart Cummings of ferret racing; Mick Veitch.

After I'd been told about Mick I had tracked down a bloke called Norm Robb, the organiser of the Geelong Ferret Racing Cup, who was eager to give me all the information I needed about the event. He told me that ferrets would come from near and far to try and win the Cup. 'They'll come from all over the place,' Norm enthused, 'from all over the place.'

Then, lowering his voice to reinforce the seriousness of what he was about to say, he continued earnestly, 'And, oh mate, there'll be some good ferrets here.'

When I asked Norm how I would find Mick, he chuckled. 'You'll find him, don't you worry.'

Norm was right. No-one could miss Mick. Standing about five foot six, Mick weighed in at around 20 stone, 'in the old currency, mate'.

His ancient, wide-brimmed hat was bent down at the front, up at the back and sat on the top of a chaos of black hair. A long, knotty beard drooped from his chin and a blue singlet stretched over his large gut while the waistband of his blue shorts disappeared under it.

Mick walked towards me on short, dumpy legs stuck in old workboots that hadn't seen polish since they were new, and stuck out his hand. 'G'day mate,' he said, his mouth appearing through the mass of hair that made him look like an armpit with eyes. 'Welcome to the world's best sport.'

After offering me a beer, which I regretfully declined as it was about 10 a.m., Mick leant on a pole and regaled me with stories about ferrets while we waited for the competitors to arrive.

'They're great fun,' he cackled raucously, 'the best fun you can have with your pants on. They can git ya a feed of rabbits, you can leave 'em in a box on the back of ya truck while ya have a few beers in the pub and when ya come out they never go crook. Try that with ya missus!'

Mick was still cackling to himself as he went to help a racer fill out an entry form.

The racetrack itself was laid out inside a big square of pink, fluorescent fence, the kind that council workers use so you don't fall in any of the holes they leave scattered about.

It consisted of four lengths of plumbers' pipe, just wide enough for a ferret to run through, that were angled every four metres so the ferrets had to think about what they were doing and not just run in a straight line.

Outside the fence at one end of the track was a small corrugated-iron shack with a notice hanging on it that proudly proclaimed Ferret Racing Office. Standing underneath the sign was a small blackboard where the names of the ferrets in each race would be scrawled once all the entries were in.

I watched Mick as he greeted each person who came to the shed. He beamed when they showed him their ferrets and I suspected he knew every one—ferrets and people.

'It's a great family sport, ferreting,' Mick enthused, 'either racing 'em or rabbiting. Mum, Dad, the kids, all out together in the fresh air . . . what more could ya want?'

As Mick and I stood there, ruminating on the wonders of owning ferrets, a traction engine, the kind with pulleys whizzing around on its side and making phut-phut noises, clanked to a halt near the track.

The driver was a tall man dressed in blue overalls that were streaked with grease. Grey hair crept out from under his old floppy hat and drooping precariously from his bottom lip was a cigarette-holder with a roll-your-own stuck in it. Mick introduced me to Norm Robb.

'Glad you could come.' Norm was genuine. 'I suppose Mick's kept you occupied.'

'Bloody oath I have,' exclaimed Mick. 'I'm the best bloke for the job too.'

Norm was a retired policeman who had two great interests; vintage engines and ferrets. 'Had ferrets since I was a lad,' he told me, his mind wandering back through the years. 'My Dad used to have 'em. We'd sit out in the shed together in the evenings and talk while he made their cages.'

I asked Norm if he was racing one of his ferrets in the Cup. 'No,' he replied, waving his hand towards the engine that was still choofing away in the background. 'I'm too busy organising these things. But I'll stick my head in during the day.'

With that, he climbed onto the platform of his engine, and with a push and a pull of a few levers, clanked off towards the displays, the cigarette-holder never moving from his lip.

The entries were now rolling in steadily, with all manner of people turning up with boxes or cages in their hands. The person who seemed to be doing the most talking, apart from Mick, was Andrew Heywood, a distinguished looking character whose corduroy waistcoat matched his hat with an enormous number of badges pinned to it. He also wore a beard, although his was flecked with grey and a lot more neatly trimmed than Mick's.

According to Mick, Andrew, who carried the grand title of President of the Victorian Ferret Society, and looked the part, could tell me some very interesting things about ferrets.

'Did you know that the Egyptians used ferrets to keep rats and mice out of their grain store?' I confessed that I didn't so Andrew pressed on, 'And that they've helped science because they are susceptible to some human diseases.'

I learned that apparently ferrets helped with research into illnesses such as leukaemia, measles, cancer and AIDS. They also helped in developing the IVF program and the contraceptive pill—not something with which you would readily associate them.

Andrew also informed me that there was a portrait of Queen Elizabeth I holding a ferret and that there had been none in the wild for over 2000 years.

'And,' he continued, 'they were used at Princess Diana's wedding.'

I didn't hang around to find out how, as all this was a bit much to absorb, so I wandered over to one of the bench-type seats alongside the racetrack and sat down, waiting for the first race. On the way I collected an entry form from the office to acquaint myself with all the rules. A youngster was scratching on the blackboard which showed that Psycho, Snowballs, Insomniac and George would contest the first heat.

The format for the weekend's racing was simple. There would be heats until all the ferrets had raced and the winners would then race off on a knockout basis until there was only one left, and that would be declared the reserve champion. On Sunday the same format applied until there were only three ferrets left and they would race against the reserve champion, with the winner being presented with the Geelong Ferret Racing Cup. It all seemed straightforward enough to me.

Mick came over to see if I was going alright and I asked him about the rules.

'Gotta go by the rules,' he insisted. 'Anyone who doesn't is out.'

The rules stated:

Handler to stand at end of pipe entrance with ferret aloft and at signal, place ferret in pipe.
Handlers to run along the left-hand side of pipe but pipe not to be touched during the race.
At exit, handlers may encourage ferrets by calling or whistling, or tapping on the ground but no lures to be used.
Ferret must be totally clear of pipe to win.

As the runners in the first heat gathered at the starting ends of the pipes, I wondered if Mick and his ferrets were the favourite for the event.

'Mate, with ferrets you never know,' he replied, watching the starters with their ferrets flapping in the air. 'They can be nearly out of the pipe and then they'll double back. So a lot of it's luck.'

They were prophetic words. Psycho did exactly that.

'Just like his name,' yelled Mick to the spectators.

Snowballs emerged from the pipe first while Insomniac just wouldn't come out.

'Typical bloody ferret,' Mick told me before yelling again to the crowd: 'Perhaps he's gone to sleep.'

The onlookers laughed along with Mick as he pulled a section of pipe apart, raised it, and sent Insomniac sliding toward the end, where he emerged, tumbling over and looking rather startled.

As Insomniac was taken away I asked Mick what made a good or a bad ferret. He looked at the ground for a while, deep in thought, as if I'd just asked him what the meaning of life was. Then he made up his mind.

'People,' he told me emphatically. 'I shampoo mine two or three times a week and keep their cages clean and they never give me any worries. They're like kids. There's no such thing as a bad kid, it's just the way ya treat 'em.'

The next few heats had runners with names such as Mother's Worry, Top Gun, Bandit, Oracle, Nipper and Fang.

Fang looked like a sure winner, with everything out of the pipe but his tail, until he did a complete U-turn and eventually returned to the starting point, much to the disgust of his owner.

Mick and I watched the heats together while he let a couple of youngsters race some of his ferrets. It didn't seem to matter that he didn't have a runner, he was just happy to watch the kids have a bit of fun.

Kids were important to Mick, he worried about them.

'Mate,' he sighed, 'I just wish I could get more kids around here interested in ferrets. It might help 'em.'

As we watched one of his ferrets emerge from the race pipe in last place I asked him what made him the ferret king.

His answer seemed fair enough. 'Cos I am,' he laughed, throwing his arms out wide and making his belly wobble under his singlet like an uncontrolled jelly.

*

Mick Veitch was a retired wharfie. He told me that he had to stop work after being run over 'by a sheila on her way to work'.

Mick cackled again. 'She reckoned she didn't see me. I told her, "How the bloody hell did ya miss me, hairy as this and twenty bloody stone? I'm not a real missable person." So nowadays I spend me time with me kids, me grandkids and me ferrets.'

He had been rabbiting with ferrets for over 40 years and said that with five kids to feed and clothe, food was pretty important in the early years. 'And anyway I love eating 'em. Baked, fried, stewed, curried, the only way I won't eat 'em is runnin'.'

About an hour later, it happened. The racing was going along quite nicely. Everyone, as well as the ferrets, was happy, until a whisper swept through the crowd. 'Bad Bart's here.'

Owners threw knowing glances at each other while spectators wondered what was going on. Even the ferrets looked anxious.

'This is the ferret to watch, this Bad Bart,' Mick told me knowingly.

Nick Nelson, Bad Bart's owner, filled out his entry form. He was a gangly youth, pimply faced and he spoke in words of single syllables. That is when he spoke at all. I wanted to find out more about Bad Bart, but Nick was a bit reluctant and his mum spoke for him.

'He doesn't talk much about his ferrets.'

Instead, I turned to Mick to explain what was different about this particular ferret. It looked fairly much like all the rest.

'Shit!' exclaimed Mick disdainfully. 'It's won the last two Colac Cups.'

Well, that explained everything.

Apparently the Colac Cup is the Melbourne Cup of ferret racing, even to the point that it is run on the same day, and Bad Bart had streeted them in the last two years. Mick grinned and his belly rolled again as he remembered. 'I bloody well told 'em to check him for drugs. But the silly buggers wouldn't.'

Mick reckoned that Bad Bart must have been specially trained but was still to work out how. He suspected they must have put his food at the end of a pipe so he had to run down it to get a feed, but he wasn't sure.

Nick stood around with his mum as a couple more heats were run and then it was his turn.

There was silence as Nick held Bad Bart aloft and thrust him into the pipe on the starter's orders. In what was by far the shortest time of any ferret that had raced, Bad Bart showed his head at the finish line and Nick grabbed him and triumphantly pulled him clear.

The crowd erupted. The favourite had won. But then Mick waddled over and informed a disconsolate Nick that he was disqualified because he didn't let the ferret clear the end of the pipe.

But, Mick being Mick, and in the true spirit of ferret racing everywhere, Mick proclaimed in a loud voice that Bad Bart could have another chance in a heat later on. This seemed to please Nick and he wandered off to feed his prized associate.

In between heats, Mick, Andrew and I stood in the ferret-racing office and talked at length about ferrets. I asked Mick what was the best ferret he had owned.

He thought momentarily and then said, 'Jeff, I reckon. He won me a Colac Cup.'

That seemed a bit of an ordinary name for a ferret but Mick had his reasons. 'I named him after the premier, Kennett,' he boasted.

I didn't want to ask why, but I did.

Mick's grin appeared through his beard. 'No balls,' he answered. 'Prick took me guns off me. And anyway he's a bloody politician.'

There didn't appear to be any love lost between the ferret-racing fraternity and politicians. Even Andrew bought into the discussion. He told me that he had a discussion at one race meeting with a couple of Democrats who asked him what he thought of the political scene. 'I told them that there was a species of otter in the Amazon jungle that grew up to three metres long and as it was in the same family as ferrets I though I'd try to breed a ferret that big so I could go to Canberra and hunt a few of them out of their burrows.'

Mick and Andrew were chuckling to themselves as I left the office and went over to watch the start of the next heat. The runners were Pond's Power, Drake, Granny and a white ferret named Teegan, owned by the association's treasurer Jinty Gordon.

Teegan looked as though she was a bit of a pampered ferret as she walked to the start on a leash and, before she was placed in the pipe, was kissed gently by her owner.

It must have done the trick as Teegan emerged a clear winner.

After the heat I followed Jinty to where she placed Teegan into a string enclosure and tied her leash to a wire stake so she couldn't run away. She also adjusted a golf umbrella and stuck it into the ground to shade Teegan from the warm sun.

A small thin woman, Jinty had close-cropped hair and long dangling earrings. Dressed in bright red pants with a purple top and a red baseball cap, she smiled gently when I mentioned that I thought her ferrets were spoiled.

'Not really,' she answered in a soft, refined voice. 'I think that's the way everything should be treated.'

Jinty told me that she started life in Borneo, where her Australian father was an engineer. They moved to England when she was young and it was then that her father decided to come back to this country. 'He bought a seventy-foot yacht and we set off to sail it out here,' Jinty told me. 'But we only got to Gibraltar when the Arabs and Israelis decided to have their Seven Day War, so we sold up and moved back to England.'

They eventually came back to Australia and now, Jinty said, she and her family were refugees from the city. They had bought a property in the country where they could be closer to nature and she fell in love with ferrets when they tried to clear their land of rabbits.

Jinty had been treasurer of the association for three years and the enjoyment she got from racing them was only matched by her love of operettas, ballet and painting.

'I'm also a witch,' she informed me quite bluntly.

I must have looked surprised, so she explained that a witch to her meant a 'wise woman', not one with spells and chants.

I breathed a sigh of relief. After all, I didn't want to ask any wrong questions.

'I treat my ferrets with herbs and potions. Lavender and vitamin C are my favourites,' she said matter of factly. 'Alternative therapies work and I try to be aware of what the land and the insects are telling me.'

Just as I was coming to terms with all that, Mick—whistling to himself, and with a ferret grasped by the neck swinging from one hand and a bottle of beer from the other—walked past. I made an excuse to Jinty and followed him to the starting area for the day's last race, the one that would decide the reserve champion.

The race was between Whitey, owned by Paul Schefferle and raced by his son Owen, Snowballs, who was still dangling from Mick's hand, Bad Bart who had won the heat he was allowed to run again, and Teegan, who Jinty had to organise quickly.

As we waited for all the runners to arrive I asked Nick if he did anything special for training. 'Nah,' he replied.

I tried again by asking if there was any special feeding. 'Nah,' he replied again.

'I told you he doesn't say much,' his mum piped up.

The ferrets were held aloft and on the starter's order were poked into the pipes. Bad Bart went in first, followed by Whitey as Owen was closer to the ground. Mick took some time to bend over to shove Snowballs in and Teegan was still being kissed by Jinty after all the others had disappeared.

First to emerge was Whitey, and shortly after Bad Bart stuck his head out. The race was on to get completely clear, with Nick not game to get anywhere near Bad Bart for fear of being thrown out again. Suddenly, to the cheers of the crowd and the dismay of Nick, Whitey ran completely out of the pipe and was declared the winner.

I watched as Mick laughed at the good-natured ribbing from all the competitors who joked about Snowballs' effort. 'Youse wait till I get it full of steroids,' he cackled. 'Then I'll bloody show youse.'

After the presentation of the reserve champion's trophy, the owners gathered up their cages and headed off with the promise of a good day's racing ahead.

As Mick and I sat down to have a beer and discuss the merits of the runners so far and who should be established as the favourite, he called out to Owen, who was about to leave with Whitey and his dad.

'Hey, Owen, it's true aint it, the worst days ferreting is still miles better than the best day of school.'

Owen smiled and Mick roared with laughter, his big belly wobbling again as he passed me the bottle.

I arrived early the next morning to find the only change in Mick was that he now wore a blue singlet that said Daly Waters Hotel.

'G'day mate, wanna a beer,' was his greeting as he leant against the wall of the ferret-racing office.

Once again I declined because of the hour.

'Shit,' he exclaimed laughingly, 'You've bin to bloody church haven't ya? It should be okay with the Lord now.'

Andrew was also in the office in earnest discussion with a little, thin-faced man with a pointy nose and small eyes. He was the president of the English ferret racing association who was out here on holiday and came across the races by accident. He and Andrew had been discussing ferrets on the Internet.

Andrew introduced us, although I didn't hear his name and I reckoned Andrew forgot it anyway, and I asked if the English had much ferret racing.

In his high-pitched voice he informed me that he had once spent over four hours on the Net reading information about ferrets. 'It was astonishing,' he squeaked, 'jolly astonishing, and I still have loads more to read.'

Mick, who was standing back a bit, took off his hat, scratched his head and, after putting his hat back on, scratched his stomach, shook his head and walked away.

After the Englishman left, Andrew turned to me. 'They pulled the TV cables through pipes. Diana's wedding, I forgot to tell you, they attached cables to ferrets and made them run through the pipes they layed in the cathedral.'

Soon enough all the ferrets and their owners arrived, keen and ready for the new day's racing. Owen and his dad had come back, Jinty told me that all her ferrets had rested well and Gryffen, Snail, Clumper and George were new entries.

As well, there was a new announcer. Andrew had handled the microphone reasonably well but the new man, David Verhagen, was a natural spruiker. Shaved head, earrings, grunge trousers and singlet, loud voice and a repertoire of one-liners to keep the crowd amused.

David also raced ferrets, although he found it hard to describe the race they were in, which was hardly surprising since they were running down a length of pipe he couldn't see into.

The heats eventually started with a black ferret named V8 winning the first and Insomniac again failing to emerge and again being the butt of Mick's fast-asleep joke.

In between heats Mick sidled up to me. 'I reckon I've got me chance,' he whispered. 'Bad Bart hasn't turned up.'

It was true, and soon the word spread amongst the onlookers.

'Musn't've understood that he could have another run,' said Mick.

The rules stated that all the ferrets could race again, but the reserve champion from the previous day was the only one assured a start in the grand final.

'Oh well,' said Mick with a grin. 'That's his problem, but at least it makes it a bit easier.'

As everyone waited for the start of the third heat, Norm Robb rolled up on his clanking tractor holding a cage with one of his ferrets inside, eyes rolling, wondering what all the noise was about.

'I named her Judy,' Norm told me as he took the ferret from its cage, 'after my wife.'

I didn't ask how impressed his wife had been.

Cigarette-holder still dangling from his lip and with overalls more greasy than they had been the previous day, Norm took his place at the start. Judy wasn't a very good racer and Norm spent quite a few minutes on his knees, posterior pointed to the sky while he gazed up the pipe from near the ground and whistled and stamped his hands.

Judy wouldn't appear, so Mick again broke the pipe and sent her tumbling out of the end.

Norm was talking, laughing and smoking at the same time. He then scratched his head, rolled a new smoke and stuck it in the holder before striding off with Judy in the cage for another trip on the clanking monster.

The crowd started to build up as the time for the final approached and Mick walked around the track talking to everyone he knew, which seemed to be everyone. He stopped to drop pearls of ferret wisdom to the kids, and to inspect their ferrets. He triumphed in the adulation afforded the king of the ferrets.

'Geez, mate, don't ya just love it,' he blurted out at me as the finalists approached the starting end of the pipe.

There was Cuddles, owned by a bloke called Gavin Murphy who had been keeping a low profile, Whitey, of course, with Owen holding him gently and two others, Misty and The Phantom, that were both raced by David Verhagen, the spruiker.

David could hardly contain himself as he introduced the contestants. The prospect of being known as the winner of the Geelong Ferret Racing Cup was obviously getting the better of him.

I considered that this may be his hardest call and wondered how he would describe four ferrets, two of which were his own, racing down pipes when he, and everyone else, couldn't see them. How was he to keep the excitement up?

I needn't have worried. He was magnificent. He could see the pipes move slightly as the ferrets ran along and the way he jumped up and down willing his charges on was reminiscent of some of the great Melbourne Cup calls.

All four runners reached the end of the pipe at a similar time. Four pink noses and sets of eyes sneaking a look round the corner to make sure it was okay to come out.

While the crowd yelled at their favourites, Mick was laughing at all the carrying on. 'Seen it all before,' he explained. 'They'll come out when they're ready.'

David was trying to encourage his ferrets out while telling the others to go back into the pipe. None seemed to be listening. He became more anxious as each minute passed but as Whitey emerged first he was nearly choking.

The crowd roared as David sat down laughing while Owen

smiled shyly. Jinty kissed Teegan, who she had hooked up to a stylish leather lead and walked around the crowd while the final was on, and told her she was a good girl.

Mick's belly shook for about five minutes.

It wasn't long before the presentation of the Geelong Ferret Racing Cup was made to Owen, and shortly afterwards the ferrets and their owners all wandered off home. Soon there was only Mick and me left and as I shook his hand he grinned at me through a mass of hair. 'Told ya it was the best thing that God invented, didn't I?'

You did Mick, you did.

CHAPTER TWO

ENOUGH TO GET YOUR GOATS

I'd always been interested in seeing what went on in Lightning Ridge.
It was such an intriguing name and a place that always cropped up in
conversations about the Outback.
But no-one I knew had ever been there.
So when I found out that one of their biggest events, in a town not known for
big events, was goat-racing, I headed off.

The sign at the entrance to town declared: 'Lightning Ridge—
Population ?'

I wondered why no-one had ever bothered to count the people.
Perhaps nobody cared. People came and went and no-one was any
the wiser. Some used their real names, others didn't really exist.

Just past the sign, behind a clump of emaciated, almost leafless
gum trees, a broken concrete path staggered from a wilting wire
fence through a garden of brown grass and dead bushes towards a
dilapidated weatherboard house that leaned precariously to one
side.

Sheets of tin were missing from its roof, like the teeth in the
mouth of the old man wearing his best blue singlet, who sat on an
decaying wooden chair on the verandah. A soon-to-be-finished beer
bottle balanced on one of the few remaining boards, and as he
dragged on his smoke he didn't appear concerned about anything.

Tall weeds and short survived in the nature strips attached to the
main bitumen street. Nothing grew in the dirt streets that bisected
them.

Lightning Ridge looked tired. Apart from the bowling club—a two-storey redbrick testament to the power of poker machines.

The only pub in town was the Digger's Rest, that announced itself with a large, signwritten fibro sheet attached to the sloping tin roof.

An old but freshly painted building, it looked slightly uncomfortable with its timber walls soaked in the past rising from a batch of new and badly layed modern pavers.

Stuck lopsidedly on one of the pub windows was a poster proclaiming, 'The Great Goat Race of Lightning Ridge—over $3000 in prize money'.

Inside, in the corner, a few Aborigines were playing pool and drinking. Nasally sounding country and western music blared from the jukebox while the bar was lined with flinty looking individuals, all with long, daggy hair protruding from underneath their dirty hats. They sat, or stood, staring straight ahead, with the silence, other than the music, broken only occasionally by the odd word.

The bar had a smooth wide laminex top nailed onto the old wooden one and the barman, who stood next to what appeared to be the world's largest esky, slid stubbies up and down the bar to the thirsty drinkers like a bartender in a Cisco Kid movie.

A notice behind the bar warned patrons, 'If you think our barmaids are attractive, don't drive home'. A triangular stack of bottles sat next to it containing a dangerous-looking brown liquid. Their labels simply stated, 'Fucking Good Port'.

'What're you here for?' the barman enquired.

'For the goat races,' I answered.

The bloke sitting on a bar stool next to where I stood turned and searched my face through eyes as tough as black, shiny opals. 'Goat races,' he scoffed before turning away again and sucking on his beer while studying some point behind the bar that was unnoticeable to me. He wasn't all that old, but his hair looked like it badly needed a wash and his shapeless towelling hat flopped over his head. Every few seconds he scratched furiously at his beard, then examined his fingers when he stopped as though he had caught something wandering through it.

It must have been a minute before he spoke again. 'You ever seen 'em before?' he asked without looking at me.

I told him that I'd never heard of it before.

'You a goat racer?' I asked him back.

'Nah. Used to be. Can't do much since I done me back.'

I wondered what a bad back had to do with racing goats but I didn't ask. Perhaps it would be more sensible to ask later, after I'd been there a while.

He stood up and pointed out of the window to an old man sitting on a bench selling raffle tickets for the local fire brigade. 'Go and see him,' he said with a sardonic grin. 'He'll tell you about goats, he knows the lot about every bloody thing.'

With that, he walked from the front bar of the pub, out a door marked 'oilets', and around to what must have been the lounge.

Through the opening behind the bar I saw him sit down and look past the barman again.

I walked out of the pub and across the road.

Toby Chesworth was 73 years old and had lived in the Ridge for 41 of them. He walked with a limp, the legacy of a fall from a buck-jumper when he was younger. Shortish, grey-haired, limping and with his hand cupped to his ear to funnel in the sounds, Toby was known to everyone in Lightning Ridge.

'Came here as a shearer.' Toby didn't open his mouth very wide so his words, after having had to fight their way out through clenched teeth, had a problem sounding as they were supposed to.

He wrote another raffle ticket. 'Done a bit of mining for a while, and now I train a few racehorses. Still ride trackwork too.'

I mentioned that I'd been told he knew about the goat races.

'Know about 'em,' he snorted disdainfully. 'Know about 'em!'

I apologised quickly and asked him to tell me how they came to be.

'Well now, that's a good story,' Toby nodded knowingly. I had a feeling it might be.

Folding his arms and leaning back on the bench he continued, 'I'll tell you about it.'

Toby, whose real name was Rupert Henry but he didn't want any-one to know it, had started the races with a few other blokes in 1976.

'We reckoned that it was a bit quiet around the Ridge so we thought we'd cause a bit of a stir and have a big, mad goat race with wild goats. So we had a meeting and came up with the name, The Great Goat Race. It was the first organised goat race in Australia.'

Toby then told me that the first thing that you need if you are going to have a goat race is goats. I nodded in agreement but didn't say a word.

'And the goats came from a place out the road called Billy Goat Hill,' he continued.

Where else? I thought.

'There was hundreds of the bastards out there but we didn't know how to get 'em rounded up, so we got a bloke with a plane. There was me, someone else and another bloke. Then we went and brought back a dozen or so, and we let the rest of 'em go.'

The men then made a couple of small carts, called gigs, hooked up the goats and the first Great Goat Race was under way.

The goat races are held on the bitumen of Morilla Street, named after the Aboriginal word for the pebbly ridges in the area. No fancy grass or dirt tracks for these animals, they just pound away down the tar.

'We had eight goats that eventually raced that first year,' Toby's voice was full of pride. 'Now we have around 40.'

As Toby and I sat there in the afternoon sun a stockily built, blond-haired, fair-skinned and fit-looking bloke came to join us. A bit younger than Toby, but also with a limp, Trevor Darling held one of the two most prestigious positions in the hierarchy of the Lightning Ridge Goat Racing fraternity. He was the official runner, the person who takes the results from the judges to the official table and who generally runs around the place. Toby was, according to Toby, the main man because he was the official starter.

Toby and Trevor were mates, although constantly at each other. Trevor was the more placid of the two. He would say something and Toby, the fiery one, more often than not would correct him.

Trevor was a builder by trade and got his limp from an accident on a site. Apart from his love of goats, he was also president of the Lightning Ridge Nudist Society.

'You're only a bloody perv,' sneered Toby.

'You're jealous, and anyway you won't take your clothes off,' was Trevor's retort.

Toby raised his voice. 'I just don't want to walk around with you bastards.'

I didn't like where this was heading. A fight between a 60-something nudist and a 70-something ex-buckjumper could have been quite nasty, so I suggested that we all go for a beer.

'Okay,' Toby was suddenly placid. 'But I've got no money on me.'

'Didn't think you would have,' murmured Trevor to himself.

The bar at the Digger's Rest was occupied by the same people who were there when I arrived, although in a slightly different condition. The Aborigines were still playing pool, although not quite as well or as quietly, and listening to the same songs. The blokes at the bar were still staring straight ahead.

Stubbies were slid along the bar when I ordered and Toby suggested we adjourn to the lounge and sit down.

We picked a table from the three or so that were out there and I noticed the bloke I'd spoken too earlier was still in the same spot. I reckoned he'd be there a lot longer. As we sat down I asked how the town came by its name.

'It's shifted, you know.' Trevor was full of local knowledge. I said that I didn't.

'Yeah, it was out on the highway originally, and when the mines opened up here the buildings followed.'

The story goes that a woman named Katie Langloh Parker, who was the manager's wife on nearby Bangate Station during the 1880s, had written that the town was so named because during one of the terrible storms that the interior sometimes experience, one bolt of lightning killed 600 sheep, the shepherd and his dog.

As I contemplated how that could happen and Trevor and Toby debated how many sheep there really were, I looked around at the old photos on the wall.

Lightning Ridge history looked back at me. Old blokes in mines, rugby teams and group pictures of people long gone. Another was of the pub years ago with an old, old box tree out the front.

'That's the tree of knowledge,' Toby informed me.

I wasn't sure I understood, so he went on, 'For years it was the only tree in the Ridge, the rabbits and such seen to that. They reckoned it must have had all the knowledge to be able to grow. The Ridge hasn't been the same since they cut it down.'

'Do they race in other towns?' I asked, changing the subject.

'Bloody oath they do,' Toby replied emphatically. 'Gilgandra, Gulargambone, Collarenabri.'

Then he added, 'They race at Roma too, but that's over the border, so we don't worry too much about them, even though they're trying to pinch our name.' The words were almost spat out in contempt.

I wondered how the goat races were organised and whether there were stewards, or even rules for that matter.

From his pocket Toby produced a crumpled piece of paper. It was a nomination form. 'There's the rules on it as well.' He smoothed the form out on the table before handing it to me. 'So no bastard can say they didn't know about 'em'.

The form stated the obvious, like the committee taking no responsibility for anything and a disclaimer saying that the racers were urged to take out private insurance, an option I thought would be sensible.

There were strict rules for the goats, as well. All goats had to be in training for two weeks prior to the event, goats had to be on time for the races and there were to be no whips, cruelty or abusive language.

I couldn't imagine what you'd do if a goat was late. Keep him in after the races? And had there been any goats that had taken offence to anything that was said to them during a race?

'The RSPCA made us put that one in,' Toby told me before pointing triumphantly to the last line. 'But that's the most important one.'

The line simply said, 'Starter to have the last say on everything.'

Toby was impressed with that, but then I asked him about the two-week clause.

'They used to get 'em straight out of the scrub,' Trevor butted in. 'But we get 'em to give a couple of weeks training now.'

That seemed logical to me. After all, two weeks should be ample time to train a wild goat.

I asked when the goats arrived.

'Most of 'em'll be here tomorrow, I reckon.' Toby took the stubbie I had ordered. 'But some'll be at the Crocodile tonight, maybe.'

I knew I shouldn't have asked what the Crocodile was, but I did.

'Well now,' Toby leant back and folded his arms again. 'That's a good story too.'

The Crocodile was a caravan park named after one of Toby's escapades with Trevor and a couple of mates. 'We'd built this tin fence, see, and dug a hole in the ground at the park and we decided to get a crocodile and put in it.'

I wondered where they would get a crocodile in Lightning Ridge.

'Well, we got him fr . . .' Toby stopped abruptly in mid-sentence. 'Never you bloody mind where we got him from!

'Anyway, we got him. And we got a couple of wedgetails in a cage and a couple of big sand goannas. It was going to be a bit of a zoo. But then we had a flood and the croc got away. Funny as buggery it was. The whole town looking for this bloody croc. Tourists shittin' 'emselves and everything.'

'We found him in the old swamp and we had to get rid of him after we told a tourist lady that it had eaten a couple of her kids.'

Trevor and Toby chuckled for a while before Toby announced that he had to go, but if I wanted I could meet him outside the pub in an hour and we'd mark out the race track ready for the big event.

Trevor had to leave as well, so I wandered off too. I walked up to the supermarket where the owner was writing a few specials on the blackboard out the front. We chatted for a while under one of the tamarix trees that lined the streets. He told me it was his biggest weekend of the year. 'Love them tourists,' he chortled.

The young girl serving in one of the shops a bit further down the street agreed. 'There's not much else here.'

Her neck was covered in love bites, so there must have been something else. 'But it's not too bad,' she continued as if she had something to hide. 'No-one knows about you, or wants to know about you.'

Marking out the racetrack consisted of walking with Toby as he limped about 150 metres down the street, painted a somewhat crooked line across the road and wrote 'Start' in lettering about as straight as the line.

He then limped back to the pub, abusing the motorists who dared to venture too close to him, and marked another, similarly shaped line across the street and wrote along it 'Finish'.

As we walked along I asked Toby how many people would come for the races. 'We used to get 30 or 40 busloads, but not now. They don't come as much anywhere now.'

Toby talked about the changes he'd seen during the years. About how the Ridge was different. 'That'll show you,' he lamented, pointing out a sandstone building with a large cross protruding from the roof. 'That's called the Holy Spirit Church. It used to be a brothel.'

The average temperature in the Ridge during summer is about 43 degrees, with days of around 50 degrees not uncommon. It wasn't quite that hot, but as the dust settled and what breeze there was died, it left a breathless, still evening.

Trevor watched us from outside the pub and when we'd finished marking the track the three of us stood under the old tin verandah and talked for a while as the burning sun vanished from the sky.

'Looks good doesn't it.' Trevor watched me watching the sunset. 'It's a special place, the Ridge.'

'Well, that's it for tonight,' Toby announced loudly, as he hobbled off. 'Get here early.'

'You ever have goats?' I inquired of Toby as he leant on his ute in the early morning sun, waiting somewhat impatiently for some other workers to arrive.

'A few, but the one I remember most had little beady eyes, one big horn and couldn't run straight. Know what I called him?'

I couldn't even hazard a guess, nor did I want to.

'Bob Hawke.' Toby laughed uproariously, before exclaiming again, 'Bob Hawke!'

I left Toby still chuckling and wandered over to where some SES blokes were tying up a two-foot-high hessian barrier around the track. The barriers were to keep the goats in and the crowd out, they explained. 'It's not much,' the man in charge told me, 'but at least it's something.'

He was right. The hessian sagged and fell down in places, but it didn't appear to matter much to anyone.

On the other side of the road a big truck was manoeuvred into position and a microphone set up on the tray. 'For the auction,' the SES man told me.

Then the goats arrived. Slowly, almost solemnly, they appeared from around the corner and into the main street, looking fiercely out of cages in trailers being towed behind a selection of utes and old cars that carried gigs on their roof. They parked in the closed-off street about 30 metres past the finish line.

Each trailer held four or five goats which were unloaded, simply, with a rope around the horns, followed by a test of strength as the owners pulled them out and tied them to the side of the trailers. There they stood, their eyes daring people to come close.

I was studying the faces of the goats, and didn't notice Trevor behind me. He pointed to one of the trailers. 'That's Redback. He's won the last three years.'

Redback was probably the least fierce looking of all the goats. He was small and a light colour with a pale brownish stripe that ran part the way down his back. Actually, it was more a discolouration than a stripe and his colour was more dirty white than anything, as though he'd spent all his life rolling in the dirt. He was hunched over, almost as if he was waiting to explode down the street and show everyone his talent.

His owner was a small, young-looking bloke named Dave Lamb, who went about unloading his gear quietly. He ran a carpet-cleaning and pest-control business in nearby Gilgandra and his eyes were covered by sunglasses and his head by a red baseball cap. He told me

how everyone laughed when he first turned up to race Redback at
Deepwater, a few hundred kilometres away towards the coast.

'They reckoned he was too small,' Dave remembered proudly.
'They were all racing big billygoats, but this bloke beat 'em all.'

He told me he'd had Redback for about eight years and that the
thing that made him special was simply that he was strong and could
run straight. Dave seemed to have a way with his goats. 'Oh, I don't
know,' he sounded almost shy, 'but Redback knows me. If I call him
he'll come to me.'

As if to prove the point he called out, 'Won't you Redback',
whereupon the small, dirty-looking goat's ears pricked up and he
turned toward the voice.

While I watched the goats, the thought crossed my mind that perhaps they objected to being tied up the way they were. 'I don't think
so,' Dave said. 'Not much seems to change them. They're just cranky
most of the time.'

The trailers held goats of varying size and colour, but in one there
were goats that were all black. Here was a goat called Midnight, a wild-
looking animal with eyes that followed you. His horns had been lopped
a bit shorter so he wouldn't butt too much, he was missing a few lumps
of hair from a few too many fights and he wore what appeared to be a
cynical smile, as if he knew that everyone was a bit wary of him.

Trevor Marchant, a tall, thickset farmer, owned Midnight. His
ute was parked close enough to the footpath to allow a woman, who
was obviously not a student of goat behaviour, to lean over and take
a photo.

The flash of the camera sent the goats into a frenzy. They clat-
tered around the trailer and when the startled lady screamed and
threw herself backwards, Midnight's grin seemed to be even wider.

A couple of minutes later, after all the goats and gigs had been
unloaded, Toby shuffled around the mob collecting entry forms and
trying to hurry everyone up. 'Come on, come on,' he yelled, 'we need
to get the Calcutta going.'

I wasn't sure what a Calcutta was and Toby tried to explain it,
but after about 10 attempts he gave up and the auctioneer stepped in
to help. A Calcutta is an auction on a race of any sort where people

can buy one of the entries. A percentage of the pool of money goes to whatever the fundraiser is for and the balance to the people who bought the eventual winner. The auctioneer was the local stock and station agent and he had set himself up on the back of the truck with a board that showed the names of all the entered goats.

The bidding was fast and furious and after about an hour all the goats had been sold with a healthy amount of money for the local fire brigade and SES.

'Now we can get on with it.' Toby was impatient. I wanted to ask him why people would buy one goat and not another, but I thought the time might not be quite right, and he may not have an answer anyway.

The crowd had built up by now, locals as well as tourists, and there was a buzz around the place as the goats prepared for the running of the first heat.

The local police had arrived as well and Stewart Gordon, a young senior constable, came across to where Toby was standing to ask if everything was going according to plan.

'Now here's what I want you to do,' Toby told the policeman in his usual organising way.

'Are you asking me or telling me?' replied the copper testily.

Toby was suitably admonished and for a moment was stuck for words. Just for a moment, that was, until Stewart smiled and winked at him.

'You bastard,' Toby growled when he knew he was being had. 'Piss off and do ya job.'

Stewart and his assistants who had joined the group then set about clearing everyone from the street to behind the hessian. It wasn't a problem, the crowd only had to be told once. I suspected none of them wanted to be standing in the way of rampaging wild goats anyway.

Stewart Gordon was a tall, imposing young man, with short fair hair and a ready smile under the peaked cap that was pulled down over his eyes. He came from the inner city of Sydney, had been in Lightning Ridge for about two years, and was enjoying the experience.

'I know this is a fair bit different to the suburbs, but a cop's life is much the same everywhere,' he told me candidly. 'Trouble is trouble, it's just the amount of people that vary.'

I asked him if he knew what the population of the Ridge was.

'Mate, that's anyone's guess,' he grinned, 'but they all get on with each other most of the time, that's the main thing.'

When I left the cops they were deliberating whether they should go over to the corner near the pub where a group of young blokes had gathered to drink stubbies and watch the races from under a sign that said 'No drinking on the street'. Stewart decided instead to tell the publican to watch out for it.

'No need to make a fuss this early.'

Toby had hobbled his way to the starting line to await the arrival of the first goats. I'd gone with him as he'd told me to. You tended to do what Toby asked.

He held up a two-way radio. 'I'll find out from Trev what's goin' on,' he announced to no-one in particular. 'Trevor, testing, testing, can you hear me?'

In the distance, down near the finish line we could see Trevor stop, turn towards the start and speak into his radio. Nothing came through. 'Bloody hell,' exclaimed Toby. 'What's bloody wrong with him?'

Then Trevor's voice came through loud and clear. 'Toby, can you hear me?'

''Course I can bloody hear you,' an exasperated Toby yelled at the radio.

'Can you hear me,' Trevor's voice crackled through again. 'Toby, is everything okay?'

Toby spluttered as he shook the offending equipment fiercely. I grabbed the radio from him before he pitched it into the bitumen and hurried towards an SES man whose radios they were.

He showed me, with a smile, that Toby had pressed the wrong button. Toby was not pleased with this news. 'Bloody nudists, you can't trust 'em,' he muttered as he finally answered Trevor's call as sweetly and innocently as he could, 'Trev, you there mate? Everything's okay here.'

The gigs had been hooked to the goats for the first heat and the drivers, none of whom appeared to be much over 12 years old, walked up the street to the start. The goats were somewhat more reluctant and the handlers had to almost drag them the length of the track. At the starting line they held them by the horns and tried to aim them while the drivers mounted the gigs and waited.

Toby, in a great imitation of an Olympic 100 metres starter, eventually sent them on their way. With the loud bang of his starting pistol, the handlers let go and goats ran in every direction. Some straight down the bitumen while others headed for the hessian. Spectators who were close to the action were screaming; others further away were laughing like mad.

That's the thing about goats. No-one has any control. The drivers just grab hold of the rope, usually tied to the goat's horns, and hang on for dear life.

I asked Alan King from Gulargambone what constituted a good goat. His entry, Red Handed, was one of the favourites to knock off Redback.

'That's a bit of a mystery,' he replied, scratching his head. 'I suppose one that has got the sense to run fast and straight.'

As the goats charged down the street the handlers prepared to catch them. That's the other thing about goats. They don't know when to stop, so at the finish line they'll just keep running if some brave people don't get in front of them and catch them by the horns, bridle or anything else they can lay their hands on.

A goat named Costly was the winner of the first heat, driven by a youngster called Darren Lohse. I walked over to him after the goat was caught to find out how old he was. 'I'm 10,' came the reply.

I was amazed as I looked around me. All the drivers were young. Blake King, Alan's son, looked up at me from somewhere around my knee. Underneath a bike helmet that was too large for his small head and made him look like a large roofing nail was a freckly face split by a mischievous grin. 'I've just turned nine,' he said proudly. And what about weight? 'I'm nearly three stone.'

Alan came over as Blake was telling me the good thing about racing goats was the money and the trophies. Alan didn't necessarily agree.

'I don't reckon you'd know about the money,' he smiled at his son as he rapped on the top of his helmet. 'There's not a great deal of money. It's more for the kids to enjoy, really. A bit of fun together, you know. It's good out here together, isn't it mate, eh?'

Blake looked out from under his shell-like helmet, still grinning.

Before the next heat started I studied the draw with an old bloke, Charlie Walker, who had turned up with two goats called Round-about and Snow. Charlie was a globular shaped 60-year-old whose ruddy weatherbeaten face was streaked with conniving. He wasn't very talkative, but when I asked him how good his goats were his eyes sparkled.

'Don't really know,' he grinned. 'Never had 'em in the cart before.'

Charlie's driver was a mate of his, a panel beater called Ron who had driven over from Port Macquarie for the weekend. Ron was thirty, skinny, and nearly six feet tall. He was gulping cans of VB as quickly as he could. 'I need 'em, mate.' His high-pitched staccato laugh was tinged with nerves. 'I need a bit of courage.'

I wasn't sure if they knew what they were doing. I couldn't see how the goats were going to pull him down the track faster than the others.

'We'll just have to wait and see about that,' said Charlie almost defiantly.

Snow didn't particularly like the walk to the start and when Toby's gun went off he sat down on the track. Nothing would budge him. A couple of gentle pokes to the stomach and a couple of not so gentle ones failed to move him. Ron tried to pull him to his feet but Snow was having none of it. He was staying put. He wasn't going to pull a cart down a street for anyone.

Charlie had waddled down to the scene by this stage and in sheer exasperation they took the harness off Snow and lifted him onto the cart, whereupon Ron grabbed the gig's handles and proceeded to run down the track with Snow lying nonchalantly behind him. The crowd roared their approval.

After that, Ron and Charlie decided not to run Roundabout. Instead, they grabbed their esky and became spectators.

'This is more like it,' Ron claimed.

*

Redback and Red Handed had been drawn in the same heat and as they and the other runners were coaxed to the starting line I talked to Dave Lamb's wife Karen, who was as small and quiet as her husband. She looked on proudly as her son Adrian walked to the start with Redback.

'Yeah I get a bit worried about them.' Karen sounded a bit hesitant, as though she wasn't quite sure how dangerous it was. 'Any sport's like that I suppose, but this isn't that bad—do you think?'

I didn't answer. Instead I asked about the ladies' event later on.

'Yeah, I'll have a go but it'll only be my second time in a race, so I'm not sure how I'll do.'

We talked for a few minutes while Toby got organised. Among other things, Karen mentioned how she liked knitting.

Knitting and goat-racing—what every good housewife should do!

A minute or so later and the crack of Toby's gun sent the goats on their way. Two ran almost at right angles to the track, one breaching the hessian and running headlong into a fence, while another cut straight across Redback's track, causing him to slow down for a few metres. Red Handed stormed straight down the track to win.

'That's what it's like.' Dave's voice was full of resignation. 'That's what happens. Still, Karen can drive him in the ladies', so we're still a chance to get some money.'

The ladies' race was the last before the final and Trevor called for volunteers.

Surprisingly, to me at least, there were plenty of takers and they milled around trying to get the nod.

Meanwhile, Toby had arrived where all the young ladies had gathered to choose their goats and be fitted out with helmets. His lecherous looking smile told the story.

'It's my job to make sure they're all okay and they understand what's goin' on.' After studying the form he continued, still with the same smile, 'Then I'll go back to the start and I'll help 'em on to the carts.'

Trevor just stood there shaking his head in disbelief.

'What's wrong with you?' snapped Toby.

'Nothing at all, mate,' Trevor replied.

After a couple of minutes they were sorted out. A young blonde woman named Colleen was to drive Ding Dong and as she placed the helmet on her head she muttered, 'I got the best named goat, didn't I?'

Kim, who had four earrings and two nose studs and was obviously not from the Ridge, was allocated Mr Smith. Her friend Bec, who told me her experience of goats extended to wanting one for a pet when she was small, was given Midnight, who stood placidly next to her, a small sneer on his face. I wouldn't have been surprised to hear him say, 'Watch this.'

A girl named Renee was to drive Thunder, and Karen was behind Redback.

After walking the length of Morilla Street acknowledging the whistles and cheers as good country girls should, they mounted the gigs without any help from Toby, who seemed somewhat disappointed but also resigned, and awaited the shot.

With a great flourish of the starting pistol, Toby sent them on their way. Redback ran straight down the track with Karen hanging on grimly, while Mr Smith ran directly sideways. Twice during the trip he dumped Kim off the gig and twice she bravely climbed back on.

Midnight thumped down the track at breakneck speed but couldn't catch Redback who flashed over the finish line, with Karen waving excitedly, leaving tipped-over gigs and very sore ladies in his wake. Midnight wasn't watching proceedings too carefully though, as he ploughed straight through the catchers and into the back of a trailer. The gig tipped over, Bec spilled out and Midnight staggered around like a punch-drunk boxer. Midnight, I said to myself, you're not the goat I thought you were.

At last the big moment had arrived and Toby was now in his element. He made sure the judges were in the right place, that the goats were in the right place and, of course, that Trevor was in the right place.

With great ceremony the goats in the final struggled with their handlers all the way down the track, each being cheered by the crowd.

All eyes were turned toward the start where, eventually and in dramatic fashion, knowing that everyone was watching him, Toby fired his pistol.

Red Handed strode away from the start and was heading for certain victory when Mr Todd, who was racing next to him, edged across a bit too far, causing him to run a bit off-track.

The crowd yelled as they flew down the bitumen with Red Handed trying in vain to make up ground on The Rat, which had swept past in great style. At the finish it was The Rat by a short horn from Red Handed.

After everyone had calmed down the presentations were made. There were cheques for heat winners as well as the finalists.

'A bit of petrol money,' Alan King called it, although young Blake was a bit keener.

'Hey, Dad,' he offered, 'Now we're cashed up can we go to the pokies?'

It wasn't long before the goats were loaded up and driven away. Toby was limping around offering his goodbyes and thanks as the crowd drifted off. The SES people started to remove the hessian and cars, once again, drove along Morilla Street.

The Ridge was returning to normal.

A little while later I decided to head off, but I was feeling a bit dry so I went back to the pub. There he was. He glanced out the corner of his eye as I walked in but he didn't take his eyes from behind the bar when I sidled up to him.

'What didya reckon?' he asked.

I told him what I thought and then asked if he had watched.

'Nah. Seen it all before.'

As I walked towards my car I heard Toby and Trevor talking over the events of the day. 'Went okay, don't you reckon?' asked Trevor.

'S'pose so,' Toby replied grudgingly. 'Want a drink?'

'It's your shout then,' Trevor demanded.

'What'dya mean, I shouted yest'day.' Toby sounded offended.

I jumped in the car and drove out of the Ridge.

CHAPTER THREE

OF MINERS AND MEN

After the ferrets and the goats I was in need of a something a bit more mainstream.
Aussie Rules is a religion in the southern part of the country and most of the time it's played on good, hard grounds.
But rarely so in Tasmania. The climate sees to that. And then there are grounds like the one at Queenstown. They say that you haven't really played footy until you've played there.
I wondered if that was true.

The entrance to the Queenstown footy ground was over a rattling, old wooden bridge that just made it across a small mountain stream. Lined with ferns and with icy water struggling over a bed of rocks, the Queen River was not very wide and perhaps too grandly named.

At one end of the bridge was a small tin shed where the gate-keeper, his neck wrapped in a long knitted scarf and his face peeking out from under a woollen beanie, sheltered from the cold.

A young boy in shorts, with apparently no feeling, stood outside, handing out programs and taking entrance money to the old man.

Occasionally a car clunked across the bridge that shook and shuddered before regaining its composure and waiting for its next test of strength.

As the wind rushed in from the Antarctic, raising swirls of dust from around the ground, the shutters on the tin-walled canteen, with their paint falling off in strips, were pushed open and the fire under the hot-dog urn quickly lit.

A couple of youngsters kicked a football between them and the five sheds around the oval—one in each forward pocket, two on the wings and one underneath the grandstand—all had smoking chimneys.

Just another football Saturday on the West Coast of Tasmania.

I had driven to Queenstown on a road that snaked around the mountains like the stripe on a barber's pole. The radio played only static, so my company was the metronomic flap of the wipers as they flicked away the rain to show the path the lights cut through the darkness.

The first sign of civilisation was the town's copper mine, which leapt from the side of the mountain as I rounded a hairpin bend, lit up like a nuclear missile station. I half-expected to see security guards with rifles checking anyone who came too close. A kilometre or so further on and round a few more bends, Queenstown materialised through the gloom.

The place where I was staying looked like a refugee camp. Rows of long fibro huts that had been built for the single men who migrated during the '50s, seeking work on the hydro-electricity schemes or the mines.

Inside the office, with a faded Father Christmas surrounded by snow still on the window in mid-June, was Gerry Mircea. As I stamped my feet and warmed my hands on the radiator he smiled. 'Is a little bit cold today?'

Gerry, a serious but friendly man, had come to Queenstown from Romania as a fitter and turner when he was twenty-two. He told me that the mine retrenched about a thousand workers during one week in the 1970s. He was one. But after winning a tender for the superfluous buildings Gerry converted them into units.

Even though it was almost the middle of the night, he wanted to show me around. I thought I was going to freeze as we stood in the bistro of the motel and looked at the memorabilia and old photos on the walls.

Gerry, his voice with its gentle trace of a European accent, explained the significance of them while pointing across the laminex-topped tables. One of the photos was of the Old Soldiers' Football

Club—Unbeaten Premiers of 1922. Young faces staring proudly into the lens were flanked by officials as well as trainers, one of whom wore a bow tie and a waistcoat, and had a towel thrown casually over his shoulder. The club treasurer, a John Cleese lookalike, gazed, as though alarmed, out of the left-hand side of the frame.

I asked what happened to the club. 'Probably stopped when no more old soldiers,' thought Gerry wistfully.

With that, he gave me a key and pointed out what I hoped would be a nice warm room.

Queenstown appeared to be have been deposited at the foot of the bare-topped mountains that surrounded the town like a serrated edged granite wall.

As I stood looking at the ground, trying to come to terms with the fact that they actually played footy there, Gerry's son-in-law, Sterle Welling, introduced himself. The president of the club, Sterle was a middle-aged man who wore glasses that sat on the lower part of his nose while the frames disappeared into a shock of greying hair that protruded from under his hat.

'What'dya reckon?' he asked, pushing his specs into a more comfortable position. I didn't answer. I couldn't. Before me was a ground like no other, a surface of gravel that had been rolled together with silica sand.

At either end, the goalposts rose starkly from the bare earth. The goal and centre squares were marked with a substance which looked suspiciously like sump oil and a sloping bitumen bike track circumnavigated the playing surface.

To reach the ground meant climbing two or three concrete steps and then walking down across the bike track. It made the whole place appear like a gigantic dinner plate.

'We've only lost one game here in about five years,' Sterle told me proudly. I could see why.

As Sterle wandered away to do the many things that presidents have to do on match days, I watched a young bloke tying big pads on to the goalposts so players wouldn't get hurt if they ran into them. It seemed a funny thing to be doing.

Curtis Doherty was a tough-looking 12-year-old who wore a Melbourne Football Club jumper, tracksuit pants and a crewcut. He informed me that he was the scoreboard manager and got $20 for doing it. 'An' I have to put these on,' he added.

I thought it was easy money and told him so.

'Nah,' sneered Curtis. 'The other kids have got the easy job, gettin' the footies when they're kicked over the fence. But it's better than runnin' the bound'ry.'

Curtis was looking forward to going up to Burnie the next day to play in an under-12 carnival. If he was an example of his team, I pitied the opposition.

I headed around the boundary towards the dressing sheds.

The visitors for the day were Yeoman, a side from Burnie on the north-west coast who played in Essendon colours but were called the Robins. They were the league leaders who also had a point to prove.

The previous year the team had travelled to Queenstown with their position secure in the top four and looking forward to the finals that were to be played on 'real football grounds'. Queenstown were on top of the ladder at the time and handed out a 20-goal thumping which resulted in Yeoman, who suffered a couple of nasty injuries during the game, having an earlier than planned finish to their season. Queenstown went on to be premiers.

Earlier this year Queenstown had travelled the three hours up to Burnie and had been flogged by over 100 points, as well as having a few players dropped behind the play. Now, they too were looking forward to repaying a few compliments.

As I was talking to Curtis the Yeoman bus edged its way across the bridge and as it circled the ground there was none of the skylarking apparent on most team buses. Instead, every set of eyes peered from the windows while their owners studied the ground in silence.

Just inside the doors of the Queenstown footy sheds stood a large stack of neatly cut timber, waiting to feed the fire that kept the footballers warm.

Stuck to the wall with trainer's tape were a couple of notices. One told the players how to stretch their muscles correctly, although I suspected not many read it. The other gave information about the blood rule. 'To be sent from the field, players must be bleeding to a significant extent,' it declared, a suggestion I found sensible as perhaps there mightn't be too many left playing under the rules at other, more traditional grounds.

The Queenstown reserves were changing when I entered. Most of them that is, as some were still being rounded up.

Just about all the players were miners, or were employed by the mining company in other capacities, and had worked their 12-hour shift to eight o'clock that morning. They would play footy, watch the senior game, have maybe one or two beers and then head back underground for another 12 hours. The senior side would do the same but at least their players would have a couple of hours sleep as their game started later.

The Queenstown jumpers were a cross between those worn by the Adelaide Crows and a Ken Done painting. Over in the corner, pulling one over his head and exhorting everyone to 'think about it' was an old, tattooed bald bloke with the long hair he did have plaited and flapping around his back below his shoulder blades. Mark Bowen was the team urger. He was also known as Fruitloop.

Just before they ran out, Seeny, their Barney Rubble-shaped coach, sat them down in the corner and proceeded to tell them, with every second word an expletive, what he thought of Yeoman, who like Queenstown had only lost one reserves game but were second on percentages, and what he wanted his side to do with them.

With loud rallying cries and with Fruitloop at the front, they charged out the door and into the fray.

Queenstown played in the Darwin Football Association, named for reasons no-one seemed to know. The league had been in existence for five years and was formed from the remnants of the West Tasmanian Football League. Further back still there was the Queenstown Football Association, with six teams from the district including three from Queenstown itself—City, named for obvious reasons; Lyell, after the mine; and Smelters, a club formed from the workers who cut down the timber and organised the smelting of the copper and tin.

And in Gormiston, a town four miles away on the other side of the mountain, another team played on a ground similar to Queeny's. Legend has it that Gormiston players were even tougher than those who played in Queenstown. That, so the legend goes, was proved in the Gormy clubrooms after home games. Players, who were suitably lubricated, would run at each other and butt heads like big billygoats until someone dropped.

Now, after years of decreasing populations, a series of amalgamations of clubs and leagues had resulted in the birth of the Queenstown Crows.

Two minutes into the reserves match a voice from in front of the Queeny bench yelled out, 'Why don't you open your eyes you big, fat cockhead?'

The umpire, who wore skin-tight shorts, not for the fashion but because his body fitted in them that way, turned to the voice and raised his middle finger.

'You concentrate on the umpiring and I'll concentrate on the abuse,' the voice scolded him.

The umpire waddled away. His shirt, that didn't quite reach the shorts he was hitching up, flapped gently as it rested on his generous stomach.

The Yeoman boys, some of whom seemed a bit reluctant to fall on the ground, were not all that competitive, although they were kept in the match by the Crows' bad kicking.

'Jesus fuckin' Christ!' yelled Seeny at quarter time. 'Youse'll have to start fuckin' kickin' straight.'

But they didn't, although they were in total control at half time. Fruitloop was in top form during the break. 'They don't like it, fellas,' he yelled. 'They're soft.'

A bloke next to me, who was new to the area, asked his companion why they called him Fruitloop. The reply was concise, 'Cos that's what he fuckin' is.'

As the players stormed through the second half I made my way over to a small silver-haired figure standing by himself near the grandstand. Bill Wedd had been involved in football in the area for 52 of his 67 years and the rover's twinkle in his eye had not dimmed with the years.

Bill was a walking football historian. 'It's not as tough playing here as it used to be,' he assured me, wondering what the world was coming to. 'In the early days it was all real gravel, now they roll in a bit of sand every now and again. Jesus!'

The grounds at Gormiston and Queenstown had developed because it was just too wet to grow grass. That, combined with the sulphur residues from the smelters, made gravel grounds the answer. 'All the other leagues used to be dead frightened to come,' grinned Bill. 'Even the TFL. We beat most of 'em here in the '50s.' But then, as Bill added, they'd get walloped when they played away.

In the '40s and '50s, according to Bill, quite a few VFL teams played in Queenstown. 'Hawthorn come over, and Fitzroy. And in 1954 we drew with South Fremantle.' He paused to reflect, his hand at his mouth, 'Or was it West Fremantle?' When Fitzroy visited, there was only a skeleton crew working at the mine. 'Everyone come down to the ground,' Bill remembered. 'I didn't know there was so many people lived here that day.'

Bill also told me about the big carnivals that would take place over the three days of the eight-hour weekend. The foot running and the bike riding.

'We had Patterson here once,' Bill told me proudly. 'Cost 'em 100 quid to get him over.'

Apparently Sid Patterson had said to the organisers before the final of the wheel race that he hadn't given the crowd much to get excited about during the heats but in the final it would be different.

'He come round that bottom corner at 100 mile an hour,' Bill laughed, 'and had a blowout.'

The great Sid Patterson, Australian bike-riding legend, had flown off the upward-sloping bitumen track and hit the pine trees at the end of the ground about 10 feet in the air.

Bill had worked in the mines all his life. 'We all had jobs in them days,' he told me, 'and those that weren't lucky enough to go the tech schools got jobs with the mines as nippers.'

Furthering my knowledge about mining in Tasmania, Bill explained that Nippers were the blokes who looked after the crib-houses where the skilled workers ate the lunch they took to work in their cribs. They also kept the fires stoked up in the smelters, boiled the billies and made the tea.

Bill looked nostalgically up at the mountains. 'Bit different now.'

Halfway through the last quarter of the reserves match and nothing had changed. The Crows were still kicking badly, Fruitloop was still in full voice and the umpire was still copping it, although his reaction to it had changed.

Chooka, a wiry ruck rover for Queeny, who had his almost shaven head, as well his socks, permanently down, had a firm grip of a Yeoman player's ankle in a pack that formed in front of the Crows' bench. The umpire blew his whistle to award the free kick. However, Chooka looked at him mournfully, said that he was sorry and wouldn't do it again. The umpire, sensing the proximity of the Queenstown supporters and being suddenly pragmatic, said, 'That's okay, mate' and had a ball-up.

The timekeeper's signal at Queenstown is an old warning device from the mine and its high-pitched wail sounded like an air-raid siren. When it blew to indicate the end of the game the Queenstown players trooped off the ground in high spirits after their 10-goal win. Frootloop joining them after shaking hands with the umpire, who seemed more than happy that it was over.

There wasn't much of a crowd at Queenstown. There seldom is. A few cars were dotted round the fence while some hardy souls braved the elements alongside the small tin enclosure that served as the coaches' box. Scattered through the grandstand and making a lot of noise as they raced along the rows of seats were a group of the local lads.

On the opposite side of the ground, on the side of a hill alongside the scoreboard where Curtis plied his trade, were the old City clubrooms.

Here about 30 barrackers warmed themselves round a fire made from a 44-gallon drum that had been laid on its side and a pipe that staggered towards the roof stuck in for a chimney. In one corner was the bar—a large battered fridge almost covered in stickers—that was trading briskly while the drinkers waited for the main game to start.

Just around from there were the old Smelters' rooms where the visiting teams changed. Inside, the Yeoman players sat on the frail-slatted benches that ran along the tin walls or stood on the bare, stained concrete floor. Their clothes hung behind them on hooks sticking out from the rough wooden posts like crooked, beckoning fingers.

Pacing up an down in front of them was the coach, Owen Johnstone.

'I want you to remember last year,' he told them firmly. 'And,' he paused for effect, 'don't worry about the ground.'

Owen's lantern jaw stuck out while he spoke. His powerful, six foot five frame dwarfed everyone in the room. He gave instructions to each player and again told them not to worry about the ground. A few furtive glances amongst the players told me that his message mightn't be getting through.

Owen Johnstone coached well. Perhaps too well. He had spent a couple of years at Essendon, playing half a season in the seniors, and had represented Tasmania on more than one occasion. But none of that helps when you play at Queeny.

He was trying to cut out all the negative talk on the trip down, he told me, but 'when they drive through the gate and see it, it's hard to convince them'.

I left the rooms as he admitted that it was perhaps the ultimate in home-ground advantages.

In the Queenstown rooms the reserves mixed with the seniors as they prepared for battle. 'They don't like it, boys,' was the cry. 'They're bloody soft when they come here.' Confidence was high.

I stood in the corner out of harm's way and, besides, it was warmer next to the fire. I didn't think the wind could reach me there as it probed everywhere searching out places to freeze, but I wasn't sure.

Queenstown had a few players out for the match, including the coach, but not through injury. The 12-hour shifts at the mines had made it harder for the players, as Grant Barwick, a genial bloke with a big nose, told me. 'There's six to eight players out every week, but then their jobs are more important to them than football.'

Seeny was organising the team, assisted by Johnno, whose arms bulged out of his sleeveless jumper while his shorts seemed as if they would split when he flexed his quads.

Johnno spoke logically and clearly to the team while Seeny assured them that 'They don't fuckin' like it down here.'

The teams hit the ground at the same time.

As the gaggle of supporters followed them from the sheds I was probably the only person to notice the sky. Fearsome black clouds had blocked out the tops of the mountains and the wind was even colder than before, if such a thing was possible.

The marrow in my bones was screaming and I wasn't sure if I still possessed toes. Sterle, who was standing next to me, sensed my discomfort and informed me with just a touch of sarcasm, 'Mate, it's not cold yet.'

Sterle loved the West Coast. 'They reckon we're a bit different down here and I suppose we are,' he conceded. 'But everything you do here is hard, you have to brave the elements to do it. Society is tough, always has been. Life's tough, and people are the same.'

In Queenstown, if you want to play sport then you play no matter what the conditions. Hail or snow, raining or dry, they still play. 'Training's the same,' Sterle told me matter of factly. 'Kids too. If they didn't do that they'd never get a game.'

As I looked around at the mountains showing signs of regeneration after being stripped of all their trees for the smelters in the early part of the century, he told me about his great-grandfather who landed at Trial Harbour in a sailing ship and walked a bullock team across the mountains into Zeehan to begin a new life.

'What those people did was unbelievable.' Sterle was suitably impressed at the feat, but not nearly as much as me. 'I suppose we're a separate entity down here, a bit like a society within a society.'

They have played footy in Queenstown with three inches of snow covering the gravel and the older blokes reckoned it made the ground a bit easier to fall on. And once, in nearby Roseberry, the umpire officiated in a final wearing a greatcoat it was so cold.

Bill Wedd sidled up beside me. 'Now, this is nothin',' he informed me, his eyes sparkling, 'Gormiston can get really cold.'

Sterle agreed and said we could drive over later, if I wanted. I declined gracefully.

As the teams warmed up with a couple of laps of the centre square, the Crows looked, well, like miners with their normal haircuts, occasional tattoos and socks down, while Yeoman players, who looked more like office workers, wore bandages that I suspect supported more than the knees they were wrapped around. Bicycle shorts, gloves and thigh pads were also very popular among the Yeoman team.

At the opening bounce there was plenty of pushing and shoving, followed by a call from centre half-back, 'Give it to 'im if he wants it. Don't stuff around.'

The advice was heeded and the game got under way with a free kick to Yeoman.

But Queenstown ran at them from the jump. Fierce tackling, some of it legal, made the Yeoman players look around a bit. And every Yeoman player got one behind the ear no matter what, although free kicks were awarded only rarely. I sensed that the football saying about earning your free kicks originated at this ground.

The Crows had much more of the play but kept Yeoman in the game by thinking more about how the Robins didn't like it and less about how they played.

One of those in charge was a small, moustachioed man called Lenny Boxhall who had been umpiring for 20 years and who knew he was in for a hard time. He told me before the game that it was always hard at Queeny. 'They're fairly passionate about it here,' he said, wondering what sort of day he was in for. 'And you know it's going to be on behind you. But if you concentrate only on what you see, it's okay.'

His partner was a tall, slight youngster, Travis Crisp, who hadn't been there before. He reckoned he'd rather be doing the under-18s somewhere.

'Shit no,' exclaimed Lenny. 'Most of them are smartarses.'

At quarter time with the Crows about four goals up, the message from Seeny was the same. 'Let's not kid ourselves, fellas, we hate these bastards, don't we?' The roared answer was followed by the statement, 'Let's bury 'em.'

The second quarter saw much of the same and halfway through it the Crows led by almost five goals. Six of their seven goals were kicked from impossible angles on the boundary. Most by Doggie, a 40-year-old, scrawny, half-bald left-footer whose grace under pressure was admirable.

Yeoman's solitary point during that time was followed by their version of the zone defence. Six of their players stood on one side of the ground with both hands in the air, the way they do on TV, while the Crows fullback kicked out to his players standing alone on the other side.

The Queeny players had let their good start go to their heads however, and at the signal that either meant an invasion or half time Yeoman had come back to be only four points behind.

Naturally, it had nothing to do with the players. According to the crowd it was all the umpires' fault. Lenny and Travis were under siege. As they headed towards their change rooms, Bill Wedd, arms swinging fiercely, shuffled after them and explained exactly where they were going wrong.

After they disappeared into their rooms, Bill joined me, red-faced, stuttering and almost apoplectic. 'Shit, they even sent a bloke off for bloody blood.'

That was true. The Crows ruckman had taken a fall and was bleeding from around the knee. So, after a lengthy inspection, Lenny took the bit between his teeth and sent him to the bench, whereupon the ruckman splattered his leg with liquid from one of the players' drink bottles and stormed back on. Lenny let the matter rest.

*

44

During the half-time break Owen Johnstone spoke softly and calmly to his players who, although they appeared to need some time to themselves, were once again sitting on the benches listening to their coach.

He told them they had performed well in coming back and that as long as they didn't worry too much about the ground they could win. He also spoke about deeefence. In Queenstown it seemed out of place.

Over in the Crows' rooms the blokes were having a smoke and a chat and feeling pretty good about their first half. Small nicks and cuts were being treated by Robyn Faulds, one of two women trainers. Her roundish body was covered in white overalls, a towel surrounded her neck and she carried a bottle of iodine.

As she dabbed the purple liquid around she told me she had been a trainer for the five years the club had existed, missing only two matches in that time. 'Me mother died,' she explained, before adding, 'She coulda done it on a Monday.' I left her laughing at the look on my face.

During the break Sterle stood with me in the corner next to the fire. I wondered if he was being polite or if he was cold. I asked him if any of the players get paid.

'We have done sometimes,' he admitted. 'Twenty dollars a win or so. But not now, only if there's something left at the end of the season.'

But there wasn't much chance of that. 'We spend around $6000 a year just on buses.'

The second half started as the first finished, with a fight. It seemed that Yeoman decided they needed to be a bit more aggressive and Johnno, the Crows stand-in coach, was poleaxed behind the play.

Seeny, barrel chest puffed out and arms pumping, ran as fast as his little legs could carry him towards the action. He was accompanied, among others, by Lathy, the Crows centre half-forward, whose long arms reached into the pack taking swift vengeance. Johnno was groggy but got up and played on.

As the game became more willing and the free kicks became fewer and fewer, Yeoman were lifted by one of their wingmen. With long black sleeves and gloves, combined with bicycle shorts, he looked like a stealth bomber as he raced up and down the ground.

He played a bit like Essendon's Darren Bewick, but unfortunately for him he had a haircut like Billy Idol and the Queeny girls let him have it when he started to get some kicks. 'Give us the name of your hairdresser, sweetie,' was the high-pitched call followed by cackles of amusement from under the umbrellas.

As the cans started to take effect, the boys on the hill became louder and the advice for the umpires was given more frequently. Yeoman were finding out what it was like here in a tight contest. But along with the physical part of the game there was a lot of good footy, it was just that I felt a lot safer where I was.

Yeoman didn't seem too keen to be thrown on the ground and I tended to agree with them. Bill Wedd had told me, 'If you roll when you hit it, it's not bad.' I wasn't so sure.

Johnno's unfortunate accident meant that he wandered around in the forward pocket for a while, leaving the side with no direction. After one of the Yeoman goals a slight disagreement broke out between the Queenstown players in the centre square as they waited for Lenny to restart play. Straightaway the runner raced out and stood at the edge of the square and yelled to the players to shut up. 'How many of youse blokes wants to coach the fuckin' side any-way?' was his direct question.

At the end of the quarter there were only four points in it.

Standing away from the pack at three-quarter time was one of the sporting heroes of the West Coast. At least to this part of it.

David 'Squizzy' Taylor wore ragged jeans, a baseball cap that sat on his dark, permanently smiling head and an old leather jacket. The can of beer that he carried seemed at home in his fist and his hand-shake was like putting your fingers into a clamp.

Squizzy had served his apprenticeship here with the mining company, but had returned to his home town of Zeehan where he had coached a premiership in 1985 with a side that had not won a game in two years. 'All local players,' he told me proudly.

The following two years brought premierships as well, but Squizzy liked the first one best. 'Then we won the thing again in '88 and I came here to Lyell Gormiston in '89.' He coached Lyell Gormy to the flag in each year up till 1993.

'Eight premierships in a row and never took a cent,' he said without a hint of boasting.

'Just honest,' was Squizzy's reply when I asked him his secret. 'West Coasters are just honest.' His teams didn't take any prisoners but there was no sniping. 'Just straight at it mate, straight at it.'

Darell Baldock, who he had met through their mutual love of horses, had told him that it was no use being fit if you didn't have any skills, and if you had no skills then fitness wouldn't help much either. Squizzy said he worked on both those aspects of his players.

Squizzy had also been a champion boxer, winning three Australian titles and eight Tasmanian during a time when he won 82 consecutive fights. In 1976, aged 15, he fought in the Olympic trials, beating a bloke named Robert Dawe for the Australian title. 'They reckoned I was too young to go, so they took him.' He sounded a little bitter as he swayed and slurred his words.

He'd started his boxing career in Roseberry and was beaten in his first three fights, all with the same bloke. Then an old man named Tiger Daniels came to Zeehan and took boys off the street and taught them to fight. Squizzy was one. 'I asked him about his record,' he recalled. 'He told me he'd had 177 fights and never won one of 'em, but shit he was a good teacher.'

Squizzy spends his time these days at Strahan, either cray fishing or in the pub. 'After I finished footy, the piss and the sheilas got me,' he admitted.

But he was happy. 'Mate, when you're on the West Coast, you should be.'

The last quarter was on in earnest as Squizzy headed back to the bar. About 10 minutes into the term Lathy took a mark after pushing his opponent in the back. Free kick.

The ball came back a few minutes later and this time Lathy took the mark legally but belted his opponent behind the ear after he'd done it. Free kick. The same thing happened a couple more times as Lathy became more physical.

The women spectators were furious, screaming at Lenny and Travis, and Bill Wedd was almost convulsing with rage. The blokes around the coaches' box weren't quite as subtle.

Suddenly Lenny paid a free to Lathy right in front of goal about 30 metres out. The crowed applauded wildly. Lenny was congratulated. 'Well done, lettuce head.'

The Crows' confidence soared, not only because Lathy's presence was being felt, but because Yeoman started to run towards the ball, rather than at it. They seemed to be losing the heart for battle even though they were perhaps the more skilful team. Passion was taking the Queeny boys to victory.

In the last few minutes, Queenstown ran away with the game. Doggie kicked one from about five metres up the bike track, Seeny dobbed one from the flank and one of the boys on the hill tumbled down and couldn't make his way up again, much to the delight of the other drinkers.

I felt a bit sorry for Yeoman. There was only a minute to go and the insults were still flying. 'It's a long trip home when you haven't had a go,' was one. 'There's no drinking on the bus, Yeoman,' another.

And a few seconds before the siren, 'Just because it's near the end doesn't mean you shouldn't give 'em one.'

When the siren sounded Queenstown were ahead by six goals. After shaking hands with the gleeful opposition, Yeoman sidled off to the cold showers and the long trip home while Queenstown strode off to the cheers of the spectators. Curtis had the numbers off the board in a flash and headed for his pay as well as somewhere warm to spend it.

In the rooms the players linked arms and, to the tune of 'The Road to Gundagai', sang with unbridled enthusiasm: 'Hear the roar when we score, from Gormiston to Strahan . . .'

The noise was only bettered by the fizz of a hundred cans being opened.

Later that night before the miners went back to work, Sterle stood on a chair and handed out the day's awards to plenty of booing, while Bill Wedd was hard at work behind the bar serving everyone gallons of 'the world's best beer'.

In the corner, leaning against the wall and somewhat the worse for wear, was Squizzy Taylor.

'It's okay this place, ain't it?' he asked me, not wanting an answer. 'You can watch all the footy you like on telly, but this is real, ain't it?'

This chapter is dedicated to the memory of Squizzy Taylor, who sadly passed away three weeks after my visit.

Squizzy had come in from his fishing job to his caravan via the pub and may have knocked over a heater. Fumes overcame him and when passers-by found him it was too late.

Sterle Welling told me that when the cortege passed through Queenstown, people came out of houses and shops to line the streets. Mourners came to the wake from all over the West Coast to pay their respects at the footy club.

'Did eight barrels that night,' Sterle told me.

I thought Squizzy would have liked that.

CHAPTER FOUR

RAIN ALMOST STOPS PLAY

I've always loved Russell Drysdale's painting, *The Cricketers*.
The desolation of the buildings, the colour of the dirt and the interest shown by
the two players and the single spectator were, to me, typical of the way we feel
about cricket.
That's why I went to Tilpa.
To try and find the feeling of another sort of cricket.
Mind you, the trip, like the cricket, was different.

I wasn't cold but I was miserable. I dodged the lightning, or rather the lightning dodged me as I slipped and slid my way along the dirt track. Mud stuck to my shoes, making them hard to lift, and there were no signs of life anywhere.

All I had wanted to do was to see a game of outback cricket and here I was, drenched, desperate and lonely, and stuck in the middle of nowhere.

It was five in the afternoon but as I plodded on, with no idea how I was going to get out of the mess I was in, the heavy, black clouds made it seem like midnight. The trip had started so well and promised so much, but now I started to question its worth.

I blamed Justin McClure. It wasn't his fault, really. After all, I was the one who had driven into the causeway. The crunch as the car hit the loose rocks had startled me and a few hundred metres down the track the petrol gauge tumbled to empty as the car glided to a halt. I stepped out into the gathering gloom, looked around at the isolation and murmured to myself, 'What now?'

Receiving no answer, I gathered my thoughts and set off, hoping to find civilisation. Swearing under my breath occasionally, and at the top of my voice otherwise, I pondered the fact that if I'd never heard of Justin McClure I'd never have been in this situation.

But Justin was the cricket-mad bloke who had enticed me to make the trip to Tilpa. He had given me directions on how to get there. 'Just turn left at Bourke and follow the river for a couple of hours,' he'd laughed.

It wasn't far from the truth. In the far west of New South Wales midway between Wilcannia and Bourke and nestled on the banks of the Darling, Tilpa is nothing if not out of the way.

As the rain pelted onto the top of my head, I stopped for a moment, yelled foolishly at the sky and remembered how different the weather had been a couple of days earlier.

I'd arrived in Tilpa about six o'clock on a blistering Friday summer evening when the temperature was coming down from the mid-forties and breathing in meant another layer of hot dust on my throat.

The road I was now standing on, with small pools forming and rivulets creating small canyons, had been a mixture of dirt, rocks and holes and as I crossed the bridge and drove into Tilpa's dusty street I felt like I'd spent a day holding a pneumatic drill. Justin had told me not to expect too much. He was right.

There are only four buildings in Tilpa. One is an old house that was once a store, another used to be the post office, but after a hundred years it closed a decade ago and is now falling down. Then there is the community centre and, of course, the pub.

The Tilpa pub didn't seem as though it had changed much since it was licensed in 1894. It was corrugated iron mainly, weatherboards at the front, with a small attached residence. There were a couple of rooms, corrugated iron of course, at the side, unsurprisingly unoccupied in summer. It stood close to the site of the old punt that was the only means of crossing the river until the bridge was opened in 1963.

Pubs in the outback are popular places and Tilpa's is no exception. Its popularity not only due to the dryness of the countryside but the fact that it is the only drinking spot for 120 kilometres.

I parked out the front and headed for the door, such as it was. The weatherboards had been cut away and a frame with glass had been put in their place. I wondered how they would lock it but I needn't have; the pub didn't seem to close.

As I wandered in I noticed the walls, corrugated iron again, were almost covered with graffiti. On closer inspection I discovered they were the signatures of people who paid $2 to the Flying Doctor fund for the privilege of scrawling their name on them.

The few drinkers at the bar glanced in my direction, surveyed me, and then went back to more important business. The barmaid, a middle-aged woman with a round, country-mum face, smiled as she looked at me inquiringly.

'A beer,' I gasped, hoping that answered the question she was about to ask. 'Big and cold.'

Lowering the glass and pausing for breath, I asked the bloke standing next to me where the cricket ground was. He stared at me for a few seconds.

'Now why the bloody hell would you want to know that?'

His broad-brimmed hat sat on top of a weatherbeaten face that could have been carved from an old tree stump. His caterpillar-like eyebrows rose slightly as I explained.

'You've come to Tilpa to watch a bloody cricket game?' He shook his head, trying to absorb this revelation before nodding in the direction of the back room. 'Well, the bloke you're after is over there.'

If Justin McClure was a ship he would have been a tanker. Like Warwick Armstrong, captain of Australia in the 1920s, a big ship. His friendly face and fair skin had been reddened by the sun far from any sea. In his mid-thirties, I imagined, with a strong, gnarled right hand that engulfed mine when we shook. He owned Killara, a grazing property and what remained of one of the first great river runs opened up in the 1840s. He introduced me to the man in the hat, Mike Smith, who was friendly enough and prepared to overlook the eccentricities of strangers, as well as to a younger bloke who worked for him, Stewie Maud.

'And this here's Beryl,' said Mike, pointing to the barmaid after Justin had forgotten to introduce her.

'Got here alright then,' Justin said as he asked Beryl for a couple more without looking at either her, me or the others. Then, 'We'll have to wait for a few more blokes to turn up before we go for practice.'

Practice, I thought. They actually practice.

'Yeah, well tomorrow's a big game for us,' said Justin, reading my mind. 'We have to win to make the finals, and we haven't had a hit for a while.'

An hour or so and a few beers later we gave up on any stragglers and wandered across the road to the community centre where there was a half-length practice wicket of artificial turf in a wire-netting enclosure.

Mike Smith had come over to the nets with us, as well as Stewie and a couple of others I hadn't met. 'This here's Andy and that's his brother Luke.' Justin pointed to a roundish, fresh-faced young man whose work trousers were held up by a belt with a huge brass buckle, and who stood next to a clone of his with a hat that could have come straight out of Dallas.

The Farnsworth brothers had shifted to a nearby station with their father a few years previously and had never been sportsmen of any sort until Justin had convinced them to play cricket. They were unlikely looking athletes but were keen enough. Justin told me that they weren't selected for many matches but were always there if needed. Andy reckoned that they didn't have to be in the team to be a part of it.

Luke took off his hat, rested his stubbie inside to keep it out of the sun, and grabbed a ball with a seam split like a clown's mouth. 'Watch this,' he whispered as he walked past me.

Mike buckled on the only serviceable pads that he'd found in the bag lying behind the drum of oil and the two shovels on the back of Justin's ute. After he'd swished around the inside of the net to belt down some of the weeds he settled over his bat. The first ball from Luke sailed right over the top of the net and out into the dusty street. 'Shit!' he said as he stomped off to retrieve it. He returned to try again, with the same result.

It went on like that for a while. A couple got close to the pitch but none actually hit it, and after each ball Luke took his stubbie out of the hat, had a swig and then returned it to safety before heading back to his mark.

In between watching Luke's ball flying over the net, Mike, a left-hander, was batting with some authority while Jake, Stewie and another bloke, Jethro, who had missed us at the pub and had turned up late, bowled at him from about two or three metres past the bowler's stump.

Left-handers have a tendency to look graceful and Mike, who must have been around 40 and was batting in work boots, denim shorts and his hat, was no exception. Some of his drives whistled out of the net along the uneven dirt run-ups, causing the bowlers to jump all over the place for fear of copping one in the ankle. He looked as though, at some stage of his life, he had played a bit.

'Piss off,' said Jethro after one drive nearly got him. 'You've had enough.'

Mike retired to the pub.

Justin had disappeared to the pub as well, allegedly to answer the phone, so from the six that had started practice we were now down to four. Stewie didn't feel like a bowl, or a bat, so Andy put the pads on. Andy was about as good a batsmen as Luke was a bowler, and as hard as Luke tried to get the ball on the pitch, so Andy tried to hit Jethro's bowling.

It was not a sight to strike terror into the hearts of any of Tilpa's opponents. Jethro steaming in, expertly missing all the holes and bumps and bowling thunderbolts, Andy never getting close to hitting any of them and Luke trying in vain to land one on the pitch.

Luke was philosophical. 'Anyway,' he confided to me while taking a swig, 'It's not whether we win or lose, it's about how pissed we get.'

In the distance, as practice continued, a cloud of dust was moving slowly across the vast expanse. Stewie, who was leaning on the side of the net with a stubbie, said to no-one in particular, 'They reckon that Paul's gone off the rails.'

There was silence, and a few more balls bowled, as the others considered this remark.

Jethro, in what must have been his thirtieth over, grunted, 'Tell the stupid prick that if we ever find out where they are,' he stopped as he got to the wicket, clean bowled Andy, and then continued, 'we'll put him back on.'

Paul's dust cloud disappeared over the horizon. Who Paul was or what he'd done was never explained. Nor was how they knew his dust from anyone else's.

Practice continued until Justin's wife, Julie, appeared at the nets to report that the opposition for the next day's game had thought of pulling out as they were scratching for a side.

'Mongrel bastards,' said Luke.

'Bloody wankers,' said Jethro.

'Don't it give you the shits,' said Julie, picking up a ball and, barefoot, bowling it down where it pitched just outside Andy's off stump and took his middle one clean out. 'Don't it just give you the shits.'

'Seeing you do that gives me the shits,' said Luke.

It seemed a fitting end to the practice session, so we all trooped back across the road to the pub.

Cricket has been played in Tilpa since around the turn of the century when locals took part in social games, the first of which was recorded as being played at a nearby station in 1896.

The first inter-town game was against Louth, a small place further along the river, and over the years games were arranged with other towns in the district, all of which were at least a few hours away.

One famous game was against a team from Cultowa, a small place further east, in the early 1950s. Tilpa batted first and were dismissed for the grand total of 9! The captain was a bloke called Ken Plant who, after the innings ended, took his team aside and told them, 'We've got 'em. Now they've got to get 'em.'

Cultowa were all out for six.

These days Tilpa plays in the Cobar and District Cricket Association, a league that has a couple of teams in Cobar, Bourke and various other places scattered around the area.

It may be Outback cricket but, as Justin told me, it has to be played the right way.

*

While we were at practice, a young bloke called Wellsy had turned up to help behind the bar. He was on the small side, but powerfully built and he wore the only earring I saw in Tilpa. He'd never wanted to be a farmer, even though his family had a station, so he worked at the pub.

As Wellsy took my order I asked Stewie what Friday nights were like in the pub.

'Depends what's goin' on around the place,' he answered, 'but usually fairly solid.'

'Solid's bloody right,' said Wellsy with a knowing grin as he went to serve some road contractors who were working in the area.

'Buggered if I know what they think they're doing sometimes,' growled Justin as he looked at the contractors.

Roads are a vital part of life in the Outback, even if they are rough, and the cause of his concern was fairly obvious. The workmen were grading the main roads and bringing in dirt from another area to use as fill. Trouble was their trucks were wrecking the road they were using to collect it, so they were causing more problems while they fixed one.

Justin was called away to the phone again, leaving just me and Stewie. Small and wiry with hair as closely cropped as one of the sheep he occasionally sheared, Stewie came from Melbourne originally, went to Ivanhoe for a while and had been in Tilpa working for Justin, for a couple of years.

'I love it here,' he claimed. 'You're doing somethin' different all the time and I just sorta fitted in. Nobody bothers you as long as you work. It's the first place I've ever felt at home.'

Stewie couldn't see himself ever bothering to go back to the city, although he had contemplated taking a couple of the other young blokes in the area down to Melbourne for a week or so. 'Just to show 'em what they've got here. I reckon they'll be ready to come back in about two days.'

Justin reappeared and confirmed that the game next day against Helmans Tank, a team closer to Cobar, was definitely a goer.

'Shit hot,' declared Stewie. Everyone agreed.

*

It was about midnight and we were sitting out the front of the pub on some old logs when she arrived. We sat facing each other, three blokes either side, and she walked between us. For a minute I thought I was the only one who noticed her. Jethro, who, as a batsman was a fairly good bowler, at least for someone who lived in Tilpa, was still talking about his greatest innings.

'I was last man in and I batted for about 25 overs and got 19,' he told us all proudly.

'Yeah, but what happened then?' asked Julie, who was still around but was toying with the idea of taking the kids home.

Jethro laughed without feeling. 'Snicked one to the keeper, and we lost by three runs.' Then he looked up. 'Ow yer going, Irish?'

'G'day Irish,' was the mournful cry from Stewie, who hadn't bothered to look up as he peered into his stubbie trying to understand why there was none left.

Luke chimed in as well. 'Evenin', Irish.'

I just watched her walk into the bar.

She was not something I expected to see out here—a young, beautiful, unmarried woman from across the sea. She bought her own stubbie and came out to join us.

'This here's Irish,' was the formal introduction.

I asked the obvious question. It turned out she had been in Melbourne on a year's work visa from Ireland when she had met up with a shearer who was on his way to Tilpa, so she asked could she go too.

How could any self-respecting shearer say no?

I asked Irish how she was accepted. I knew the answer, although she added that it wasn't only that she was young 'and I suppose a bit attractive. But it's also a novelty', she said with the lilt in her voice going up on the last words, 'having an Irish person out here.'

We were talking about the contribution that Ireland made towards world music and world peace when her rangy, blond-haired boyfriend made his way over to us. His blue singlet barely hid the little chest hair he possessed but made his shoulders and arms seem all the more powerful.

Irish introduced him as Peter. He wasn't the bloke she had come with and his eyes had that 'keep away' untrusting look in them. I suspected that he had become her boyfriend when she arrived and would cease to be so when the shearing team, or she, moved on. We had a couple of beers together while Irish complained about the pub having no Guinness.

I tried to talk to Peter but he was having none of it. Instead, he stared at me while I did the sensible thing and kept my eyes off Irish. Fairly soon they wandered off into the blackness. Irish still lamenting the fact that there was no Guinness and Peter with other things on his mind.

About three in the morning the crowd in the pub started to thin out. Farmers and shearers jumped in their four-wheel drives and headed home. Some had to drive just a few kilometres, others a lot more.

'They're used to it,' said Wellsy. 'They'll be okay, and when they're buggered they'll pull over for a sleep.'

I'd parked my car on the banks of the river about 500 metres past the pub and I was about to sneak away and throw my swag out when three sets of lights appeared down the track. Soon three utes had pulled up at the front of the pub.

'It's a couple of the Louth blokes,' said Wellsy.

The drivers headed for the bar and ordered stubbies.

'What's the go?' asked Wellsy as he took the tops off the bottles.

'You know what the silly old prick's like,' said one of the Louth men, talking about their local publican. 'The bastard hates it when we look like getting pissed, so we headed here.'

At the time it seemed logical. Louth was, after all, only 120 kilometres away.

I was awake early the next morning, the peace and quiet disturbed by a flock of galahs wheeling and screeching in the sky. As I rolled gingerly out of my swag, they landed in the gum trees that lined the river and perched there, looking down at me in mocking silence.

Through the fog that was my eyes, I watched the muddied water of the Darling drift slowly by as I strolled back to the pub where Beryl, also up early, was cleaning up after the previous night's revelry. As she busied herself with cloths and bins I listened to the weather forecast on the scratchy old radio. The prediction was for rain.

Justin had rung the pub to see if I was still alive and he agreed with the forecast. He also thought it might rain, although not enough to interrupt the cricket match. 'It'll need a couple of inches to stop us playing,' he told me. 'The ground's so bloody thirsty it'll soak up anything less.'

But, nevertheless, he'd sent a fax to a number that faxed back a weather chart showing whatever it is that weather charts show. I remembered thinking that even though Tilpa couldn't reach the world easily, the world could reach Tilpa.

But that was yesterday and now, after walking for what seemed like hours, I had finally made it to the bitumen highway that ran between Wilcannia and Cobar. I stood there, dripping onto the road. I reckoned that I was about 130 kilometres from Tilpa, about 200 from Wilcannia, 220 from Ivanhoe and God knows how many from anywhere else. It was dark now, and silent. Unbelievably silent. The rain had stopped and the breeze, that had been making me hear all kinds of noises in the trees, had dropped.

Suddenly, a couple of wild goats raced out of the scrub, ran around in a circle, stopped at the side of the road, made strange-sounding goat noises and rushed back in. I wondered if that was how my life was to end, struck by lightning and gnawed to death by wild goats.

Then I remembered Beryl telling me the morning before, while she hosed out the toilets and the front of the pub, how valuable the goats were.

Beryl had told me that she was from Wanaaring, a dot on the map about 140 k's nearer the Queensland border, where she and her husband owned a property. She'd come down to Tilpa to help out for a few days while the publicans were away on business. Her hair was tinged with grey and her hands and face reflected the harsh years.

'We've been doing it fairly tough over the past few years, but we'd never want to leave the Outback. It's our way of life.'

She smiled at me as she spoke. In fact I can't remember a time when she wasn't smiling. And, like all farmers' wives, she wasn't afraid to get her hands dirty. 'We can't afford too many workers, so we do what needs to be done, most of the time, by ourselves.'

Beryl and her husband had sons away at university, hoping they would qualify as something or other so they wouldn't have to live on the land. 'The money isn't real good these days,' said Beryl, 'but there's heaps of wild goats around here and if you can catch 'em they're worth a bit. We get a ute load every now and again.'

I watched her while she finished mopping the cracked and broken concrete floor in the bar and collected the empty cans and stubbies laying around in the dirt outside. Then she called to me. 'Come and have a look at this.'

She was standing beside a small grave with a headstone that read: 'In loving memory of our Little Jessie'.

Jessie was the ten-month-old daughter of Arthur and Mary Cotton, who owned the post office (now the pub) during the 1880s. She died in November 1882 and, as presumably there was no consecrated ground, they buried her next to what was the mail receiving door.

I studied the grave for a few moments and then looked up, but Beryl had gone back to work.

Wellsy had risen by this time after what must have been a very long night for him.

'Want to come to the tip?' he asked as he filled the back of his beat-up ute with the rubbish Beryl had collected.

He leant back and kicked open my door from his side. I sat amongst an assortment of old cans, books and other odds and ends that are generally carried around in utes for years. As I tried to brush away the countless flies that had descended upon the ute, I asked him if he'd ever played cricket.

'Nah,' he said. 'It's not bad, but league was my game till I did me knee.'

Wellsy had been quite a player according to some of the blokes. He'd signed with Parramatta in the Sydney competition but had broken down during a regional match and didn't think he'd ever play again. 'I dunno,' he said ruefully. 'It was a bit of a problem when I was playing, what with the travel and all.'

'You're still young enough,' I volunteered.

'Maybe, but I'm happy enough being here.'

On our return, Wellsy parked the ute next to a petrol bowser shaded under the canopy of an ancient coolabah tree just as a four-wheel drive pulled up with Justin, looking slightly the worse for wear, leaning out of the window.

'I've got a meeting for the Catchment Area Committee at nine, then I'll be back,' he called out before pulling his head back inside and driving off, clouds of dust billowing from his tyres.

As I coughed and spluttered, I asked Wellsy what the Catchment Area Committee was.

'Mate,' he told me gravely, 'it's all the main codgers from around here, who talk about what we do with the little bit of water we get. Like from the river and the rain. They're pretty serious.'

As Justin drove away so the mailman from Bourke headed in. 'Bloody roads,' he said, obviously not impressed with the contractors either. 'There's a bloody road train bogged in the bloody bulldust out there.' After passing on wishes of good luck to the cricketers, he had a cool drink and headed off, still concerned with the state of the roads, as a man who drives around 800 kilometres a day has a right to be.

A couple of hours later Justin swung his ute round to the front of the pub and flung open the passenger's side door. 'Hop in,' he called out. 'We've got a couple of hours before the game, so I'll take you for a look 'round Killara.'

About ten minutes out of Tilpa, Justin told me that before the white man came the Aborigines who lived along the river were the Baakandji, feared by other tribes as well as explorers. Local historians say that Tilpa comes from the Baakandji word *thulpa*, meaning floodwaters. I could see why as we drove for miles on the grey mudflats stretching endlessly to the horizon.

The first white man in the Tilpa area was Thomas Mitchell on his journey down the Darling in 1835. Soon after his trip, the lands in the area were opened up to the squatters and the river runs—Killara being one such place.

His large frame occupying more than its share of the cabin, Justin drove with his left hand on the top of the steering wheel while his right arm, with elbow bent, was resting halfway out of the window. Every now and again he would change hands and wave his arm in front of me to point out some item of interest. I asked him how big the property was.

'About 160,000 acres now,' he replied. 'It used to be close to a million, but it was nothing like some of them around here. Momba was two and a half million.'

Owners of properties such as these were encouraged by the government to break up and sell off blocks of their holdings as part of the soldier settlements after the First World War. Those who didn't do so voluntarily had it done for them.

Like most stations, Killara was once almost a self-sufficient town. It had its own store, its own church and school, even its own policeman for a time. And its own graveyard. As we walked around the small fenced-off area resting peacefully under the spreading arms of a peppercorn tree, Justin pointed to a headstone that simply read: 'John Brown, shearer, drowned 21 November 1889'.

In the old store that was still intact, Justin showed me the cellar where he had found some beef jerky that had been there since the store closed. The shelves and counter were still there, as well as some other wooden boxes that, cleaned and varnished, would have brought a good price at a suburban trash 'n' treasure sale. Most of these were nearly hidden under a selection of stuff that farmers leave lying where they last put it.

'Have a look at these stables,' said Justin as we walked towards the skeleton of a once-proud building. 'They had hundreds of horses here up till the '50s.'

Looking round the stables he told me about Mrs Jessie Crowe, born in Tilpa in 1885, who could remember, as a young girl, being fascinated by all the horsebreakers who came to the stations. There were letters, in which she wrote about 'an Englishman, Harry Morant, who was breaking in horses right round the area. My Father and Mr Morant would spend evenings together talking about "back home in

England". He was very much a gentleman and an educated man. You could never convince my parents that there was anything wrong with Harry Morant upon hearing of his shooting in South Africa.'

By now Justin was becoming anxious. It seemed his nerves were getting the better of him.

'We'd better head back,' he said. 'I can't be late for the toss.'

The cricket ground at Tilpa has changed locations over the years, but hasn't changed its look. It is now about 500 metres down the track from the pub with the pitch—artificial turf on concrete in the middle of an expanse of barren ground—baked by the sun.

There are the occasional native grasses and weeds that grow there, but they are soon eaten off by rabbits, emus and the odd grazing kangaroo. The only time the ground sees water is when it rains, and with an annual rainfall of eight inches that is not very often. I asked Justin if he ever needed to mow it.

'We get plenty of burrs sometimes that I have to knock down,' he told me. 'So I drag a couple of old wagon-wheel rims behind the ute and it flattens the ground out a bit as well as fixing up the weeds. It does a pretty good job.'

The boys from Helmans Tank, so named because that was where a bloke called Helman had a water tank years and years ago, turned up with only 10 men but were ready to play and, after winning the toss, invited Tilpa to bat.

Tilpa's team contained a few expatriates who lived in Cobar but still played with the club. These blokes were in the unique position of travelling 120 kilometres further for home matches than they did for away games.

Justin told me that the selected team for the vital match was fairly strong. The Farnsworth boys weren't required, Stewie and Mike had to work, and Jethro wasn't available for the game, so there was no-one in the team, except Justin, from practice the night before.

After a quick talk amongst themselves as to the importance of the match, Justin opened with Peter Brien, the local Telstra man. Local in this area meaning anywhere within 200 kilometres.

*

Umpire Fraser, from Bourke and resplendent in white shirt and black trousers, called play and the game to decide whether Tilpa would participate in the final series was under way.

The openers walked to wicket and took guard. Two vastly differently shaped cricketers but both with white trousers neatly tucked away behind snowy white pads, red Tilpa club hats perched on their heads and determination set on their faces.

They didn't take long to establish their authority, soon bringing up a century partnership. Shortly after, however, Justin was run out for a stylish 44.

After he'd cooled down and had the usual inquest with the rest of the team as to whose fault it was, he came and sat next to me on a fold-up chair.

'We've had the Primary Club here, you know,' he told me. 'Do you know the Primary Club, that you can join if you get a first-ball duck?'

I said that I didn't know they'd visited but, yes, I did know what they were.

An old captain of Tilpa, Peter Luffman, who had the distinction of batting in nine Tilpa matches and scoring 505 runs before he was dismissed, was living in Sydney and in 1983 had organised a Primary Club team to journey to the Outback. The team boasted ex-Test players John Dyson and Peter Toohey as well as the English cricket fanatic and scorer, Bill Frindall.

'We won, what's more,' boasted Justin. 'Got 'em out for 134 and passed 'em with only one wicket down. Not bad, eh? It was prob'ly the heat and the night before, but they took us too lightly I reckon.'

My head was throbbing as I sat in the sun and I tended to think of it being the night before.

Tilpa had lost a couple of quick wickets by now, but were handily placed at 3 for 146. Patrick O'Keefe, the Tilpa number five, was batting with aplomb, but was also in the process of running out two of his partners.

An elegant batsmen, he made 65, which included some handsome drives that bobbled down the ground raising little clouds of dust as they went. He was the subject of much derision when he finally ran himself out as well.

The Helmans Tank bowlers could do nothing right and fielding on the Tilpa ground was hazardous enough without the added burden of being a man short.

As we watched the fieldsman rushing through the dust after the ball had been thumped yet again, Justin and the others were laughing about a person called Michael who had once played for them.

'He wasn't much good, but he was bloody enthusiastic,' recalled Justin. 'One day he's chased a ball to the boundary and dived through the dirt and the burrs to stop a four. There's a big cloud of dust and he's stood up and thrown it behind him over the boundary! They'd already run three so it was the only seven ever at Tilpa.'

All matches in the competition are one-day affairs and after their allocated 50 overs Tilpa had made 6 for 270. Everyone agreed that it should be more than enough.

During the afternoon tea break we feasted on chocolate cakes about a foot high and laden with cream, home-made biscuits and thick sweet tea.

They had worked it out one year, Justin told me. 'The average distance for the players to travel is 100 k's round trip for training and home games, and every other week it's the same for training but about 500 k's for the match. And don't forget that's just the average.' He paused. 'When we play at Nymagee, it's about 700 kilometres.'

Even though I could understand their love of the game, I thought there must be something better to do with their time. I asked Justin what he put it down to.

'It's about a lot of things,' he said quietly. 'I know it sounds funny, but it's for pride in our little place and letting the rest of the world know that they can't forget we're out here.

'And anyway, that's the way it is. It's just what we do.'

Tea was over and the Helmans Tank openers were ready to face up. They were never in the hunt and lost their first three wickets for 15.

Terry Prince, a medium-pacer who made the ball dart around on the artificial turf, and Tommy Tumeth, who was fairly slippery, did the early damage. Peter Brien chipped in later by clean bowling a couple of the middle order. Helmans Tank captain and number three, John Carswell, was the only batsman to trouble the scorers with a polished 56.

During the innings Patrick O'Keefe showed that he was not only a good batsman, he was an even better wicket-keeper. He'd already taken a couple of catches and made a couple of smart stumpings when there was a loud appeal for a third. The square-leg umpire, a member of the batting side of course, was unmoved. 'Not out,' he said firmly. 'Jeez, how could it not be bloody out?' screamed the third man, knowingly. The umpire remained unmoved.

The argument was quite heated for a while but then a voice from the slips called out, 'Let's have another look' and all heads turned toward an imaginary electronic scoreboard, situated somewhere in the mulga trees, waiting for the replay.

The Tilpa players were in a light-hearted mood and could afford to be humorous, but the laughter eased the tension.

Pretty soon the game finished with Helmans Tank being all out for 109. The last wicket fell to the most raucous, enthusiastic appeal ever heard as Patrick O'Keefe stumped the Helmans Tank number 10 from the bowling of Steve Townsend. There were handshakes all round, as well as calls of congratulations and bad luck, and the players sat around, or leant against their utes and drank stubbies while discussing the match in detail.

During the post-mortem I spoke to Terry McCabe, a 56-year-old ex-cropduster who fielded at short leg and, although he dropped a couple of easy catches, also took a couple of blinders. According to Justin, he sort of 'floated around the area'.

Bald except for a couple of strips of white hair that stretched over each ear, Terry was a happy-go-lucky sort of bloke who had lived in the Outback all his life. He told me he would love to get city people out into the bush and show them how great the life was. He was definite about his feelings. 'When the city snoozers think about us, if they ever do,' he told me firmly but not nastily, 'they reckon we must be different. Well, we're not.'

The celebrations continued at the ground until the stubbies ran out, so we adjourned to the pub. The talk for most of the evening centred on how the team needed to practise and look after themselves so they could have a real go at the finals. The night at the pub, with some of the Helmans Tank players and most of the Tilpa boys was, again, solid.

Sunday morning came around and after a recovery barbecue at the pub, the weather started to change. 'I reckon you'd better go,' said Justin. 'We get 50 points and you won't leave for a week.'

My constitution couldn't handle that so I said my goodbyes and drove off ahead of the approaching storm.

The road to Ivanhoe hadn't improved at all during the last two days and the pneumatic drill was again in action. My head wasn't working well enough to notice and it was so full of thoughts I probably wasn't concentrating when I hit the causeway. And the rest, as they say, is history.

So there I was. By now the rain had started again and as I stood in the silence, waiting, I wondered if they'd all get rained in at the pub. I didn't think they'd have enough grog if that happened.

About half an hour later a light appeared in the distance.

As it approached I stood as close as I dared to the middle of the road so the driver could see me. I watched the lights coming closer and closer, and the noise become louder and louder until the car roared by, tyres drumming on the wet bitumen. I watched as the tail-lights and the noise faded and, once again, the silence returned. The desolation then seemed greater than before.

Soon enough another set of lights appeared and this time, although there was still a reluctance to stop, I managed to scrounge a lift towards civilisation.

Around eight o'clock and some 20 kilometres down the highway towards Cobar they dropped me off at a roadside mailbox and I walked towards the house I could see in the distance.

Mick Ryan was the manager of the station and he appeared to be a bit wary as he saw me plodding towards the house.

'You'd better come in,' he said when he saw how I looked.

He found the phone number of the NRMA man in Cobar and I rang.

'Come on,' said Mick. 'We'll go and pull your car back onto the bitumen, cos if it rains any more you'll never get it out.'

We grabbed a couple of ropes and hopped into Mick's old Bedford truck and headed back to my car. As we bumped along in the rain I asked Mick if he'd always lived in the area.

'Nah, I've bin 'round a bit. Bit of shearin', bit of truck drivin'. Bin manager here for about three years now.'

There was silence for a while. Then I asked, 'You get many idiots like me around here?'

His gaze didn't move from the road as he stared out the small, cracked windscreen that was barely being cleared by the almost rubberless wipers.

'No.'

We measured the distance from the highway to the car at about 15 kilometres. 'A fair walk,' Mick smiled smugly.

The rain had nearly stopped by the time we got back to Mick's mailbox, and after leaving me on the side of the road he drove away, promising to tell my rescuers where I was.

It was now nearing 11 o'clock and once again the silence and the darkness were with me.

I woke to a knocking on the window and a torch being shone in my face. 'Ow yer going?' said the voice behind the beam.

I replied that I wasn't going too well.

'You'll be right, mate. We'll hook you up and piss off into Cobar.'

Geoff, the tow-truck driver, was a happy bloke, even allowing for the fact that he'd had a horror night. He'd started at seven o'clock and here he was still going at 2.30 in the morning. The radio in the truck was blaring out Tammy Wynette and Slim Dusty as he organised the towing chains.

'I reckon I'll take to you to the Ampol servo,' nodded Geoff, knowing what to do and who to see. 'Lawrence'll be able to fix you up, I reckon.'

We talked, or rather Geoff talked, for the hour and a half it took to travel to Cobar and when he finally dropped me and the car off just after 4 a.m. I lay on the back seat and tried to sleep. It had been a long night.

Lawrence woke me a couple of hours later while opening the doors to his workshop. He inspected the car on the hoist and found the bent fuel pick-up line. But with the use of a jerry can I bought from him, I could make my way home.

The trip from there was uneventful. I listened to the cricket on the radio for a while. Australia were playing New Zealand in a one-day match and the commentators remarked how wonderful the scene was at the ground and how cricket was so much a part of the Australian way of life.

I smiled to myself and drove on.

CHAPTER FIVE

GETTING IT OFF WITH SHEEP

South Australia was my next stop.
I had met a lot of shearers in my travels and found out that most of them don't
have time for the more traditional sports.
Moving around the country following the sheds sees to that.
They followed sport keenly enough, though, and when it came to actually
playing something, they had a sport of their own.

Sheep, generally, are pretty vacant. Not too many brains amongst the whole lot of them. At least that's what farmers and shearers will tell you.

The bleating mob that were being unloaded from the back of a truck looked to be in that mould. As they trotted up the wooden incline into the holding yards they stopped and started as though they couldn't quite make up their minds which way to go.

'Get in there you dopey bastards.' The tanned and tattooed truck driver leaned on a gate and encouraged the last of the sheep through by resting his foot, as gently as truck drivers can, on its woolly backside.

Peter Hamilton, or Hammo—which was the name he answered to—was one of the organisers of the Keith Sportshear in the south-east of South Australia and, after rubbing his dark, stubbly goatee beard and poking his blue singlet back into his frayed jeans, he shut the gate behind the sheep.

'Go in round there.' He motioned to the corner of the shed as he followed the baa-ing beasts. 'I'll go in this way.'

Inside the shed, in front of the holding pens, and under a large net that was designed to keep birds from flying or depositing excess weight on the competitors, a two-foot-high stage was set up. Four small motors which drove the shearers' handpieces were mounted on a large board that ran across the top of the stage, while four numbered swinging gates flapped between the sheep and the shearers. Next to the drive mechanisms on the top board were small screens that displayed illuminated red numbers.

'They're scoreboards,' Hammo explained as he emerged from the labyrinth of wooden channelling behind the stage. 'The judges press a button for every mistake and the numbers come up there so the people watching can tell how each shearer's goin'.'

The Keith Sportshear was scheduled to start at eight in the morning but Hammo was not confident it would. 'It's like anything,' he growled as he checked his watch that told him there were 10 minutes to go. 'There's always some bastard that can't get 'imself organised.'

After he had busied himself testing the machinery and checking the stage out, Hammo mounted a wooden object shaped like an old-fashioned school desk but built up so the occupant looked down over the assembled masses, and started taking entry money from the shearers who were drifting into the shed.

Twenty-five bucks got you into the competition, gave you a free singlet with Keith Sportshear on the back and also a ticket in the raffle for a new handpiece. A bargain as far as I was concerned.

All around me, lining up at the desk where Hammo sat with pen in hand, rough and ready looking types straight from a Henry Lawson story milled around. They muttered greetings to each other and shook hands with grips like Stillsons before they put down their equipment and, a bit like cricketers inspecting the pitch, jumped up on the boards to have a look at the sheep.

Actually, to the uneducated, they jumped up on the stage, but I knew the stage was really called the boards because Hammo had told me so, and because I knew the words to 'Click Go the Shears'.

All the men wore singlets—the colour and condition of which varied from shearer to shearer—and they all had haircuts that looked like they had run the handpiece over their heads that morning. They were true sheep men.

The only experience I had with sheep, apart from eating legs of lamb, was watching them as they played follow the leader around fallow and stubble paddocks. And I knew a bit less than nothing about shearing. But nearly all the shearers that I had spoken to, and that wasn't many, had assured me there was no more backbreaking work. So I was somewhat bemused by the fact that there were shearers around who actually took their work home with them and used it as a sport as well.

According to Hammo shearing as a sport had been around since the turn of the century. 'Shearers have always had this sort of thing goin'. It's just gettin' a bit more in the public eye these days, that's all.'

Hammo had to shift the truck that had brought the sheep in, so he handed his job over to the president of the club who was also the tallest man in the shed, probably the broadest, and whose thick eyebrows looked like they may form part of the competition.

Craig Rowsell divided his time between talking to me, writing out raffle tickets and taking the entries. In between chats I stood at the front of the holding pens watching the sheep, whose expressionless faces all looked back at me, and listened to the baas.

'We've got a fair bit on terday,' Craig explained when he had a spare minute. 'We've got the speedshear, the quickshear and the one that all of 'em want is the place in the team to represent the state for the Australian title.'

The first event for the day, Craig told me, was to be for the learners. 'That's for them that haven't shorn more than 500 in the sheds.

'After the learners, they go to intermediate, then senior and then on to the open,' he continued as he moved a couple of the wool tables in front of the boards. 'Once you've won an event in one grade you have to move up.'

As the first entrants made their way to the boards the commentator for the day, dressed in jeans and a blue singlet, naturally, and whose luxuriant body hair did not continue above the eyes, tested the microphone. When I asked him how he got the job he replied honestly, 'Cos I'm the bloke that can dribble the most shit.'

Apart from his loquacious talents, Woody was a good bloke, vice-president of the club, popular with all the shearers, a more than adequate shearer himself and, with his glasses bobbing around on his nose as he jumped around, he kept the spectators entertained.

By now Hammo and a couple of others had funnelled two sheep into each of the small holding pens behind the swinging doors where they stood waiting, looking around in blank astonishment.

'Learners get two each,' Woody revealed as we watched the contestants oil their gear and attach it to the long, swinging, tentacle-like arms of the drive shafts. 'Their time starts when they pull 'em out of the pen and finishes when the last one gets pushed through the porthole.'

I'd learned about the porthole too. That was the little hole beside the swinging gate where the sheep were dispatched after they'd been shorn.

By now a dozen or so onlookers had gathered to watch. They sat on planks of wood that were mounted on a steel frame behind a barrier in front of the tables. The barrier was to keep the crowd away from the stage rather than to keep the wild sheep in.

Woody was pleased with the turn-out. 'We'll get a lot more this arvo,' he predicted confidently as he looked around.

By this time Hammo had returned with five blue-coated judges who mounted the platform. But there were only four shearers.

'Yeah,' said Hammo. 'They rotate so that everyone gets the whole range of judges and what one bloke reckons is okay another one might not.'

Fair enough, I reckoned, but what was there to look at when judging shearing a sheep.

'You get judged on time, obviously.' Hammo was being patient with me. 'And you can't nick 'em too much or make second cuts where you have to go back over a bit you've already done.'

Shortly it was all ready and the four learners, a couple of long-haired youngsters, an older farmer who was showing he cared about the sport by joining in, and a shapely young blonde woman, were away.

One of the young shearers had arrived in a pair of football shorts, matching socks and a silky leopardskin top.

'Shit,' exclaimed Woody through the mike. 'It's a bloody shearing competition, not a fashion show.'

The young fellow grinned and took his place on the stand while Woody turned his attention to the more serious business of watching the young woman very carefully. Not, of course, because she was young and attractive but because she was the nearest to where he stood at the end of the stage. Or at least that's what he reckoned. Everyone else thought he was a perv. Woody reckoned he just needed a woman.

'Anyway let's get on with it,' he said dismissing all the derisive comments as he took two paces towards a portable stereo system and pressed a button.

Loud rock music filled the shed and he yelled so I could hear him, 'It keeps everyone in time. Shearing to a beat makes it a lot easier.'

The blonde pushed through the swinging gate and emerged partially dragging and partially pushing a bemused looking sheep that was bigger than she was.

It looked to be a big job for a young woman to shear that sized animal.

'I s'pose,' Woody bellowed over the top of the sound of Creedence Clearwater Revival, 'but they're only crossbreds. They're a bit easier for 'em to handle and the wool comes off a bit better. The learners get them. Everyone else gets merinos.'

My face must have carried an expression similar to the sheep because he motioned towards another mob at the back of the boards. 'They're merinos.'

When I went over to have a look they were all looking stunned. I wasn't sure if it was their usual look or whether they just didn't like John Fogerty.

Two other woman were in the next heat and Hammo told me they were wool handlers who wanted to see what it was like on the other end of the business. 'About 70 per cent of the shedhands now are women,' he estimated as he gave me a quick lesson in what it means to be a roustabout.

I learned that rousties take the wool from the feet of the shearers and throw it onto a wool table. They then trim the sides, which is called skirting, pull off all the stained and dirty wool from the edges, then gather it all up and take it to the wool classers.

Hammo was of the opinion that the women were best at it. 'It's their soft hands. The wool doesn't get damaged and the good stuff doesn't get taken off. Blokes can get a bit rough.'

The blonde won her event easily and, sweating elegantly, she left the boards to wait for her turn in the wool-handling event later. Woody's gaze followed her. I thought I heard him panting but I wasn't sure.

During the second heat of the learners' section, Hammo and Craig handed over their position at the desk to Kate Stiles, the newly appointed secretary of the club. Kate wasn't so much flustered as late for the start, but she soon had her fair hair pinned back and her attractive frame perched behind the desk.

And she was organised. A box for the entries, another for the results and a tin for the money. 'About a bloody day!' she exclaimed when I asked her how long she had been secretary. Apparently the previous incumbent had resigned a couple of days before and Kate, being Kate, took it on. 'I suppose it's about being a part of the place. It's something I thought I should do.'

Kate was born in Keith but had moved around Australia after her father had joined the air force. Twenty-five years later she had returned.

She had a shearer for a partner and admired them as well as loving the country lifestyle. 'I love their teamwork,' she told me as she took another entry. 'I worked in Myers before I came back here and they pay thousands of dollars to teach their staff what these blokes do every day.'

The learners were finished and the young blonde, who was the fastest of the lot and appeared to be odds-on to win the final, had cleaned up all the blokes. It made me realise that Hammo was right when he told me that shearing was about finesse, not about strength.

She had been quick and efficient while the sheep from her opponents had departed through the portholes looking like, well, shorn sheep, with little pieces of red all over their bodies. They stood in the pen bleating. When one head turned they all turned. When one tried to turn around, they all did.

'Have a look at the bastards will ya,' muttered Hammo, shaking his head.

I went back to the desk where Kate was looking around the crowd. 'The big guns are here now,' she informed me.

I'd never known a gun shearer so Kate pointed to a wide back. 'He's the biggest gun of the lot.'

On the back was a blue singlet but, stylishly, this one had red ribbing.

It stretched almost to its limit across the ginger-haired shoulders as the owner turned to meet me. His head was drooped so his eyes were always looking up. His arms looked like the legs of one of the lambs out the back and the shoulders under the singlet about as wide as a sheep is long.

Trevor Bacon held the Australian record for shearing crossbred lambs. He'd done 707 of them in eight hours. I told him that I couldn't count that many in eight hours. He laughed self-consciously.

'I've bin shearing for 18 years now. But I don't do much in the sheds any more, I go instructin'.'

Trev reckoned that things had changed a fair bit in the sheds over the years. That farmers and shearers had learned to get along a bit better.

'Like there was once when we was out in New South and they had a long drop out the back with a dead roo at the bottom,' he remembered, vaguely amused. 'Geez it bloody stunk and every time anyone went for a crap they got crook. But nowadays that sort of thing doesn't happen. They look after us.'

When Trev instructed in the sheds he taught shearers where to stand, where to make their blows and how to best handle sheep. 'The main fault with any shearer is their gear,' he thought. 'They've got to take care of it.'

I'd learned about blows as well. Hammo had told me they were the runs along the sheep with the handpiece. I was becoming an authority!

As I spoke to Trev I had to remind myself this was shearing we were talking about, not cricket or football. Still, it was important to them. 'This *is* our footy and our cricket,' Trev asserted. 'We don't get too much time for that, but we can do this.'

And he said it was important for the shearers to be involved if they wanted to be better at their chosen profession. 'You get into a shed and you'll soon see who the shearers are that go to the competitions. The farmers like it too. They get better sheep that are done quicker.'

Even though Trev was amongst the best there was, he considered he was still a long way from the real top. 'One of my heroes is Dave Fagan, and Jackie Howe of course, but he's a legend more than a hero.'

Dave Fagan was the New Zealand world champion who could shear sheep like combing his hair, and Jackie Howe was the Queenslander gun shearer who, in 1892, sheared 321 sheep in seven and a half hours. With blade shears!

'Sheep were a lot smaller then,' Trev said, 'and a lot less wool. But shit, that's still bloody amazing.'

Trev was under pressure in the event and knew he had the job ahead of him. 'Everyone is here to knock me off, so I'll have to be at my best.'

Craig Rowsell was shearing in the intermediate class. He removed the check shirt he was wearing to reveal a green polo top with an emblem on the pocket declaring that he had been part of the Australian team at the world championships. 'I was in the wool handling,' he explained proudly as I thought he must have been the only man there without a blue singlet. 'I come second.'

Craig had started wool handling about three years previously after, as he put it, 'having a go and finding out I wasn't too bad at it'.

He was a left-handed shearer, something that was unusual in the sheds. 'Bastard of a thing to be,' Woody had told me. 'Everything's on the wrong side. They have to do everything backwards. It makes it awkward for everyone else too when they're shearin' next to ya.'

So Craig had turned to handling and became so good that he ended up in Ireland. 'We're competing in this big shed and there's

5000 people watching.' He shook his head slowly as the memory came back. He was still amazed by it all. It didn't matter that it wasn't a headline sport. 'You know, when you think about it, it's not just shearing, it's representing your country and all that.'

Craig, who restored my faith by taking off his polo shirt to reveal a blue singlet underneath, finished his five sheep in third fastest time in his heat, a long way from making the final. I wondered if he'd ever get further up the ladder. 'Not sure,' he grinned as he shrugged his shoulders.

With that he walked over to a blackboard standing next to Kate's desk and scratched his name in chalk at the bottom of a long list of them. 'That's for the quickshear,' he told me. 'That's the race.'

The quickshear was an event for all comers who compete against the clock. 'All you have to do is get it off,' Craig remarked. I realised he meant the wool.

Near the top of the list was one T. Bacon. 'He'll be bloody hard to beat,' Craig was emphatic, 'but there's a couple around that'll give him a shake-up.'

I couldn't understand why anyone would enter an event that they had no hope of winning.

'Prestige, mate,' Craig smiled. 'And you're only testing yourself out to see how good you are. Doesn't matter about winning it.'

The seniors were about to start and the five bald sheep in the pens had been exchanged for five woolly ones. Woody had dropped the microphone and had changed into his shearing outfit. Although he was in the open event he wanted to be ready early, to get himself psyched up.

As he oiled his handpiece and waited for the seniors to start I asked him about his trousers. 'They're called dungas, mate,' he advised me. 'Special jeans with double fronts.'

I could see why they would need those but I wasn't sure about the shoes, which appeared to be two bits of sheepskin wound around the feet and done up with a bit of leather thonging.

'Sheepskin slippers, comfortable as bugg'ry,' Woody told me. Fairly comfortable, I presumed as he continued. 'In the old days blokes would use scrap bits of the wool packs and stuff some wool inside, but we've gone all modern.'

He reached over to press the button on the stereo, filling the shed with the sound of the Doobie Brothers as the seniors reached up and pulled the cord to start their machines.

It wasn't long before the two heats of the seniors had sheared their way through their five sheep each, and as they left the boards Hammo, who had taken over the mike, announced the starters in the open heats.

There were four heats in the open and Hammo reckoned the standard was high. 'We've got a couple of blokes come down from north of Port Augusta and a few over from Victoria, so us locals'll have to watch out.'

Woody proved that he was more than just a shit dribbler by winning his heat quite easily. On the way he had to contend with some disparaging remarks from Hammo, who had the opportunity to get a few back. Woody's body was covered in hair and Hammo thought he should have a full body wax or a perm. Woody concentrated on the sheep, although I suspected a slight grin, both on him and the merino.

Trevor Bacon got through his five sheep in under five minutes, a feat I thought astonishing.

'Nah,' he remarked. 'Fairly ordinary time.'

He would know, of course, but the wool had rolled off his shears like the peel from a banana. The sheep trotted off his stand proudly, as though they had just left a hairdressing salon.

After he'd poked the last sheep back into the pens, Trev stood next to the gate watching the others as they finished. I wasn't sure whether he was being critical or just getting a closer look, but Hammo set me straight. 'It's just manners. You don't leave the boards till everyone is finished.'

Unusual, I thought, shearers with manners, being polite.

'We do have some social skills y'know,' claimed Hammo as though he had been hurt. 'I know that everyone thinks shearers are all just pissheads and rough bastards, and some are, but not all.'

Hammo ran three shearing teams and was amazed at the way things had changed in the shearing game. He goes to work now with a mobile phone and a briefcase. 'I've got about twenty shearers as well as shedhands to look after. It's all big business.'

And what about the famous shearers unions and the argument about the comb sizes?

'That's all changed too. Not much blueing these days.'

With that he raised the mike and announced a half-hour break for lunch with the finals immediately afterwards, followed by the quickshear.

The first final was the learners and during the lunch break I'd found out that Jo Roper, the blonde, had been following her boyfriend around the sheds working as a roustie and had decided that it was time to have a go at shearing as well. 'We don't get much chance in the sheds to shear so these competitions are good fun.'

Jo took up her position on the boards and, luckily for Woody, she drew the stand nearest the end once more. I wasn't sure that it was just coincidence.

'Trust me, it was,' Woody confided to me as Jo ripped through her allocation of three sheep, 'but I'd rather be shearin' behind her.'

Woody had calmed down a bit by the time Jo had finished her third sheep, and he explained about the extra sheep. 'There's always more for the finals. The others'll do eight and the open'll do ten.'

Jo, blonde hair tied in a ponytail and T-shirt hugging her body, won the final by a convincing margin. She was neat, quick and the sheep weren't cut a lot.

As they changed the sheep around in the pens, I went to see what Kate thought about the equality of it all.

'Fantastic,' she said. 'But it's been like that for a while, really.'

Kate had worked the sheds herself. 'Well, you have to don't you? I mean, things aren't that great on the farms so we all have to help out when we can.'

She was six months pregnant when the shearing started at the farm a few years ago. 'I'd go down and work on the boards and then two weeks after I'd had the baby I went back. I'd do some roustying, make the tea and then sit down on the boards and breast feed.'

She pointed out a woman who was standing near the wool press examining each fleece as it came over. 'That's Stephie Brooker Jones, she'll tell you all about pioneer women in this game.'

In her own words, Stephie was voluptuous. She admitted to being nearly 40 and had been a wool classer for 20-odd years, the first woman in South Australia to be one. When she was 18 Stephie decided she wanted to travel as well as work in something to do with agriculture but in the careers booklet she saw there were not many jobs that suited. 'There were things like governessing which didn't appeal to me, artificial insemination which appealed even less, so it came down to wool classing.' She admitted to it being tough early. 'I mean here I was, the only woman in what had been a male-dominated industry for 100 years or more and I was trying to get accepted. It wasn't easy.'

In those days women weren't allowed in the shearing sheds. Even the farmers' wives didn't venture too close. 'Shearers were supposed to all be rough and uncouth and they couldn't have ladies exposed to that sort of person.'

Stephie laughed when I suggested it was okay now as the woman were all rough and uncouth as well. 'I don't know about that.' A grin split her round warm face. 'We can be a bit like that I suppose but we're really all very ladylike.' Then she added, 'but I've seen some bloody rough ones too.'

Stephie's first outing as a wool classer was in a 10-stand shed north of Port Augusta. 'That was, how should I put it?' Stephie struggled for the right words. 'Let's say I persevered.'

They tested her out a bit. 'But I've never put up with a lot of shit at all, so once they realised that, it was okay. Some realised it quickly, others took a bit longer.'

The sheds have changed a lot since Stephie started in them, but basically there was still the same principle. 'Generally, if you can get the work done then it doesn't matter what you are, you're accepted.'

Now Stephie is a wool buyer. 'I came here a while ago classing, met a shearer and married him.' She laughed out loud. 'Poor bastard's never been the same.'

*

The intermediate final was won by a bloke from Kangaroo Island who, when he was at home, sheared in bare feet. Why, I had no idea. Nor did he. 'Aw, I dunno,' was his answer. 'Bit more comfortable?' He was concerned that, because the officials made him wear shoes, he mightn't do too well. But it didn't affect him at all.

The winner of the senior event had wild hair that sprouted from his head as though it had been electrified. He was from W.A. and his shock of curls and acne-covered face made him look more like a teenage surfer than a shearer.

Bruce Springsteen accompanied him with 'Born to Run'. I was becoming more impressed with Woody's selection of music.

After he had left the boards I caught up with the surfie as he sat in his ute that boasted more lights and more aerials than Cape Canaveral. 'I was in New Zealand shearing before I went to the west. Then I worked me way back and I'm off to New Zealand again as soon as I can get some money together.' Good life. I thought.

Then it was time for the open.

The finalists were Woody, Trevor Bacon, Stephie's husband—the poor bastard Dave Brooker—and long, thin, black-haired Tim Walter.

Hammo was on the mike and the final started to the sounds of Kylie Minogue. I suddenly changed my mind about Woody's music. Halfway through the contest Trevor Bacon led by a whole sheep and at the end he was two ahead, completing the whole thing in around four and a half minutes.

The others battled on but he was simply too good. I reckon the sheep appreciated him too, although he did get a couple of kickers.

One was trying to free himself while being dragged onto the boards but settled down as Trev rolled him over, but the other one leapt around and wouldn't keep still until a couple of forceful movements on the top of his head slowed him down considerably.

Some of the other shearers had got kickers during the day but their response was generally less subtle. 'Bloody kickin' bastard,' was the usual cry, followed by a few thumps to the guts which, more often than not, got the message through. It was never cruel, it was just that sheep generally didn't respond to meaningful discussions with shearers.

'We'll have a bit of a spell then we'll get into the State Reps in both the shearing and the wool handling. Then it'll be the quick-shear,' Hammo announced over the top of Kylie, who was going through the umpteenth rendition of 'Locomotion'.

The qualifiers for the rep spot were the same as for the open final except that Trevor Bacon couldn't compete because he was from across the border in Victoria.

Tim Walter reckoned he could improve his speed a bit when I spoke to him while he was sharpening his handpiece. The small electric grinder he was using threw long orange lines of sparks across the area that was separated from the shed by a canvas tarpaulin hanging from the rafters.

He finished the sharpening job by whipping his combs on a leather razor strop like you saw in the old barbers. 'I reckon with Bacon out of the way I've got a good show,' he said as he felt the smoothness of his blade. 'Anyhow, we'll see.'

Both the wool handling and the State Reps shearing were run together, with the finalists in the wool handling being all women except for Craig Rowsell who went about his work quietly and without fuss. The women seemed to be doing everything a lot quicker but Craig was the more efficient.

The three shearers worked smoothly and calmly to the sounds of Bob Seger's 'Against the Wind'.

After three sheep they were almost level, but after five Dave Brooker had edged ahead by about a good roast leg, I reckoned. Tim was trying his best but the sheep weren't cooperating while Craig waited at their feet for the signal to start his time.

As the wool tumbled off the sheep he cleaned up a bit of the rubbish that fell from the blades. Then, when it was ready, he gathered up the whole fleece in his large hands and flicked it out across the table as though he was throwing a sheet across a bed. The fleece seemed to hang in midair for a second and then it fell gracefully and laid across the table like a cloth.

Quickly, Craig walked around the table skirting the fleece before gathering it up once more and depositing it onto the classing table.

He then had to hurry back to the table and gather all the little bits of skirting up and throw them into boxes before sweeping the floor clean. His time finished when the broom was placed onto the table.

'Not too bad,' Craig acknowledged when I asked what he thought of his effort, 'but I'll have to improve when I get to the Australian titles.'

Meanwhile the gap between the shearers was closing with even Woody making a move. The music was blaring as I watched with Kate.

'Have a look at their feet.' She pointed at the shearing slippers. 'It's like ballroom dancing.'

That threw me a bit but after a couple of minutes I could see what she could see. The shearers' feet went to almost the exact places with each step. Every movement was the same as for the previous sheep. 'I can watch 'em for hours,' Kate admitted. 'Their rhythm gets me, but you don't think about it unless you're a shearer.'

I hadn't.

At the end of the 10 sheep Dave Brooker had won the title in the incredible time of just over 10 minutes and Stephie was suitably proud.

'He's not such a poor bastard after all,' she said, smiling.

Finally it was time for the quickshear. Woody explained the rules to all the watchers. The main one being that the wool had to come off to shed quality, which meant not too many cuts on the sheep and reasonably neat. 'The better you can do it the better for you, the farmer, and the sheep,' he stated.

As Woody was holding the centre stage, Hammo was hanging up a set of traffic lights. 'They're not bloody traffic lights, they're red and greens for this.' He sounded despairing.

It was like weightlifting. Three judges would watch each shearer and then press the appropriate buttons. Two greens and it was okay, two reds and they were out.

The third shearer up on the stand was Trevor Bacon. He brushed through the gate and chose a sheep from the five in the pen. When he brought it back on its hind legs through the gate, the merino stood a good six inches over Trev's head and had wool as thick and curly as Jimi Hendrix.

I thought he was going a bit slow but Hammo explained that in this event they start when they've got the sheep positioned and when they pull into gear. When the big dopey looking merino was plugged firmly between his legs, Trev reached around for the cord to start the machinery.

He was incredible. His hand disappeared under the wool, a small bump travelling along the various parts of the body the only way you could tell what he was up to. Every now and again it emerged to start on another part.

On the mike, Woody was excited. 'Shit, he's up the neck in 10 seconds, he's into the side in 30 and now he's into the long blow in 38 seconds. He's Smokin' Bacon, can you believe it?'

No, I couldn't. But I had to because the sheep was thrust back out of the porthole slightly dizzy, with all his wool gone, and without a cut anywhere. And all this in 42 seconds. I was stunned. It couldn't be that quick.

'Well,' Hammo told me, 'that Dave Fagan does his in about 28.'

I thought that if they had eight green lights, or even 100, Trev would have got them all.

From then on it was a procession of blokes trying to get close. Most of them couldn't get within a bull's roar, or a sheep's bleat as seemed more appropriate.

One good effort was by the solid George Parker, who had won a contest at Crystal Brook a few weeks earlier in 44 seconds. The prize was his weight in beer. They sat him on a seesaw and cartons of beer were stacked on the other end until it tipped up. It took 14 slabs before the seesaw moved.

A couple of places later came Woody. He selected his sheep, dragged it out and then made a plea over the mike, which Hammo had taken off him, for a woman, 'If there's any lovely lady out there who is as desperate as me I'd love to meet 'em. Even if there isn't any desperate ones I'd still like to meet ya.'

'You should be like those New Zealander shearers,' Hammo chided him as he wrested the microphone back. 'They never go without.'

With half the shed laughing out loud, Woody reached over for the cord, but before he pulled it Hammo pressed the stereo into life, and to the tune of Woody's own choice of Donna Summer belting out 'Want Some Hot Love, Baby, This Evening', he started.

Fifty-five seconds from Woody wasn't a bad time in the whole scheme of things, and when Hammo's turn came Trevor Bacon was in the crowd, timing all the main challengers with his own watch.

He needn't have worried. Even Hammo, who some had picked to be the most likely to take the first place, could only manage 51 seconds.

After a while all the shearers had finished. None came anywhere near Woody's time, let alone Hammo's, George's, and Trevor's, but they all had a go.

Later, as the cans came out and the discussions started, I realised the pride they had. I could see there was something totally and brutally honest about them. With others and with themselves.

'This is us, mate,' Craig remarked later as we watched the sheep trot back up the wooden plank to the truck. 'It's only about gettin' better. There's no egos in a shearin' shed.'

CHAPTER SIX

WITH BANJO AT MY KNEE

One of the great loves of Australians is the country's poetry.
Banjo Paterson in particular.
In almost every country pub, or city one for that matter, you will find someone
who can recite some lines.
And in the mountains there are still men living the life that Banjo made
immortal.
I wanted to find out how they felt about the great man so I headed off to the
High Country.

> *There was movement at the station, for the word had passed*
> *around*
> *That the colt from old Regret had got away,*
> *And had joined the wild bush horses—he was worth a thousand*
> *pound,*
> *So all the cracks had gathered to the fray.*

The words of the poem rushed around in my head as I drove towards
Corryong. On either side of the road the mountains rose and fell like
some great velvet ocean, their colours changing from the darkness of
the valleys and gulleys to vivid greens where the sunlight fell. White
clouds whispered their way across an otherwise clear blue sky and
the smoke from an old cabin's chimney meandered slowly to the
heavens.

I pulled over and for a couple of minutes stood and watched an
eagle floating overhead, aided only occasionally by a single flap of its

wings. As I watched it I thought I understood why Banjo loved coming here.

The office I was looking for was in the main street, posters about the weekend's events stuck all over its windows.

Vicki Melrose, a small woman with short dark hair and dressed completely in denim, handed me a brochure which had written boldly on the front, 'The Man From Snowy River Challenge—Where Legends Ride'.

'It's simply the greatest test of horsemanship there is.' Vicki's words left no room for debate as the drover's daughter and I discussed the legend of Jack Riley, who some say the poem was written about, and the horsemen of his time.

After a glance at the program, I set out on foot for Horseman's Hollow, the arena alongside the Corryong Showgrounds where the Challenge was to start, to see if what she told me was true.

Inside the showground camps had been set up by those who had travelled to take part in the Challenge. Billy cans hung from blackened tripods, their contents bubbling above small fires while tethered horses stamped their hooves to signify their impatience and snorted long plumes of hot, white air.

Nearby, men on horseback practised their stops and turns on an expanse of ploughed dirt, while chasing imaginary cattle.

Everyone I could see wore large hats and huge belt buckles, even the kids, and whenever anyone walked, the sound of clanking spurs went with them.

I negotiated my way through the milling equine throng and walked into the front of a tin shed where spectators sat on long slabs of red gum. The rear of the shed served as an office and there, standing behind one of the red-gum logs, with a clipboard and various bits of paper, was Sharon Nankervis. One of the event coordinators, she was a slim, attractive woman with long blonde hair cascading from under a large cowboy hat. As I waited for her to finish chatting to a young rider, I noticed that her hands, as well as her shirt and jeans, were of the working variety, not the designer stuff I had seen earlier.

I asked her about the Challenge.

Sharon's smile was genuine as she paused to reflect. 'Well,' she said, 'I s'pose it's what every horseman dreams of—to be known as the Man From Snowy River. Might sound a bit corny to outsiders, but I reckon they do.'

The Challenge was a series of events which were designed to reflect the work that horseman of the era would have performed in their everyday life. Things such as shoeing a horse, taking a packhorse into the mountains, cracking a stockwhip and riding bareback. Then, after points had been tallied up, the top 10 scorers would enter the final, consisting of two events—catching a wild brumby and buckjumping.

'It'll be starting in a few minutes, so you'd better head over there.' Sharon motioned to the gathering horsemen.

As I walked outside the shed, there, standing calmly while his rider watched others practising in the newly worked dirt, was an enormous pale-coloured horse with a contrasting mane. I asked the man who filled the saddle and whose legs dangled halfway down the horse's flanks, what sort it was.

From somewhere under the huge hat and out of a face that was as tough as the leather he sat in, came the curt reply, 'Palomino', as if to say, 'What're you doing here if you don't know what sort of bloody horse this is?'

I stood back while both horse and rider's eyes watched what was going on around them.

Sharon saw me standing there and came over to tell me that the man was Bill Willoughby, a previous winner of the event. Thankful that I at least knew who he was, I approached him again and asked the horse's name.

'Sir Galahad.'

It seemed fitting for such an animal and I said as much. A hint of a smile crossed Bill's face and he told me Sir Galahad was the horse he'd ridden when he won the Challenge two years ago. 'He was good enough then. Hope it's the same this year.'

Bill came from Booleroo in South Australia, where he'd left his farm in the care of his workers. He'd employed extra staff for the week and, in a bad year, he was paying them with 'stuff I haven't got—money'.

When I asked why he travelled over 1000 kilometres to compete in this event, Bill's faint smile returned. 'Well, I don't take drugs, so I've gotta do something.'

He wasn't about to expand on that so I said I'd see him later. 'I'll be around,' was the reply. He nudged Sir Galahad in the ribs and trotted off. I followed at a safe distance.

Meanwhile, the first part of the Challenge, a check on the horses' fitness and on the gear the riders would use, was going on. There was only one set of gear and one horse that could be used for the three days it took to complete the event, and dress and gear had to be relative to the Man From Snowy River era.

Most of the entrants were approved by the judges, with one or two told to tighten a strap or tuck in a flapping belt.

Soon enough, everyone had received the okay and had assembled ready to start.

The first actual riding event was stock handling, where the horsemen had to pick three head of cattle from a herd, move one of them around an invisible (to me at least) course and then take all three from one point to another. Simple, I thought, nothing to it.

I was leaning on a fence made from rough-hewn logs of odd shapes and sizes that circled the paddock where all this was happening when, in between contestants, Sharon walked her horse over to me.

'Look alright?' she asked.

She laughed when I shook my head and told her that I couldn't really follow it. 'Have a close look at this next bloke,' she said seriously. 'You'll see what he's up to, I reckon.'

Ron Connelly was a mountain man, no mistake. At 65 years of age, most of them spent on a horse, he was as tough as a mountain ash and had a face as solid as a piece of the flintstone that covered the ground.

Sharon was right. Even I could tell that Ron was in charge. He worked silently and efficiently, his sleek, glistening black horse reacting to the slightest touch. The cattle seemed in awe of the man. They moved whenever and wherever he wanted them too. As he took them through a little gate, round an enormous tree and across a small gully I could see what was supposed to be going on.

When he'd finished, a round of applause broke out from the crowd. Ron gave a slight nod of his head in recognition and rode off the course and out of the limelight.

Tall and angular, Ron was also a man of few words. I walked over to where he was standing, rubbed his horse's nose and asked him what the Challenge meant to him. Ron had come second in the event previously and he looked me straight in the eye while wondering whether to answer or not, then he quietly told me, 'It's the greatest event I've ever heard of.' Ron then excused himself and led his horse away so they could be by themselves.

By now Sharon had been joined by another woman whose horse stood quietly alongside the judges as she watched the proceedings. A couple of minutes later Sharon beckoned to me.

'This is Jenny Boardman, she's the real boss,' laughed Sharon as she introduced me to the chief coordinator of the Challenge.

The two women were similar in most aspects, although Jenny was more intense and the hair that fell from beneath her hat was brown. But she, too, was quite obviously a working woman.

'I'm heading out to Nariel to check the set-up for tomorrow,' she told me. 'You can come if you want.'

I hoped she didn't mean by horse.

Nariel was at the foot of the mountains, a short distance out of town. In the car Jenny told me about the Challenge and why people travel from all over the country to enter.

'It's Australia's greatest myth, isn't it?' she asked rhetorically. 'I mean, who wouldn't want to be known as The Man From Snowy River?'

I opened a gate, and as we drove through an avenue of elms that had turned to their autumn coat and stopped at the base of the mountains the talk drifted to the story of Jack Riley.

He was, Jenny told me, a horseman in the area in the early part of the century and one of the mountain's great characters. He had emigrated from Ireland and, after wandering around the country for a few years, he'd got a job with John Pierce up at Tom Groggin and lived in a hut on top of the mountains. He enjoyed his hermit-like existence, but anyone who came past was more than welcome to drop in, especially if they had a bottle of whisky.

Apparently Banjo Paterson had been taken to see Riley by another mountain man, Walter Mitchell, who knew Riley was a bit of a storyteller. Banjo had shared a couple of bottles with him while listening to marvellous stories about the mountains, their horses and their riders. One story was about catching a horse that had run away from a homestead.

'But not everyone thinks that "The Man" is Riley,' Jenny insisted. 'Every district up here has someone who could have been him. It just depends on who you talk to.'

I helped Jenny with some barriers that needed shifting, then we headed back to town.

That evening quite a few of the horsemen had gathered at the local sports club where the scores from the day's events were to be posted. Ron Connelly was well in the lead but he wasn't among the crowd. I suspected he was at home readying himself for the contest tomorrow.

The sun fingered its way through the mist and across the sky around Nariel early the next morning. The peace and tranquillity broken only by the sound of galloping horses and the crack of a stockwhip that echoed through the mountains.

Away from all the others, a short stocky man wearing black jeans, white shirt and wraparound sunglasses rode a brown horse for about 50 metres one way, then he'd turn around and ride him back. This ritual went on for some time and when he eventually stopped for a breather I wandered across.

'Just loosening him up, mate,' Wayne Banney told me.

Wayne was from Queensland and earned a living teaching people about horses and the way their minds worked. 'It's a bit of horse psychology I suppose. Sort of teaching horses and people how to communicate.'

I looked at the horse, but it didn't seem to understand the conversation, so instead I asked Wayne about the Challenge and about
the Man.

Wayne was himself a dedicated horseman who, judging by what
I had already seen, could get horses to do what he wanted without
any fuss. His answer summed him up.

'This is it, mate. This is Australia.'

When I left Wayne he was sitting in the saddle staring straight
ahead while the horse was walking backwards exactly where he was
supposed to. I wondered if anyone had ever tried to fit mirrors to a
horse's head, but the thought passed quickly.

All the entrants had gathered by now and were awaiting instructions
from Jenny, who would split them into groups so the different events
could be run at the same time. As they circled their horses around
her, one bloke who was hanging off his horse and finding it hard to
put on his large, shapeless hat after a hard night, looked across at
one of his mates and said, 'I'll give you the hundred bucks later.'

Neither of the two appeared as though he was among the main
contenders, but as someone had said earlier, 'You just gotta have a
go at it.'

True, I thought. Hard-working and hard-playing mountain men
have to.

But I was intrigued. What was the hundred bucks for. I started to
walk across to ask but the two of them galloped off to start their first
event.

The day's events were a bareback obstacle course, horseshoeing, a
packhorse trial, a cross-country ride and a whip-crack test. Jenny
had sorted them all out and I saw that Ron Connelly was heading for
the whip-cracking venue, so I followed him. He mustn't have wanted
to talk too much, as he galloped off when he spotted me. I let him be
and walked back to where the riders were waiting their turn at the
bareback course.

There, while not watching where I was going, I was almost run
down by a huge black horse. Its rider was dark haired and hatless,

which showed off his solid, square-jawed face that looked vaguely familiar.

'Sorry mate, but you'll have to watch out around here,' apologised The Man From Snowy River. Well, not the real one, but Gerald Egan had done all the riding and was the stand-in for the actor when the movies were made. I asked him about the poem.

'I reckon it's typical of Australians,' he told me. 'It means the underdog has always got a chance and you don't have to be the flashest to be the best.'

Fair enough, I thought, but what about his chances? With that much experience he must have a show.

'I don't know about that. It's like what I said before. But I reckon I'll go okay, won't I, Smoke.' With that he patted his horse's neck and received a long hrrumpff in reply.

I watched Gerald as he walked his horse around the arena. He looked comfortable. Like the others he appeared to be almost a part of the horse.

A small distance away, Wayne Banney was unsaddling his horse ready to start the bareback obstacle course. He was soaking up a bit of sun and nonchalantly chewing on a piece of grass when he heard his name called.

He vaulted onto his horse and went straight into the obstacles. Backwards through a line of poles without touching one, down into a gully and over a log, round a few trees, turn the horse around inside a circle of logs without disturbing any and a big figure of eight at a gallop to finish.

When he came back to retrieve his saddle the grass was gone. I asked if he'd lost it.

'Nah,' he smiled. 'Ate it.'

Over at the packhorse area, which was past the Rotary Club's barbecue and the bar that was selling more beer than soft drinks, Ron Connelly was sitting quietly on Charcoal. After extracting from him that he had 'gone orright' in the whip-crack, I asked him what he thought about the legend of Jack Riley.

Ron had a grazing property at Omeo, on the other side of the mountains, and wasn't that keen to concede that the Man may have been just one person. 'I reckon he's a bit of everyone,' Ron told me firmly. 'I've heard all the versions and I reckon that's the most likely one.'

I watched Ron as he waited his turn. His family had lived in the mountains for generations and the Challenge was just an extension of their everyday lives. Ron was a traditionalist and he scoffed when I asked him if he ever used motorbikes.

'No,' he replied. 'In the high country when you come across logs and creeks you can't take those things through 'em or over 'em without a fair bit of trouble.'

The gear the riders had to pack was laid out on a groundsheet. All the sort of stuff a horseman would have had to take with him for a journey into the mountains. Pots and pans, food, blankets, bags of salt for the cattle as well as a swag to tie on behind.

The riders were doing the event with staggered starts and the bloke with Ron looked flummoxed at the array of gear. 'Jeez,' he exclaimed, 'I didn't take this much gear when I left home.'

Ron went about his work quietly and with no great rush. Everything was packed with method. He placed the pots in the saddlebags just so, the food went in another bag and, after packing the salt, he lifted the saddlebags to test the balance, lest it upset the horse's rhythm.

Then the pack-saddles went onto the horse, there was a quick tightening of the straps and Ron was away, leading the horse behind Charcoal. He went easily through the obstacles, Charcoal picking out the way and the packhorse following dutifully behind. Pretty soon he returned, unpacked the gear again as the rules demanded, and acknowledged the judges, who seemed impressed. Then he remounted Charcoal and headed off to his camp site, the expression on his face never changing.

For most of the day, the sound of stockwhips had filled the air, along with the clanging of hammers on anvils as the horseshoeing continued.

I had watched, or rather heard, the whips from a distance, and when I saw one bloke stand on his horse and flay away with whips in both hands I thought I'd investigate a bit more closely. That, I was told, was the freehand. There were extra points awarded for flair after the riders had completed the compulsory part of the course, where they had to ride at speed and cut bits of paper from stakes with their whips.

One bloke complained when he returned from his round that the whips were only five feet long. 'They should have six-footers,' he whinged. 'I wouldn't've missed anything then.'

To a mountain man, it seemed size did matter.

By mid-afternoon most of the events had finished and the riders were gathering for the cross-country, the most difficult of the day. Earlier I had listened in on a discussion between Bill Willoughby, Ron Connelly and a couple of other horseman who had come to Ron for advice on how to approach the course. Typically, he gave it free and easily. It didn't seem to matter that he was talking to a competitor. To Ron, he was just talking to another mountain man.

After they had finished, Ron and Charcoal trotted off towards the cross-country start, but Bill walked Sir Galahad. I walked beside them.

I wondered what a South Australian thought about the Man From Snowy River.

'I believe that there are Men From Snowy River everywhere.' Bill didn't mince his words. 'Maybe they don't have mountains and maybe they haven't had a poem written about 'em, but they're still there.'

Sir Galahad broke into a canter and I ran along beside them. I was breathing rather rapidly when I asked if he thought the Challenge was important.

'Hell yeah,' was Bill's reply as he clucked his tongue and Sir Galahad trotted off.

I puffed and panted as I watched them go.

'Well, what d'ya reckon?' asked Jenny Boardman as I leant on her horse and looked up the mountain at the cross-country course. Not all of it was visible from where we stood, but what there was of it looked difficult. I told Jenny that I reckoned I was staying where I was.

The riders had to head up the mountain while jumping logs and fences, crossing creeks and ditches, and then ride back down. It was just over two kilometres that had to be ridden in about seven minutes.

I watched Ron walk Charcoal up the track, followed by Gerald Egan and Smoke. As they broke into a trot, standing there amongst the trees and the horsemen, I imagined both Ron and Gerald riding with Clancy and Harrison a hundred years ago.

But the man from Snowy River let the pony have his head,
*   And he swung his stockwhip round and gave a cheer,*
And he raced him down the mountain like a torrent down its bed
*   While the others stood and watched in very fear.*

He sent the flintstones flying, but the pony kept his feet,
*   He cleared the fallen timber in his stride,*
And the man from Snowy River never shifted in his seat—
*   It was grand to see that mountain horseman ride.*

I could feel it, whatever it was, all around me as I watched the riders disappear into the mountain scrub.

'Gets to you, doesn't it?' The observant voice came from behind me. It was Sharon who had come back to check the riders on their return. 'We've been here all our lives and it still gets to us.'

After all the riders had returned and the shadows of the mountains lengthened, we drove back to town to see who had made the final.

As the riders drifted off, the two betting blokes were at it again.

'Double or nothing,' was the call.

'Nah. It's too bloody cold and it'll drop off if I do it again,' came the shy reply.

'Geez, one bloody lap for two hundred—weak as piss.' The bloke obviously thought he was a sure thing.

But the other party was not too keen. 'Anyway, I'm not drinkin' tonight.'

'Yeah, mate, okay,' sneered the punter.

*

That night I strolled along the main street of Corryong to a vacant area that was known as 'Banjo's Block', where yarn spinners and blokes who could recite the poem had gathered.

A small crowd of people sat, warm and content, around a blazing fire. I stared into the coals and watched the sparks as they jumped into the night, illuminating the space around them until they faded and dropped back to the earth, invisible and cold.

I sat there for an hour or more, amongst the mountain people and those who wished they were, listening to the passion in the voices.

Later, I met a wonderful lady named Elynne Mitchell, author of the Silver Brumby books, who was to present an award at a local art show. Her husband, Tom, is credited with being the person who first named Jack Riley as the supposed Man From Snowy River.

She sat, her aged and gentle hands clasped and resting on the top of her walking stick in front of her, and patiently talked to me. Her lined but wise face moved softly as she told me about her father-in-law, Walter Mitchell, taking Banjo Paterson to meet Jack Riley.

'They went out from Bringabrong to Tom Groggin,' she remembered, 'and took a couple of bottles of whisky with them. They went out a couple of times, I think, so Banjo could listen to the stories Jack could tell.'

I asked whether she believed that Riley was the Man. 'No,' she said firmly, her face set. 'The Man was a composite figure, taken from everywhere, including Jack Riley.' According to Elynne, there is a letter somewhere from Banjo to her husband that explains how he came to write the poem.

What was he like, Banjo Paterson, I wondered.

'A small man with a face like a walnut.'

That night I slept with all manner of visions.

The final events were to be held back at Horseman's Hollow and as I arrived I noticed a number of what I assumed were wild brumbies pacing around in a steel corral.

I was surprised to see how small they were. Much smaller than a normal horse, with hairy faces and dull coats. I'd obviously learned quite a bit the previous night as I found myself leaning on the bars of the yard quietly talking to one brumby as I watched him circle and paw the dust.

> *He was hard and tough and wiry, just the sort that won't say die—*
>   *There was courage in his quick impatient tread;*
> *And he bore the badge of gameness in his bright and fiery eye,*
>   *And the proud and lofty carriage of his head.*

'What're you doin'? Talking to yourself?'

It was Sharon sneaking up behind me again. She'd come over to warn me not to get too close or the brumbies might charge. I was a bit startled to be caught thinking out loud.

Sharon smiled at me. 'Anyhow, come over here. I want you to meet someone.'

I had to wait a few minutes for the introduction as the man in the wheelchair, who was in charge of the brumby catch and buckjump, issued instructions to the blokes bolting the yard together.

Jim Pierce, grandson of John, was in a car accident a few years ago and had been in a wheelchair ever since. He told me it happened two days before Christmas, before adding without a touch of self-pity, 'Happy Christmas.'

As he pushed his wheels around and struggled his way through the dust, Jim acknowledged that it wasn't much fun being in a chair, but it made him see things a bit more clearly and gave him more time to devote to running things like these. His family had been in the high country for generations and his grandmother was taught to ride by Jack Riley.

'She reckoned he was the Man, but I'm not so sure,' Jim reflected. 'Have a look around at these blokes and remember that every second bloke was like them in those days.'

As expected the 10 finalists included, in the top four spots, Ron Connelly, Bill Willoughby, Wayne Banney and Gerald Egan. As they waited to be introduced to the crowd, the sounds of the theme from *Bonanza* blared from the loudspeakers.

'Geez, what the hell is that supposed to be?' muttered Bill Willoughby. 'We in bloody America now?'

The finalists sat on their horses and shook their heads, almost in unison.

The music soon stopped and I asked Jim Pierce what was going to make the difference in the final.

'Luck of the draw, to a certain extent,' he told me. 'Depends on the nature of the brumby you get.'

The brumbies were all tagged with a number and then drawn against the number of the contestant. The riders had to catch the brumby with a rope, slip on a halter and take off the catching rope, before leading them out of the yard through a gate.

Gerald Egan drew a brute. Although small in stature the thing just wouldn't be roped. Gerald rode around and around trying to drop his rope over the brumby's neck. Clouds of dust rose as the brumby ducked and weaved while Gerald and Smoke ducked and weaved after him. Eventually the rope dropped over his neck, but he struggled against it and Gerald battled to make him lead. Time was almost up as the brumby eventually settled down and was led out by a somewhat frustrated horseman.

Wayne Banney had similar luck and fared only marginally better than Gerald Egan, but Bill Willoughby's brumby was not too bad. Bill caught him quickly using a lasso which he flicked over the brumby's head from about six or seven metres. The only problem Bill had was that the brumby wouldn't go through the gate easily.

Then it was Ron Connelly's turn. The brumby he drew was placid, or that was how it appeared. I thought it may have realised Ron was going to beat it anyway and was resigned to its fate.

Ron circled the yard a couple of times sizing up his foe and then dropped his rope over the its neck without any fuss. He slipped the halter on in a trice and loosened the catching rope so the brumby walked straight out of it. It was remarkable. Ron, as ever, was in total control. His touch was light and the brumby trotted along next to Charcoal as if hypnotised. Perhaps he was. Ron, I reckoned, could do that to horses.

After letting the brumby loose in the holding pen, Ron was sitting quietly astride Charcoal as I approached, gathering his thoughts and waiting for the last event.

I thought better of disturbing him. He was, after all, a man of action not words. His quiet, determined strength was obvious. The brumbies had no chance.

And he ran them single-handed till their sides were white with
  foam;
    He followed like a bloodhound on their track,
Till they halted, cowed and beaten; then he turned their heads
  for home,
    And alone and unassisted brought them back.

Bill Willoughby's ride on the buckjumper was excellent. His father had been an all-Australian champion rodeo rider quite a few times and Bill had inherited his talent while adding some of his own.

He'd told me earlier that to ride a bucking horse was what every rider aspired to.

'Nearly every horse person I've known, whether they be jockey or show rider, that's what they've wanted to do. Ride a horse that bucks.'

Gerald Egan and Wayne Banney also rode well but when Ron Connelly's name was called the crowd fell silent. Even the competitors seemed to be riding with him. Ron had done a bit of rodeo riding in his younger days but now he faced his biggest test. Would his age be a barrier? Could he keep up with the younger blokes? As far as points went, it seemed that all he had to do was stay on and he'd win.

The gate swung open and the buckjumper with Ron aboard flew out and across the yard. The dust swirled and the crowd roared as Ron held on grimly. He didn't need to wave his hat and scream 'Yehah' to show everyone he was in charge. As a matter of fact all I could see through the dust was a horse and a figure on it with a face set so firm and determined I thought the horse could have bucked all the way to China and Ron would have still been there glued to his back. He didn't crack his whip. He didn't use his spurs. And he didn't get thrown. When he came back to the yard he walked over to where Charcoal was tied, rubbed him on the nose and told him softly, 'I reckon we might've done it.'

At the presentation Ron thanked everyone quietly and genuinely. There was, I suspected, a flicker of a smile and he certainly spoke for longer than he normally would. I started to walk towards him but then realised that I didn't need him to tell me what I already knew.

I drove out of Corryong the way I had come. With Banjo Paterson for company.

I pulled over at the spot I had stopped at on the way in and looked around once more at the mountains.

> *And down by Kosciusko, where the pine-clad ridges raise*
> > *Their torn and rugged battlements on high,*
> *Where the air is clear as crystal, and the white stars fairly blaze*
> > *At midnight in the cold and frosty sky,*
> *And where around the Overflow the reed-beds sweep and sway*
> > *To the breezes, and the rolling plains are wide,*
> *The Man From Snowy River is a household word today,*
> > *And the stockmen tell the story of his ride.*

CHAPTER SEVEN

HORSEMEN OF THE APOLOCROSSE

In the Outback there isn't much time for sport.
No grounds, too much work to do, too far to get to anywhere.
And yet when there is time they make it worthwhile.
When I was told about people in Western Australia who played
polocrosse in the middle of nowhere and who travelled thousands of kilometres
to play, I bought a plane ticket to Perth.

It was a 10-hour drive from Perth to the Murchison and when we arrived there was nothing there. Well, almost nothing. Hiding behind some overgrown wattles and melaleuca bushes were the shire offices, a couple of houses and three oblong expanses of ochre-coloured dirt that served as three polocrosse grounds.

And then there was the Murchison Roadhouse—an oblong, fibro building with a flat tin roof and small flywire windows protected by shadecloth. Decorating the walls by hanging on randomly bashed-in nails were a selection of ancient crosscut saws, rabbit traps and other rusting paraphernalia.

The frontier-style verandah, that began where the red dirt finished, was held up by poles cut from the branches of old twisted gum trees. A sign on the almost derelict petrol bowser stated simply, 'No credit cards—no cheques'.

At the rear of the roadhouse, in between a small square of grass that struggled for life and one of the polocrosse fields, was a rickety tin shed.

Like most sheds it was full of stuff, some useful, some useless. The stuff that didn't fit or wasn't quite up to being put in the shed was scattered around the yard. A young emu, wearing a perpetual look of surprise, strutted around alternately sticking his long neck into the stuff or pecking at the ground.

We drove down the track at the side of the roadhouse towards a clearing in the trees. As Bev Hammerton parked the car I asked what time it was.

'Beer o'clock,' she replied, stretching as she removed her tired body from the car.

Bev was the secretary of the Western Australian Polocrosse Association. Dark haired, olive skinned and with a motor that ran at full throttle the whole time, Bev told me earlier that she'd never played polocrosse or, for that matter, ever ridden a horse.

'I took the job because my two sons played and they gave me something to do because I was always there, hanging around,' she had explained as we waited at the Perth airport for the members of a touring English team who were to travel up to Murchison with us.

It was not an auspicious start to the trip. The plane carrying the English team landed at the international terminal instead of the domestic area, where we were looking. I suppose it was a bit presumptuous on our part to think a plane from Sydney would land at the domestic terminal. And beside that, the terminals were 12 kilometres apart.

When we arrived at the correct place, the hire bus that Bev ordered had been replaced with a smaller one and the gear the English people brought with them—and did they bring some gear!—wouldn't fit in.

A mechanic was called to remove the back seat for space and to his annoyance, just as he was finishing the job, a bigger bus arrived. The luggage, saddles, whips, spurs, polocrosse racquets and other various odds and ends were soon packed away, with the stuff that was left over thrown on the back of a ute or pushed into the cars that were making the trip as well.

Eventually the convoy—a four-wheel drive, a car, a ute, a truck carrying horses and the bus—headed for a small place near Geraldton called Walkaway, where the Polocrosse Association's state president had a farm, and where we would camp the night.

John Marriott had been involved with polocrosse most of his life. The walls of his house were almost covered with photos of him and his wife Pearl's exploits. Not to mention those of his children Jane and Sarah. John ran his farm and bred horses specifically for polocrosse but also drove grain trucks for a bit of extra money.

'This isn't a rich man's sport you know,' John explained smiling, as we stood on the track at the front of the house, where the fence-posts were half-hidden by the weeds that had flourished in the recent rains and where a couple of strands of fence wire were missing.

Walkaway acquired its name either from the Aboriginal word, *wagga wah* meaning break in the hills, or from a story about a farmer named William Cousins who planted wheat here in 1852. When the crop didn't grow he returned to Perth, disillusioned. John continued the story: 'Apparently, the next year another bloke turned up and there's this great crop. The new arrival asked the local Aborigines who planted it. They replied, "him walkaway".'

We both preferred the latter version.

That night about 30 of us dined around a blazing fire on soup and casseroles, washed down with plenty of wine, beer and polo-crosse stories, amongst the dirt and old timber in John and Pearl's stone shed, built in the 1850s.

We were off early the next morning, bound for Mullewa, a small town on the edge of the Murchison, before the last 250 kilometres took us along a dirt road where the wildflowers were just breaking from the prisons of their buds. Soon there would be a mass escape and a carpet of whites and mauves would cover the floor of the bush.

As we rattled over one of the numerous cattle grids on the track, a grey kangaroo bounded alongside the car, contemplating a quick crossing. He thought better of it, however, and wheeled away to join his companions who stood upright, ears pricked and faces set, almost waiting for the collision.

A short distance later the track eased its way over a slight sandhill. Before us the extended road narrowed into nothing while the sky seemed to sit gently on the land like a blue and white lid.

The locals had organised a large tent for the poms, as they had been christened without the slightest hint of rancour, and had started to put it up. It took shape gradually while everyone in the group stood around and watched.

Lizzie, a friend of Bev's who had been sampling a few bottles of wine she had brought with her, leant against her four-wheel drive and scrutinised the scene. A physiotherapist, she was impressed by the men's lack of exertion as they held up the poles.

'That's a great erection,' she told them in between sips.

'Wait till you see it in action,' was the reply.

The tent immediately fell down.

Meanwhile, Alan Crooks, a rangy farmer whose jeans flapped around the top of his boots and whose slicked-down hair was never out of place, had unloaded the horses and led them to a holding yard. He had come to Murchison with three other members of the Kojanup club not only to play, but to help the poms out and give them something to ride. As scattered applause marked the final erection of the tent, he threw a tarpaulin down in the back of the truck and placed a line of swags where the horses had stood.

'Mightn't be the Ritz, but it'll be comfortable.'

Alan was older than everyone else and his quiet nature a pause in the continuing bustle of the day. He was the steadying influence on some of the more playful.

'We came up here once with no horses,' he told me, 'just 20 people in the back of the truck. They had a few big Eskies and were playing cricket of a sort. But some bastard kept hitting the ball between the boards on the side.'

He laughed as he went on. 'I was stopping every couple of miles so they could get it back, but they stopped doin' it when I started to pull up a bit quick.'

On the ground behind us, a couple of the poms, two young women Ruth and Penny, had saddled their borrowed horses and

Ferrets are brought from near and far to try and win the prestigious Geelong Ferret Racing Cup.

The Ferret Racing Office is the sophisticated nerve centre of the races.

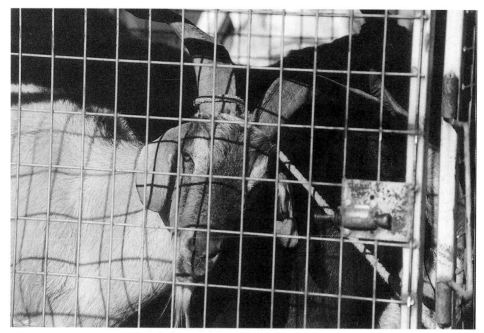

'Don't look at me like that, I'll
get out of here soon, y'know.'

Goats are not always enthusiastic about
racing and need to be encouraged all
the way up Morilla Street.

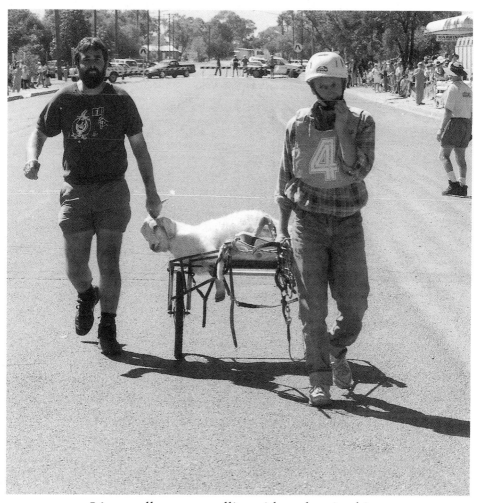

It's usually goats pulling riders, but in this case the goat refused—so what was left?

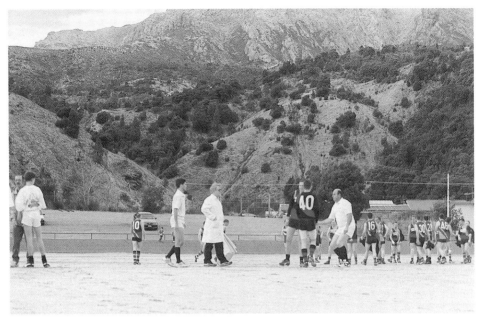

All involved leave footprints in the gravel while the bleak, bare mountains look silently down on proceedings.

Boundary umpires don't take a great deal of interest in fights at Queeny. Goal umpires occasionally wander over.

The pub is the centre for nearly everything that goes on in Tilpa, and is the almost-official home of the cricket club.

Not much room at the holding pen, but one sheep keeps an eye out for those characters who want to give it a haircut.

The results of all that shearing laid bare.

Shearers hard at work on the boards
while the judges and handlers stand by.

But the Man From Snowy River let the pony have his head, and he swung his stock-whip round and gave a cheer.

It's not easy to get a fully packed stock horse to follow you through obstacles.

Both horse and rider seem almost part of each other as they celebrate the conquest of another obstacle.

All eyes on the opposition except one, who is concentrating firmly on supporting his rider.

Polocrosse horses need to respond to anything their riders may do, even if it means leaning over and turning in six inches of dirt.

Modern line marking technology hasn't quite reached the Murchison.

The greens are called blacks in Coober Pedy, for obvious reasons.
Perhaps they should also have renamed the 'fair' ways.

You can find your way around easily in Coober Pedy,
everything is well sign-posted.

It's not easy to keep in step when your feet are hanging out of the bottom of the boat.

Dig those paddles in and don't worry if you throw a bit behind you.

The crew of the *Nauteus* takes to the river to prepare for its battle against other pirate ships.

If you are ever travelling near Eulo you'll be in
no doubt as to where the lizards race.

Sometimes, the lizards prefer to stand and look at the crowd
instead of listening to the 'Clerk of the Course' and racing.

Midafternoon and the Birdsville Hotel is a popular place to be.

Horses sweep into the straight and the dust cloud sweeps round after them.

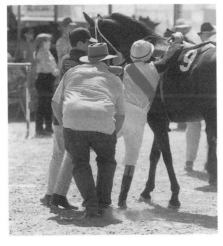

'If you're going to help me, just make sure you don't heave too hard.'

The Murrindindi Gift has not been around as long as
the pedestal that will, hopefully, support the winners.

The mountains watch as the runners
sprint a long way uphill to the finish.

Technique is everything in competitive rabbit skinning.

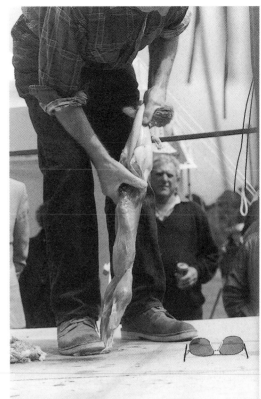

Skins must be pegged out correctly and hung in the right places.

The boxing tent stands proudly in the dirt.

The corner chair is ready and waiting for some brave challenger.

The boys are keen to take on all comers as Fred and his family look down on them with pride.

were trying them out. The horses ploughed through the dirt like equine battleships, stopping and turning in a stride, ducking their bodies and twisting around in spaces shorter than their length.

Ruth, short, fair haired and stocky, carried a ball in a net on the end of a stick and flicked it to Penny, who was shorter both in hair and size, who would catch it and ride around before flicking it back.

'It's better than polo,' Alan observed as we watched them. 'Four of these grounds fit into one of theirs. And they just hit the ball and chase after it. Here you've got limited space and you've got to pass it around.'

I wondered how many horses they were allowed as polo players seemed to have them laid on. 'They can use as many as they can afford.' It wasn't a sneer, Alan wasn't that sort of bloke. 'But with us it's one horse for one game.'

Ruth and Penny finished their practice and as they thundered to a halt declared themselves satisfied. 'They are a bit different to the horses we've used so far on the trip,' explained Ruth, 'but I'm sure we'll be okay.'

The English party had nine players, five women and four men, who had come to Australia for the experience. 'Ours is only a newish sport at home, so any knowledge we can gain will be helpful,' said Ruth.

Penny, meanwhile, was trying to grasp the enormity of where she was. 'We've come from England to the tropics of Queensland and then the hills just outside Sydney, and now this,' she said as she gazed across the bright red dirt.

Penny had been given the name Half Penny as she was smaller than another Penny who was also in the squad. At the start I'm not sure she appreciated it.

'Don't worry,' Alan reassured her as he went off to rug his horses for the night. 'You get a nickname out here and you've made it.'

Ruth and Half Penny returned to the tent. The others had lit a camp fire and, filtering through the branches of the bushes, the light from a hundred others danced on the faces of the poms, illuminating their amazement.

I wandered over to join the gathering numbers at the clubhouse where they were beginning to sample the legendary Murchison hospitality.

The Murchison Polocrosse clubhouse was a concrete brick building with a kitchen at one end and a bar at the other. Large tilting metal doors opened on one side where spectators could eat, drink or simply watch the game on the main ground. Behind the bar, three big fridges waited in anticipation, condensation dripping its way down their glass doors. I asked what I could have.

The barman's faded checked shirt couldn't quite manage to stay tucked into his dirty moleskins.

'Mate,' his hands were busy tucking things in, 'you can have a blue stubbie, a red stubbie or a yellow stubbie, and for only $2.'

I placed my money into the callused, grained hand that was extended, while the other kept tucking, and chose a blue one.

On the bottom shelf of one of the fridges lay a few lonely cans of soft drink and in the sink nearby sat a large yellow plastic drum into which bottles of rum had been poured. A long, snaking plastic tube transferred the liquid from the container to a sheep drenching gun.

For $3 you received a can of Coke that was opened and a small amount tipped out, replaced by three long pulls from the drench gun. It seemed good value.

'We ran out of rum a couple of years ago,' the barman remembered, laughing to himself as he drenched another can of Coke, 'Then one bloke staggered up and wanted to know what we were goin' to do about it.

'Well, it was late and we'd all had a bit,' he continued in the understatement of the century, 'so we whacked a pourer onto a bottle of Handy Andy that we found under the sink.'

He was grinning like a shot fox. 'Buggered if I know how he didn't cark it.' Then he added, almost solemnly, 'But you get a good profit out of that stuff.'

I promised myself not to trust these blokes as I took my beer and sat on a vacant seat next to a dark-haired, well-dressed man sitting alone outside the clubrooms.

Kim Keogh was president of the Murchison Shire and he told me that the area, about 300 kilometres inland from Geraldton, is called the Murchison after the river that flows through it. There is no town, just some 28 stations up to a million acres in size. 'We're the largest shire in Australia without a town,' Kim informed me, 'about 90,000 square kilometres with 180 people.'

As well as that there are nearly 2000 kilometres of roads in the Murchison with only a kilometre of it bitumen, half of which is either side of the one bridge that crosses the river.

Kim owned Byro, a station 100 kilometres to the north that was first settled in 1874 and which his family had been involved in since 1919, when his grandfather was appointed manager.

'He'd ridden a pushbike, with all his belongings, from Perth to take a job as a jackaroo.' Kim sounded amazed. He'd obviously known the story for years, but it still astonished him. 'No roads around here then, only tracks through the scrub. Hard to imagine, isn't it?'

I tried to, but couldn't. Instead we sat in silence, watching the shadows of evening as they slid over the earth and the sky's last pink stripe of colour turned to black.

The tournament was scheduled to start at around eight o'clock. Around, not precisely, as the good fellowship of the previous night meant that a few players considered sleep to be more important than punctuality.

Anthony Fellowes stood near the office. The wispy moustache that covered his top lip and almost hid the gap where a tooth had been missing for some time bristled with anger. The main organiser of the tournament, he ran a thin hand over the forehead that was becoming more prominent each year as the hair receded.

'Listen up, will ya,' he barked into the microphone, 'we've put the first game back to nine, so let's get going, don't stuff around.'

'That should fix 'em,' he grinned as he threw a couple of empty bottles in a large wire cage outside the rooms to join about a thousand others. 'Better go to the tip soon,' he mumbled to himself.

Anthony and his wife Anthea managed Meka, a million-acre station 130 kilometres away, but he had travelled a lot further. 'After the rain the river was too swollen for us to get through, so we came around the other way.' Around the other way meant that when he was within 30 k's of his destination he had to travel a further 400. It didn't seem to worry him greatly, 'Yeah, well, that's living out here for you.'

I wasn't surprised at his lack of concern about distance when he told me that he had 138 windmills on his property that needed checking every week. Apparently if sheep don't have water for three days or more, they die. So with some 33,000 of them to worry about, water was a priority. 'I check 'em all by plane once a week and then send a bloke round in a ute the next,' Anthony told me, 'and then I do 'em again. It goes on like that all year.'

And that wasn't the only big job. Mustering and shearing at Meka takes five months. 'I know when I go out on the first day of mustering in the middle of summer, that when I finish that one job it'll be the middle of winter.'

Anthony busied himself organising scorecards and whistles while I stood and tried to absorb what he'd told me.

Polocrosse was developed in Australia during the 1930s when horse lovers Marjorie and Edward Hirst brought an idea back from an indoor equine training school in England. They had watched riders learn control of horses by carrying a ball at full gallop from one end of the arena to the other and dunk it into what looked like an elongated basketball net.

They adapted the idea, as an amalgam of polo and lacrosse, to an open field divided into three sections with restrictions on where players can enter. Anthony, who had joined me in front of the clubhouse, reckoned that the game was as much about how smart the horses were as well as the riders. I tended to agree after seeing the horses stop and turn without so much as a tug from their riders.

'The players are still in charge, don't you worry,' he laughed. 'But they do need a good horse.'

Polocrosse in the station country, as it is everywhere else, is a family sport. Most of the lower grades were made up of the sons and daughters of the better players.

All teams, or at least the majority of them, were mixed. 'If a woman can ride well, she can generally play well,' conceded Anthony. 'It doesn't really make any difference at this level.'

As we watched the game in progress he pointed out a few rules, not that I could understand them. The only one that I thought I could see was that the sticks with their small nets on the end could only be used on one side of the body and that you could knock the ball out of the other player's net with controlled hitting if you were good enough.

I wondered what would happen if accuracy was a problem. 'Well you cop one in the ribs or the hand.' Anthony was straightforward. 'Or the mouth.'

The opening game in A grade was between Irwin, a team from near the coast about six hours away, and Walkaway. After the second of the six chukkas that make up a game, Walkaway were three goals behind and didn't look like making up the leeway. By the end the deficit had doubled.

'Good side, that Irwin.' Anthony looked over towards the other grounds and saw that games were under way there as well. 'I reckon it's out of them and Moonyoonooka for the final.'

I planned to have a look at the wonderfully named Moonyoonooka, but first I had to watch the locals in action.

Murchison were a B grade side and had been scheduled to play their first game at around mid-morning but the team wasn't very happy with one of their players, a certain Jock McSporran.

Jock's name was one that I didn't associate readily with the middle of the Outback, but when he turned up he certainly looked Outback. He hadn't shaved for a couple of days and his blond hair, that badly needed cutting, stuck out at all angles from under his greasy baseball cap. His gut could have done with a few less kilos and as he walked his arms swung across in front of it, not back and forwards. Jock had been helping out at the bar by serving customers and himself until close to dawn. His eyes rolled in their sockets, not focusing on anything in particular.

But by the time the match was due to start, Jock reckoned he was ready to go. He'd had a feed and a couple of smokes and his horse was saddled and waiting. Trouble was, Jock had difficulty getting his foot up to the stirrups. He held the reins in one hand while standing on one leg and holding the other by the calf. After three attempts, and after swaying gently back and forward a couple of times, he thrust his foot towards the stirrup where it slipped into the metal and stayed there while he heaved the rest of his body up and over the horse. He thumped down in the saddle and both he and the horse snorted, the air forced from their bodies—one from the exertion and the other from the weight that had crashed onto its back. Jock sat there for a moment gathering his thoughts and his breath before galloping off.

Most teams at the carnival turned out resplendent in their uniforms. Creamy coloured jodhpurs tucked into polished knee-high riding boots. Horses' tails plaited with the same coloured ribbons as the bandages on their legs and shirts with numbers neatly sown on.

The Murchison blokes were slightly different in appearance. A couple had riding boots, some of the horses' tails were plaited without any ribbon and the bandages were whatever could be scrounged from the backs of the trucks. Anthony wore his helmet back on his head so his forehead was even more accentuated than normal, while Simon Broad's bushy beard bulged from under the grille on his helmet.

Sandy McTaggert was a similar shape to Jock, only shorter and older, and his son Boots had his number attached to his shirt with safety pins. Jock, before his monumental effort at mounting his horse, had just turned up and strapped on his spurs.

Their opposition was Mullewa, the most local of all the rivals and the ones Anthony and the boys desperately wanted to beat. Trouble was, Mullewa could play. The Murchison boys rode like they drove their trucks, but the other mob were better polocrosse players. They had all the answers and when the last chukka ended they had flogged Murchison by 20-odd goals.

Anthony wasn't happy. I let him cool down a bit before I ventured too close. He was washing down his horse, 'I'm like it at work as well. If other stations do two k's fencing a day, we'll do three. If they use five men to muster, we'll use four. It's just the competition, it keeps me going.'

I left him to contemplate the defeat and went back to watch the poms, who were to play in the next match.

They were a young side, the poms. Their coach was a Zimbabwean track rider and jockey, Andy Maxwell, who had gone to England on a working holiday 10 years previously and stayed. Even though at 31 he was the oldest member of the touring party, his piercing eyes and his taut body made him look more like a lightweight boxer from the veldt than a jockey.

Andy had again spent the morning with his team trying out the horses that Alan Crooks had driven up in his truck. 'It's not easy getting on a strange horse.' Andy's accent was strong. He looked down and scuffed the red dirt with his boot. 'Especially around here.'

The poms had nine players, six of whom Andy picked in the team. The excess three played with Kojanup, who had only three of their own—Alan Crooks, another farmer Steve McGuire and a man whose ability to seemingly elongate his arms to catch a passing ball caused him to be known as Inspector Gadget, Colin Ednie-Brown. Colin's name sounded like he should be playing polo but Bev Hammerton reckoned he was 'as rough as guts, that's why he's with us'. But neither of us told him that.

As well as Murchison being a new experience for the poms, it was the same for the locals. After all, not too many overseas polocrosse sides have attended the Murchison carnival and interested onlookers gathered on the sidelines. I watched with Andy.

It must have been difficult trying to work strange horses through a paddock of deep churned-up soil the colour of red ochre. These were people who were used to the green swards of the English countryside. Used to having their farming fields all neatly fenced and in order, not miles and miles of paddocks that went on forever with nothing but bushland to the horizon. And beyond those horizons more of the same.

Andy had picked Half Penny in his side while Ruth was left to play with Kojanup.

'It makes 'em all think a bit more about their game,' Andy remarked when he told me the sides. 'And the competition won't hurt them.'

Indeed, the game was willing, with Alan copping a stick under the chin early and being knocked off his horse, stunned. After getting his chin fixed with a few Band Aids, he copped it again in the next chukka. This time it was the umpire at the lineout.

After a goal is scored the teams ride back to halfway and the umpire throws the ball in down the line. But this time he threw the ball straight into Alan's face and knocked him off his horse once again.

The poms in Andy's main side wanted to show the locals that they could play and the other three wanted to show Andy they should be in the side. And they all did, although they seemed to be class players outclassed by the unfamiliarity of the place.

Ruth, riding hard and fast all game, adapted with the others who played with the Kojanup team to win comfortably.

Andy smiled reflectively as he sat in the sun. 'The result doesn't matter, does it? Not everybody is this lucky, eh?'

I lunched with Sandy McTaggert, or rather I had a hot dog from the kitchen and a beer with Sandy McTaggert.

Sandy had been in the Murchison for 18 years after buying a station from his father's estate. As a youngster he'd had a 'bit of a row with the family' and left home to work on farms around the country after he had failed university 'rather spectacularly'. At one stage he was fibreglassing rainwater tanks on stations in South Australia and New South Wales, but he was brought up in this country and he always wanted to return.

Polocrosse had been his sport for 30 years or more but he confessed he'd never been all that good and had never really played it seriously. 'We're a bit more serious these days, because we have a few better players around.'

According to Sandy, the distances meant that they couldn't get together very often for practice. 'From the grounds here most of the stations would be at least 150 kilometres away.'

The Murchison tournament was in its seventeenth year. 'It's a community thing,' remarked Sandy, emphasising its importance to the people in the area. 'Everyone's involved because it's about the only thing we do all year.'

Sandy bought another beer. I asked him if he'd stay here when he retired. 'Dunno really, wool 'ed have to improve so I could buy something to retire in.'

The talk drifted to his son Boots. He didn't work on the station and Sandy wasn't sure about him ever coming back. 'He's at uni. Anyway the problem's not with the young blokes coming on, it's what you do with the old blokes.'

During the long break in mid-afternoon, the main ground was repaired. A four-wheel-drive ute, transporting two blokes in the front and two more on the sides in the back, all with stubbies, drove around the square towing a bar on a chain which, as well as raising clouds of dirt, flattened it out and filled in the holes that the horses had made.

When the ute drove off, a small young bloke in a large hat pushed a severely dented metal drum with a handle attached over the more or less level earth. White powder dropped beneath his feet from holes punched in the sides, forming a white line which marked the boundary.

I watched the workers while Anthony was huddled over his score sheets in the office trying to work out where each team was positioned in the lead-up to the finals. 'We'll play a final in each grade tomorrow on the main ground.' He swept his arm around. 'But I've got to let all these people know who looks like being in them.'

Teams had to win two matches at least to be assured of a place in the final and if teams were level, then goals for and against would decide who played.

One team that was assured of a place was John Marriott's team, Moonyoonooka. Even to the untrained eye they appeared to be a cohesive unit. John and his daughter Jane controlled the centre sections of the ground and after flicking the ball between them one or the other would gallop to their scoring end, pull up at the line they were not allowed to cross and flick the ball to Pearl, who more often than not calmly slotted it between the goalposts. Then they'd return to the centre, wait for the umpire to toss the ball back into play and they'd do it all over again.

After the match John was bit reticent to talk about their skill. 'We play a lot more than most of these people. These other blokes are basically farmers who do it for recreation.'

Indeed the Marriotts did do it all the time. Their other daughter Sarah was overseas, playing and teaching, and Jane—young, vivacious and at peace with the world—had just returned from three years touring all over, breaking-in horses and playing for a living.

Jane unsaddled her horse. 'I thought I'd better come home and see what was happening.' Then with a smile in her eyes as well as her mouth: 'But I'm not sure how long I'll stay.'

In the A grade, neither the poms or Kojanup made the final against Moony. As Anthony had predicted, Irwin were the side. In the B grade Murchison would play a rematch against Mullewa.

Just then, Anthony was called away to look for a horse that had bolted. Apparently the horse had got a scare, thrown its rider and headed for the bush. Anthony drove to the airstrip, borrowed a plane and flew around for a while until the horse was spotted.

When he got back he explained that the horse, still wearing his bridle and reins, could have got caught in trees and choked himself. 'But he'll be right now, he's only in a small paddock, and it's getting dark soon so we'll pick him up tomorrow.' I found out later that the small paddock that Anthony referred to was 40 kilometres square.

Later that night, after a sumptuous feast prepared by the ladies of the Murchison who had come to the grounds to be a part of the evening, I shared a corner with Natalie Broad, petite, round-faced, smiling wife and partner of Simon.

If there was one thing that stood out amongst the virtues of the station people it was patience. When we arrived at Murchison, Simon was standing in a hole full of water, baling it out with a bucket and a pump. He had been there since the post-hole digger went through the water pipe when they were putting up the goalposts the previous evening. 'You wouldn't read about it.' Simon sounded placid, even though it was taking forever. 'One pipe going through this bloody great area and we have to hit it.'

He had kept at it with a smile on his face and about 36 hours later, after spare parts had been driven in from Geraldton, it was fixed.

Natalie laughed. 'That's Simon for you.'

A woman's life is hard on the station, even for someone like Natalie who was born on one and knew from childhood what it was like. 'I think it's the distance that's the worst. It's not that we don't see anybody, it's just that we see the same ones.'

Then there are the children. All the kids in the area are taught by the school of the air, supervised by either their mother or by a governess for those who are lucky enough to be able to afford them. 'One time everyone had them, but nowadays we have to watch our dollars.'

And then when the kids are about 12 they are sent to boarding school in Perth. There was more resignation in Natalie's voice than sadness. 'There's nothing else we can do.'

Then again, she didn't think it was all bad. After all, it was their choice. 'There is a togetherness out here that perhaps some city couples don't have, and we're able to give the children a sense of values that hopefully will carry them through the boarding school years.'

Natalie reckoned it was a special place and she was pretty happy. 'Most of the women are. Some from away have a bit of trouble adjusting but that isn't their fault, really. It can be difficult to come here, but we all support each other.'

However, if there was one thing she could have above all else it would be time.

'Nothing material—just a bit more time. Late at night I have a bit of time to myself. I can read or just sit in the quiet on the verandah and watch the night. I wouldn't mind a bit more of that.'

The finals were going to start a bit later on Sunday and spectators placed their fold-up seats along the boundary. The ground had been levelled once more with the ute and bar and the lines-marker had again performed his job admirably.

While the lower grades played off, the Murchison boys were preparing their horses and motivating themselves for the big game. Mullewa were obviously going to be hard to beat but that wouldn't matter. Intensity was the key, according to Anthony. I asked about the rivalry and whether he thought they could win.

'If I was honest, I'd prob'ly say no.' He sounded almost resigned, and then added, 'But they'll bloody earn it.'

Bridles clanked and leather groaned as the riders swung themselves onto their horses with ease. All, that was, except Jock who once again had difficulty lifting his leg high enough. But at least he was in better shape than the previous day, although not by much.

'Had an early night,' Jock protested when asked about his nocturnal perambulations. 'Must have been about four, I reckon.'

At the moment the team was to ride out one of the barmen rushed up to Anthony and tugged at his leg as he sat on his horse. 'There's only two bottles of rum left,' he gasped in horror.

'Shit!' snorted Anthony as he held his horse steady. 'Well you'd better go and get some more, about four boxes I reckon.'

'Righto,' replied the barman and headed off to his ute.

I asked Anthony where he had it stored. 'We haven't. They'll have to nip into Mullewa.'

Nip in! It was only a five-hour round trip.

In the tradition of polocrosse, the two teams in the B-grade final lined up at opposite ends of the ground and on the umpire's command, with their sticks held over their shoulders, walked their trusty steeds towards each other like jousters, stopping in the centre where the umpires gave their instructions. 'I want a good clean game. I know you blokes are keen but no rough stuff.'

'Yeah, righto,' came the grunt from the Murchison boys, sincerely, but not convincingly so, as they turned their horses around and galloped around the ground to warm up.

The Mullewa side were decked out perfectly but the Murchison mob were the same as they were the day before, even to the point that most of them wore the same clothes.

The first chukka was close and when the teams swapped over Anthony pulled off his helmet and looked pleased. 'Not a bad start for us. Hope these blokes keep it up.'

Knocking the ball out of your opponents' net calls for a good eye as you are only allowed to hit upwards. Jock didn't quite have it right and gave a couple of penalties away by clobbering a couple of Mullewa arms. 'Won't bloody hurt 'em,' was Anthony's retort to the umpire.

At the halfway mark of three chukkas the scores were level. 'I reckon we can do it, fellas,' Anthony exhorted the rest of the team, who were equally keen.

Halfway through the fourth chukka the ball ran loose. Anthony and his opponent, a young woman, rode straight at the ball. Anthony leaned his horse in and pushed with his body to keep the Mullewa player out of the way. Harder and harder he pushed until the woman was forced to gallop over the sideline, nearly collecting the umpire and a couple of spectators who were perhaps too close. The whistle blew and Anthony was penalised. A free shot in front of goal. Anthony was not impressed and left all the Mullewa players and the umpire in no doubt as to what his thoughts were.

But it was the turning point of the game. Mullewa scored three more quick goals and Murchison went into the last chukka four behind.

Anthony's intensity wasn't behind, however, and at the end of the chukka in which he had ridden the player out, a smart comment from the Mullewa side of the ground made him see red. He charged his horse across and was about to jump off to sort the offending speaker out when Jock and Sandy rode swiftly across and grabbed him, guiding him away. As the three of them trotted off, Anthony was half-turned in the saddle still having a go. You don't mess with the boys from the Murchison.

But it was all to no avail. Mullewa won by four goals. Just a few scrappy minutes had caused the defeat.

'We didn't do too bad, considering they flogged us yesterday,' Sandy conceded.

Jock went looking for a drink while Anthony fumed for a while and then agreed with Sandy.

'Anyway,' Jock was secretive and quiet, 'now we've got all the polocrosse out of the way we can get on with the main event of the weekend—tonight.'

As we walked back from the stables to the bar the A-grade final was being decided. It turned out to be an easy win for Moon-yoonooka, with the Marriotts all starring. They played the game on another level but in doing so helped the players in the other teams to learn a bit more about the game.

The presentations were held, the speeches were made and the rum drench had been filled up, much to everyone's delight.

Jock was relieved. 'Geez, it could have been the Rum Rebellion all over again if we'da run out.'

A couple of hours later an auction was held of donated goods to aid the Flying Doctor. Bidding was way over the top but out there the Flying Doctor was like part of the family and you looked after your own.

Then Jock took the microphone for the start of what he called 'the main event'.

The night started with boat races, in which teams of drinkers sit on opposite sides of a table and see who can quaff their drinks the quickest. Females first. On one side of the table sat the locals. All fair dinkum country girls. Hands like leather, hair that was last combed on Friday and skin that still had a dry look no matter how much Oil of Ulan was used.

Opposite were the poms. Fresh-faced girls from the English countryside. Ruth and Half Penny were prominent and had a done a bit of training for the event in the previous few hours.

Half Penny was a bit of a player. Early that morning she had woken up to find herself in her swag in the centre of the grounds with no cover for 100 metres in any direction. A couple of the local boys had carried her there when, to put it delicately, she passed out. Watching a young, slightly built, English rose try to run for cover with only a swag protecting her modesty created quite a deal of amusement.

But in the boat races there was no contest. The 'sheilas' as they called themselves did the locals proud, and while the poms tried hard they didn't quite make it. Still, one of their number videoed the whole affair so back home they would actually believe that Murchison existed and they did actually carry on like this.

Jock was in rare form on the mike. Disputing decisions, re-running events and all the while trying to keep a hundred thirsty drinkers happy.

Anthony then introduced bungy drinking, where people had to attach themselves to a long rubber strap made from old tractor tyres, run towards a bench and drink through a straw from a glass before the rubber pulled them back. But the strap kept breaking.

'Shit!' said Jock. 'We'll have to work on that before next year.'

Anthony agreed.

There were representatives from every team that played in the carnival, but every game that was played resulted in a win to the Murchison mob.

Jock's hat was precariously balanced on the side of his head and his eyes were wide as he mumbled in my ear, 'Some of 'em can beat us at polocrosse, but they can't beat us at havin' fun.'

Later in the night than I realised, I excused myself and staggered away.

Most of the poms had only slept from about five o'clock and when they were woken at seven to head for Perth they were reluctant to get up. It was another 10-hour drive after which they faced a 24-hour flight back to the old country. They were in a state of shock. Andy threw luggage in the trucks, not caring how it fitted.

'It's unreal,' he said. 'We leave here and then tomorrow we may as well be on Mars, eh?'

Ruth and Half Penny were asleep in the back seat as Bev Hammerton drove back along the track to civilisation.

I watched the country passing endlessly and I thought about Sandy McTaggert.

'Mate,' he'd told me about three the morning before as we discussed isolation, 'it's not a geographical position, you know, it's a state of mind.'

CHAPTER EIGHT

PLAYING AROUND IN THE DESERT

Golf in Coober Pedy is different.
In fact, I found that most things about Coober Pedy are different.
And golf is such a trying game.
Asylums are full, I suspect, of ex-golfers sent there by the frustrations of what the game did to them.
And that's playing on a good, or even a reasonable, golf course.
But nothing compares with playing on a course like Coober Pedy.

I thought I might spot the Coober Pedy golf course from the air, but I couldn't. All I could make out were anthill-like mounds of dirt.

The plane, a large flying pencil with a black nose where the point would be, landed on a stripe of bitumen that ran like a black texta colour mark across the landscape.

As I walked across the runway towards the small tin shed that served as a terminal, I looked around when I heard my name called in an accent halfway between Scots and Australian.

'I knew it was you.' The voice belonged to Janette, a middle-aged woman wearing shapeless shorts, no make-up and whose fair hair fell as it liked across her face.

I hoped so. After all, the other passengers on the plane were a young woman, an older woman, and a barrel-shaped Chinese man dressed in a dark, sombre suit who carried a large briefcase that he never took his hand from.

I jokingly asked him during the trip if it was a bomb.

'Bomb, bomb? Bomb?' was his frenetic reply. 'You tink I fuckin' clazy. Bomb, bomb? I not mad.'

He looked at me contemptuously and then watched me out of the corner of his eye for the rest of the flight. When we landed he rushed away in short, abrupt steps, cuddling his briefcase like a baby.

Janette ushered me to an old van and we started on the short drive to town. I told her I was impressed with the service and she crunched through a couple of gears before replying. 'I wasn't doing much, so it didn't hurt me.'

Janette nodded knowingly when I explained my reason for coming to Coober Pedy, 'Oh yes, it's the Open this weekend isn't it.'

It certainly was. Actually, to be more precise and to give it the name it deserved, it was the Coober Pedy Opal Fields Golf Club Annual Open. A prestigious event.

The drive to town took us past Bob's Wrecking Yard, a rust-brown graveyard of motorised hulks in varying stages of decay. It seemed that Bob had plenty of business.

On both sides of the road the ventilating pipes of the underground houses sprouted from the small mounds of rock and dirt like periscopes. Janette told me that 60 per cent of the people in Coober Pedy lived in dugouts because of the heat. Aborigines called the place *kupa piti*—white man's burrows.

A little distance later, she pointed out the new bomb-proof police station. 'They bombed the courthouse a while ago, so everything has to be bomb-proof now.'

I wondered who 'they' were. I hoped it wasn't the Chinese.

Radeka's Underground Backpacker Inn had been converted from its days as an old mine and was now owned by four people: Janette, her Australian partner Doug, Yveline, a petite French lady with a heavy accent and her partner Tony, who was Greek. It was a volatile mixture, but warm and friendly nonetheless.

Inside the front door and past the reception area, a communal room hewn out of the rock was bathed in artificial light that caused dark pink streaks to appear like swollen veins in sandstone walls the colour of pale lemon skin.

Sitting at the plastic tables were a collection of young backpackers writing postcards, reading tour guides or listening to each other's stories of the road. I smiled as they studied me before realising that I was probably the only person in the place over 25 years of age.

Janette issued me with a blanket and a couple of sheets and I followed her down a steep set of steps carved into the rock face into the coolness of the dugout.

The silence and musty smell were how I imagined a dungeon in a mediaeval castle would be, and as we turned each corner in the tunnel I half-expected to see a long bearded skeleton chained to the wall.

We stopped in one of the alcoves where there were two sets of bunks, each one waiting to be occupied.

I dropped the bedding onto one of the lower bunks and sat there for a while, listening to the quiet. Then I climbed back into the upper world to look for Janette, who had promised to drive me out to the golfcourse.

'It's just up there.' Janette pointed up the track as I got out of the van.

Since I couldn't see anything that resembled golf, I took her on trust. Looking closely as I walked, I finally made out the flattened fairways curving gently across the ground. Some distance away, a flag displaying a yellow number 1 hung limply from a pole that rose from a large black circle on the ground.

I knew I was in the right place when I saw some people pulling golf buggies across the bleak terrain towards a flat-roofed building.

The spacious but sparsely furnished clubhouse was cut into the side of a sandstone hill and had large windows that ran the whole way along one side. At night you could look back across the front nine and see the lights of Coober Pedy sparkle in the black nothingness—the only lights for hundreds of kilometres.

Just inside the door was the captain's office where golfers picked up and returned their cards. On the shelf in front of the office window was a large cardboard box which had the word 'GRASS' scrawled across it in bold, black letters.

There didn't seem to be anyone around so I pulled out the contents. Inside were small squares of artificial turf. As I examined them, a voice from behind the bar at the far end of the room startled me.

'Know what they are?'

I had absolutely no idea.

'Come here and I'll show you.'

Bootlace was a grey-haired, balding man of about 60, small in stature but big in heart. One of those people every club needs.

'You see the fairways.'

He pointed out the window. It was a statement not a question so I didn't dispute the fact that there were actually fairways out there.

'Well they've got a groove marked down each side. If your ball's outside that you're in the rough and you have to play it where it lies, but inside and you're on the fairway and you get to pick it up and play it off those bits of grass you take with you.'

I was suddenly aware why golfers say that you have to hit it down the middle.

Bootlace had things to do, so I decided I'd wander around the course for a while and watch some of the golfers who were playing in the prelude to the next day's Open.

'Go down there,' Bootlace urged me, pointing to a group about to hit off the tenth tee. 'That's Mulga. Tell 'im Bootlace sent you.'

Mulga was 77 years old. A small man with shoulders hunched from years of work, and skin as tough as his stained felt trilby hat. I could tell he was still a miner by the way he swung his three wood, round and flat as though he was sticking a pick into the side of his diggings.

'Been around here for over 30 years.' Mulga sounded proud. 'Shearin' for a while and then chasin' opals.'

His tee shot, although not out of any textbook, scrubbed away down the fairway and we set off after it.

Mulga was dragging a buggy with no tyres. Or at least no rubber on the tyres where they touched the ground. The edges looked reasonable, but the ground had worn away the rubber towards the middle of the wheels, leaving only the wire reinforcing. Rattling around inside the buggy was an assortment of misshapen clubs, all badly scoured and worn at the bottom from years of Mulga's golf-ball being off the fairways.

Mulga chuckled while thinking about his next shot. 'There's not too many fancy sets of clubs around here.' He proceeded then to take his piece of grass from his bag, shake it like someone flicking out a handkerchief, then bend over and carefully place his ball.

Then he stood back, flexed his elbows and lined up his shot. About an eight iron, he reckoned, but took a five because he didn't have an eight, and pickaxed the ball towards the hole.

As we strode the fairway I asked Mulga about his name.

'Bootlace reckons I'm as tough as a bit of mulga,' was the reply. 'He reckons he's never seen a bastard this tough. We get down shafts, climbin' ladders, diggin', and all. But he never does any of that.'

And where did Bootlace get his name, I wondered. 'Well I've got to pick him up all the time, haven't I.'

Mulga surveyed his next shot and when he turned to me his grin was even wider. 'Watch this, straight on the black.'

'The what?' I asked, shaken.

'Well, what else do we call it?'

Mulga's question was rhetorical as well as logical. That's what they were. Blacks. A big circle of sand mixed with copious amounts of sump oil from the electric generating station in town. The windier it got, the more sump oil went on in case the sand blew away.

Mulga was right in his prediction. Straight on, about six feet from the hole. He sank the putt and shuffled away.

One of his playing partners who sulked past me, frustrated and disgusted with his golfing prowess, was a young bloke on his way to Darwin.

Julian had stopped in town for a feed and heard there was a golf tournament on, so had put aside his travel plans for a couple of days, parked the old Holden and decided to play. He told me those plans might change back pretty quickly. 'It's like playing on the fuckin' moon.'

I thought he mightn't be far wrong. All I could see were rocks. Some had been crushed and rolled flat to make the fairways while others had been left to form the rough. Bunkers consisted of shallow holes in the ground while an occasional pile of rocks formed another sort of hazard.

Dirt roads crisscrossed the course so that vehicles could make their way to the diggings, and tourist buses could meander along with their gawking, pointing, loads of city types. I thought that the whole course should be marked G.U.R.

Whoever put 18 golf holes into this place was a visionary.

There were a few more people in the clubhouse on my return. Bootlace was one of them. He may not have been a great help to his partner, but he was making up for it around the clubhouse.

Leaning on his elbow at the bar was a tall well-dressed man with neatly trimmed and combed dark hair. A rather obvious exception to the rule. Not that the others were unkempt, but he stood out.

Dennis Rowston was the treasurer of the club. 'That's right,' he remembered as we shook hands. 'Father Tony said to expect you.'

The president of the golf club was the local Catholic priest, Father Tony Redan. I hadn't met him but it was he who invited me to the Open. As he would be missing, performing his duties at a wedding in Adelaide, Father Tony had told me to look for Dennis.

Dennis managed one of the underground tourist places in Coober Pedy, hence the dress sense. He had spent quite a few years in the navy and I was surprised that an old salt would live here. 'There's an old saying,' Dennis told me: 'When you leave the navy you put an oar over your shoulder and head inland. When someone asks you what it is, that's where you stop.'

I laughed with him, and then mentioned that it was such a long way away from everything.

'I s'pose,' agreed Dennis, 'but then I don't want to go anywhere.'

There was no answer to that so I changed the subject and asked about the number of single men I had seen around the place. Dennis said that most of them weren't single, but their wife and kids might have left them there. They had probably stayed because they know that, each year, one or two out of the hundreds of miners here strike it rich. They reckon it could be them. They live the dream.

*

We stood at the bar in silence for a while and looked through the windows at the golfers returning from the desert and handing in their cards and grass. I'd seen small mines on the course, neat piles of dirt next to 40-foot holes. I asked Dennis why they allowed them, as they appeared to be dangerous.

'Well we've gotta have something for the tourists to fall down haven't we?' he grinned before falling silent again. 'Great course, though, isn't it?' he asked after a couple of minutes.

What could I say? It *was* a great course to them. I muttered something about it certainly being different while I watched a man limping towards us with a stiff, awkward gait, as though his leg was permanently straightened.

'How'd you go, Phil?' asked Dennis.

'Not too bad,' was the reply. Phil Lewis' Welsh accent had changed only slightly in the years he had been in Coober Pedy. A dark and swarthy complexion, coupled with a thick body and neck, made him look just like a Welsh five-eighth.

'I lost my leg in a mine,' he answered my question in a straightforward manner.

Phil was about 60 feet down a shaft when his legs became tangled in his machinery, one being almost torn off. 'My partner freaked out a bit.' Phil sounded as though he had remained calm, and it seems he had been: before his mate took off Phil yelled at him to get a piece of rope, 'Otherwise I may not be around when you get back.'

Phil wound the rope around his upper thigh, tightened it with a stick to stop the flow of blood, and waited. It took about an hour for the mine rescue men to get back. 'I sang an old Welsh hymn, "David of the White Rock", to keep awake.' Phil smiled to himself at the memory. 'I must have sung it a hundred times.'

The recovery was long and hard. 'It certainly gave me a new outlook on life,' he told me as his voice softened. 'And then, after I was over the worst of it, my wife died of cancer.'

I watched Phil as he told me his story and I wondered how someone gets over all that.

'I don't know really,' he answered reflectively. 'You just do.' He headed for the bar, elbowing his way through the crowd and smiling at me. 'But life's been pretty good.'

Outside the clubhouse the sunset had left the sky streaked with colours that glowed in a reflection of the opalescent earth.

I thought about Phil as I walked down the hill and out to the space that seemed to stretch away from me forever. The desert breeze tugged at my hair as I studied the small mountains that rose in the half-light like giant bumps on the flat earth. Lost in my own insignificance I watched as the night draped itself over the land, stealing the sunset and replacing it with its own billion pricks of light.

It was nearing midnight when I arrived back at my lodgings. The communal room had been taken over by a mass of European backpacking youngsters watching the FA Cup Final from England on satellite TV. I thought about it briefly, but realised I stuck out a bit and wandered off to my dungeon.

A couple of hours into a deep sleep I was awakened by movement. The other bunks were being taken up by two young women and a young man. As I lay on my side in the bunk I could make out their figures through the dimness of the security light. Their bodies were long and slim, and their quiet voices sounded Northern European, possibly German.

One of the women stood alongside my pillow and took what seemed to be an eternity to wriggle out of her jeans before slipping her foot on my bunk and levering herself above me. The others whispered to each other as they climbed into one of the other bunks.

It wasn't long before the Germanic whispering had turned to Germanic groans of pleasure, followed soon after by the man climbing into the top bunk. The silence then returned and I was left trying to get back to sleep.

I was up early the next morning, resisting the inclination to make a noise and wake my sleeping neighbours. The main street was deserted apart from a few battered utes parked in the dirt that joined the ribbon of tar winding through the town. A couple of mangy dogs sniffed around the shops hoping to find a few scraps that had been thrown away. They didn't seem interested at all when a ute with 'exxplozives' written on the tailgate backed out of the dirt and drove off.

Everything seemed to be covered in dirt. Everything was. Even the modern hotel that looked somewhat out of place, as if someone had plonked it in the middle of nowhere by mistake.

I decided to walk out to the golf course.

The Open was played over 27 holes and some of the players were already on the course as I stumbled across the small hills surrounding the area and made my way back up the fifth fairway towards the clubhouse.

The Coober Pedy Open attracted quite a number of visitors. They came down from Alice Springs, across from Woomera as well as up from Booleroo Centre and Adelaide. One of the visitors about to head out to tackle the course was a big red-headed character named Mick McMullen, although everyone called him, naturally enough, Red.

An auto electrician from Ceduna on the South Australian coast, Red was not the best dressed golfer around. He wore a black and white hooped T-shirt, frayed runners and his thin, blue shorts, with hibiscus flowers as a trim, hung just low enough to expose the crack in his buttocks.

The previous year, in his first attempt at the Open, Red had come last by a long way. In fact he sank a 15-foot putt on the last to finish with a total of 299. After he had boasted that it's not every day you can sink a monster putt to break 300, I asked Red how that sort of score was possible.

'Shit easy, mate.' Red was self-derisive. 'They can add up pretty quick around here.'

Indeed they could, but I wondered how much liquid refreshment he'd carried around with him.

'Actually not much,' was the rather pensive reply. 'I think I'm just a shithouse golfer.'

On the first tee, Red waved his two wood in the air a couple of times to loosen up and then proceeded to hit his drive about 15 metres straight into the rocks. It was going to be a long day.

He had travelled to the open with a bloke called Mark Lang, who owned the taxi service in Ceduna. Their transport was a car that Langy had named after his favourite mode of transport, the Tardis. It was an old, rusting Fairlane that had been cut in half, the roof raised, and had been used as a sort of stretch taxi. The numberplates were suitably marked: DRWHO.

The Tardis was parked outside the clubhouse, its roof appearing like a top hat amongst a row of cloth caps. 'It's a great rig,' Langy told me proudly. 'We can fit in heaps of blokes, all our golf gear and lots of grog. What more do you want?'

He also told me that the trip from Ceduna varied in the time taken to reach Coober Pedy. 'The quickest I've done it in the 20 years I've been coming here is almost seven hours. The longest was when I took three days to get home.'

I left Red and Langy when I noticed Bootlace emptying a rubbish bin. I called out and asked if he'd seen Dennis Rowston.

'He's about to hit off the twelfth, I reckon,' Bootlace told me before ushering me around the side of the clubhouse and pointing him out.

Dennis was playing with John James, the club vice-president. A small, thin-faced man with curly but receding hair, John wasn't having the best of mornings and his narrow faced clouded over as his golf became worse and worse.

John's handicap was 24 but even that many strokes were not helping. Nearly every shot he played ended up in trouble and his piece of grass stayed mostly in the buggy.

Not that Dennis was helping matters. He was a genial bloke and nothing appeared to get to him, even golf. 'You'll be right Johnno,' he said grinning at his partner's misfortune. 'You'll come good.'

John was having none of it, becoming more and more withdrawn and morose until he finally said he was feeling crook and he'd have to pull out.

'Don't do that, mate,' Dennis urged him. 'You'll be right soon.'

But John went off, back to the clubhouse.

While Dennis and I waited for another group to come along I brushed and cursed at the flies that had been hovering around all morning.

'Flies,' exclaimed Dennis. 'They're pretty good today. You should see 'em when it's hot.'

Dennis told me that in the summer you dare not take any food out on the course because the flies would get to it first. He added that when it gets to 50 degrees the Gladwrap gets a bit sticky and when you unwrap a sandwich it's black before you can get it to your mouth. 'So you've either got to chomp through 'em or chuck it away.'

It was then Dennis remembered Johnny Vidar.

During one exceptionally hot day, Johnny was standing on one of the tees, trying to line up his drive, when the flies were incredibly thick. He swore and cursed for a few minutes until in sheer exasperation he reached into his buggy, pulled out a shotgun that he always carried and blasted a couple of rounds off at the offending insects. 'Reckons he hit a few as well,' Dennis chuckled as he walked away with the threesome that had caught up.

At lunchtime the barbecue was stoked up and golfers came, ate and went back to their game at different times.

Sitting in the office and trying to organise a scoreboard was the club captain and course curator, Harry Blobel.

Harry was a big, bald German. Big gut, big voice, big opinions, but also with a big heart. He'd been in the opal fields for 30-odd years and had been club captain, on and off, for 13 of them. He was a reasonable golfer, playing off 12, but had a bad back which was the reason he was in the office. 'Ven you got a crook back, you know,' Harry informed me, 'you know about it, you know.' I was a bit confused until I worked out how he spoke.

While he was checking the scores that came in Harry listened to a cassette of loud, knee-slapping German music and demolished a couple of bottles of his favourite red. 'South Australian, the best vine, you know.'

The leader at lunchtime, as far as Harry could make out, was a visitor from Adelaide, Greg Peacock, a two handicapper who had shot 78.

A tall, likable young bloke with close-cropped hair and a big gold earring, Greg was a real golfer. His swing was a long, languid circle, transcribed from over his right shoulder, around the arc to finish over his left. He supposed he was 'hittin' 'em alright'.

Greg led a local bloke, Ronnie Sternberg, by a shot. Ronnie, who played off eight, was a talkative, stick-like plumber who hadn't played golf before he came to Coober Pedy, 20 years beforehand. He was losing his hair at the front but the moustache that drooped towards his chin more than made up for it. He leant against a table, rolling a smoke, and the grin that was perpetually on his face widened further when I suggested that this wasn't the easiest of courses on which to learn golf.

'Aw, I dunno,' he smiled as he walked off with Greg.

Harry wished them both luck as they went but he was not a happy man. Not all the golfers who had completed 18 holes were handing their cards in for him to add up and write on his display board.

'Dey piss me ov, you know,' Harry moaned, 'but vwat can you do, you know.'

I didn't know so I headed back out to the course, leaving Harry to his wine, his music and his moaning.

Paul Bourke, who was about to hit off the first, had been the Catholic priest in Coober Pedy for 10 years until Tony Redan took over about three years ago. An intense man, his unwavering eyes squinted against the glare and were set deep in his face, half-hidden behind thick eyebrows.

His playing partner, Kim Kelly, towered over him. Well over six feet tall and several stone heavier, Kim was the father of ex-Collingwood footballer and hard man Craig. There was nothing hard about Kim, though. A laughing, joking man he seemed to be enjoying whatever life and golf threw at him, although earlier in the day he had been rendered speechless, which was not an easy task.

He had been lining up a shot when suddenly Paul had thrown his clubs down and raced off as fast as he could. Kim said that all he could see was Paul disappearing around a hill and yelling over his shoulder, 'I've just remembered Tony asked me to say Mass!' A while later, after he had seen to the spiritual needs of the flock, he had returned to join Kim.

Paul drove first. Watching him I realised what the term 'agricultural' meant. His feet, head and body all moved as he crashed the ball down the fairway. It landed in a large puff of creamy coloured dust before rolling slowly into a bunker.

'Bad luck Paul,' Kim guffawed before adding a touch more solemnly. 'I suppose I shouldn't laugh.' But he did.

Kim's drive travelled about the same distance but was way off to the right. Paul said nothing but set off for the bunker, which was actually a hole in the ground.

As Kim strode over the rocky ground, he looked all wrong. This huge man in shorts and T-shirt with a fist engulfing the handle of his ancient golf buggy, barely as high as his knees, that bumped along behind him.

Kim had played footy for Port Adelaide in the last of Fos Williams' seven consecutive premierships. He remembered playing on Neil Kerley in one of his first games. 'I thought I'd show him how tough I was.' Kim smiled. 'I whacked him one in the guts. It was like hitting a steel post.' Kerley just turned around and told him, 'You stupid little boy', before knocking him out later in the game.

Both Kim and Paul made bogey on the hole and Paul's three wood from the next tee was straight down the middle once more. But then he hacked a five iron into a few stunted saltbushes. 'Shit!' He was emphatic with his choice of word as he swished his club through the air. His next shot wasn't much better. 'Shit!' he exclaimed again. Two more 'shit' shots and Paul was no nearer the hole. Eventually, he managed a good one and as we walked towards the black I asked him if human frailties showed up a bit more in a place like this.

'You realise the truths of faith a bit more here,' was his reply, either not recognising my sarcasm or choosing to ignore it.

Paul said that, out here, people had to live with themselves, with their own humanity. 'They know you and love you for what you are. In the cities people might do that too, but they don't see you after dark, they disappear into their own suburbs. We have nowhere to hide.'

I sat on a rock as Paul and Kim hit off the third, a par three up a small hill. Kim's ball wobbled towards the saltbush but Paul hit his onto the black and raised his eyes to the sky in a quiet thankyou.

From where I sat I could see most of the course. A couple of holes away were Red and Langy, who was reaching for refreshment.

Langy's buggy was a work of art. I imagined it, without the bag, sitting in some inner-suburban gallery as experts in berets and scarves discussed what it meant while sipping chardonnay and nibbling cheese held in the tips of their fingers. And in the corner, Langy would be leaning against the gallery wall, smiling to himself and swigging a stubbie.

Welded on the side of the buggy were two holders, one carrying a bottle of marsala, the other a bottle of rum. Under those was a square metal box with ice and six stubbies, while beneath the seat was another compartment 'for emergencies'. Langy looked at me earnestly. 'A bloke can get thirsty out here.'

As Langy handed him a drink, Red informed me, 'Goin' well today, goin' to beat last year's score easy.'

I wasn't quite sure which way he meant. More shots or less.

As I looked across the rocky, barren ground at the golfers wandering around in the distance, Phil Lewis flashed by. His artificial leg hadn't dampened his enthusiasm for the game, although he was aided by the fact that he drove the only motorised buggy in Coober Pedy.

Paul was right. People here were part of every heartbeat. Part of the pulse of life.

I had been sitting for a while, pondering golf in conditions such as these, when a four-wheel drive pulled up.

'Vot you doing there?' asked Harry as he leaned out of the window. He didn't wait for an answer before introducing me to Tony Redan, who had just arrived. 'Two bloody priests here now,' he said, shaking his head in mock disappointment.

Obeying Harry's instruction, I hopped in the car. 'Ve going to see Desmund Tutu,' he informed me. I was about to express surprise at the fact they had such a celebrated visitor when Harry continued, 'Kim bloody Kelly.'

When we caught up, Kim told me that he was the pacifist to Harry's redneck rantings. 'He has some weird views,' said Kim, serious for a moment, 'but we've got around fifty nationalities in Coober Pedy so there are going to be some differences.'

The two fathers were silent.

After the golfers had finished putting, Harry accidentally backed over Kim's buggy, laughed uproariously and drove off. On the next hole, Tony, Paul and I walked the fairway discussing Tutu, B. A. Santamaria, Mandela et al. until, from the rocks and saltbush, Kim's voice rang out, 'I've had nine shots on this bloody hole and I'm still not on the bloody fairway.'

Tony Redan's parish consisted of a twentieth of Australia, some half a million square kilometres. 'About 10,000 people in all,' he informed me in his clipped tone, 'around eighteen hundred Catholics.'

I thought about that for a while. Tony had one Catholic to almost 30,000 square kilometres of land.

'The four-wheel drive gets plenty of use,' he grinned.

Tony's stride was long and regimental. Longer than it should have been for his medium height, his foot reaching out before it was grounded. He had not a black hair out of place and his moustache was neat and tidy. In another life he could have been a sergeant major.

He told me that up in the Centre they don't get to see too many priests, so people of any denomination are welcome at his services. 'I don't ask too many questions and I know that Jesus is pretty understanding.'

One of Tony's first jobs after arriving in Coober Pedy was to organise the now defunct football team that consisted mainly of Aborigines. There were two distinct groups, one the religious, Christian types while the others were more inclined to drink and smoke forbidden substances.

The team had no ground so they had to travel over 400 kilometres to Woomera just for their home games. Away games were a different matter.

On one trip home an argument broke out. The smokers and

drinkers decided they wanted to stop for a little while but the Christians knew what was up and weren't too keen.

'So there I was,' Tony remembered. 'Midnight, stopped a million miles from anywhere while refereeing a fight between a group of Christian Aborigines who were screaming at another mob quietly having a bong on the side of the road.'

Tony reckoned his belief in his life's purpose was put to the test that night.

It was almost dark by the time the last of the golfers handed in their cards. Mulga was rubbing his feet as he sat with Bootlace having a quiet drink.

'They're that sore from the rocks pokin' through these shoes I reckon it would been more comfortable bein' nailed to the cross.'

Harry's scoreboard was up to date and showed that Phil Lewis had won the B grade event but didn't declare the overall winner. Harry tapped the side of his nose with his finger. 'I don't vont you to know that just yet, you know.'

Then came the announcements and presentations. Last by a long way was, once again, Red, who rose to thunderous applause to accept his trophy and make a speech. Red was glowing from not only the sun on his fair skin, but from the fact that this year wasn't one of abstinence. His shorts by now covered only half his backside but he didn't seem to mind.

Red had also won the longest drive and as he accepted the trophy he explained how a golfer of his stature could actually do that and still have 14 on the par four.

'Don't worry about that,' he roared over the bubbling noise. 'Just remember it's not every golfer who can beat last year's score by 73.'

Next was Harry's big moment. He announced that the open winner was Ronnie Sternberg.

He told the story of Greg Peacock being two shots in front with just three holes to play and parring them all. But Ronnie, in one of the great finishes in golf anywhere, not just Coober Pedy, had birdied the last three to win by a shot.

'Local knowledge,' admitted Ronnie as he spoke. And in the time-honoured way of golf he then thanked the curator, the ladies for the tea and his playing partners.

Later, I listened as Red made another speech, and then attempted another, before chatting to Kim and Paul and Tony. Over a few quiet beers they told me what a great weekend it had been. They didn't need to.

CHAPTER NINE

RED SUN AND THE SAILS SET

Alice Springs was high on the list of places to visit.
When I was driving into town I thought about how calm everything was.
No rushing about. No real stress.
It's not always like that, of course, but generally in the Outback,
things go along steadily.
They have their own problems but they never take themselves too seriously.
For instance, why would anyone want to run around dressed up as a boat
on a river that has no water.
I'd thought about that as well on the trip, and I wondered about the answer.

Mark Bushell stood in the middle of the riverbed, megaphone dangling from one of his large hands while the other ran through his short black hair. He looked around.

'Where are they all?' he asked himself without expecting an answer.

It was approaching midday and the Henley-on-Todd was scheduled to start but the competitors in the first event hadn't presented themselves.

Mark raised the megaphone to his mouth. 'All people who are going in the BYO boats come here to me!'

As he dragged his six-foot something frame towards the shade of a twisted, white-barked gum tree, Mark's work boots struggled to raise themselves from the river sand.

Under a sign that advised people not to dive in the river, he produced a handkerchief from the pocket of the long khaki shorts that left only a small exposure of skin between his knees and the top of his work boots. He wiped his sweating, chubby, red-cheeked face.

'Everything runs on time, sometimes,' he grinned as he stuffed the piece of cloth away. 'But that's the Alice for you. Not today, not tomorrow, perhaps Monday, or maybe Tuesday.'

I looked over to where the spectators had gathered—an area outside the fence line that would, on any other river, be a grassed bank where people could sit or lie and watch the water flow gently past.

But this was the Todd River in Alice Springs. It had everything other rivers have: the bank, shapely trees whose finger-like branches reached eagerly for their leaves, a winding course that meandered through the contoured land, as well as river sand that would be a treat to feel squishing beneath your toes as you waded. But there was no water.

'It doesn't look like anyone has brought their own boat,' Mark mumbled, again to himself. Up came the megaphone and the booming voice floated out over everyone within range. 'We're running the Oxford Tubs now so get yourself down here if you want a go.'

This plea looked to be a bit more successful as three or four teams made their way up to Mark, who wrote their names on the clipboard he carried under his arm.

'This is better.' He sounded eager. 'It's going. Now we won't have too many problems. And Bill'll be happy.'

Bill Van Dijk, Dutch born and still with an accent after 25 years in the Alice, was the executive director of the Henley-on-Todd, the person who made everything happen. Not actually on the day—that was Mark's job as the ringmaster—but leading up to the event.

A retired schoolteacher, Bill watched proceedings from the shade of a canvas awning at the end of the arena. 'I vork at it all year round. It's become such a big part off life in the Alice.'

The Henley-on-Todd started in the early sixties, Bill recalled. 'Reg Smith vas a Rotarian who gets the credit for the original thought.'

Reg had heard of the Henley-on-Thames, so why not a Henley-on-Todd?

Why not indeed? Just because Alice Springs was thousands of kilometres from the nearest large body of water, and their only river was mostly dry, shouldn't have been any sort of obstacle.

'They came up with all the ideas off how to do it running on the sand and holding the boats around them,' Bill continued. 'And ve are still doing it.'

Bill apologised that he had a few things to attend to, so he went one way and I went back to Mark and the start of the heats of the Oxford Tubs.

Three narrow railway lines, laid in the sand, ran along the fence in front of the grassy bank. On them were small canoe-shaped objects with railway wheels attached to the bottom.

'Now the object here,' Mark explained, 'is to paddle with those small army shovels they have like you'd paddle a canoe.'

Easy!

The first heat was between a team from the British Aerospace Centre and the Americans from Pine Gap. They knelt in the tin canoes like Red Indians and dug the paddles into the sand, propelling themselves at a rapid rate down the train tracks. At the end of the line the rules stated that they had to jump out, change positions, and paddle back.

At the finish, the Americans, whose lead paddler had a body like Arnold Schwarzenegger and an accent like John Wayne, were half a length of the line ahead.

'Man, I lark this eevent,' Arnold drawled. 'I caan use mah strength.'

He flexed his body, half-casually, which rippled like an ocean swell, and then sauntered back to where his companions, all wearing reflector wraparound sunglasses and their hats on backwards, sat under the protection of a large canvas flyover.

'Big bastard, him,' Mark said quietly as we watched him go. I nodded.

As Arnold sat in his fold-up chair that bulged as he lowered his weight into it, another group of Americans double-marched into the arena, chanting Marine slogans and carrying a large silver cup.

'That's the America's Cup,' Mark informed me as we watched them chug past. Then he added seriously, 'That's the main event. It's on later, after the final of the Whitbread maxi yachts and the Fastnet.'

Well, I thought, that would be the time to run it.

The Americans placed their trophy on the judges' table, which was situated on a truck heavily disguised as a large paddlesteamer.

Their leader, a short, confident man named Chuck, informed all and sundry that it was 'goin' to be there for just a short while, until we win it back again'. That brought great sounds of booing from everyone but the Yanks.

As they chugged out of the arena again I rejoined Mark who was studying the program on his clipboard.

Mark was the general manager for a local tour company. He had come to Alice Springs on a holiday and stayed. 'I'm like most people here. Everyone's from somewhere else.'

There was something about the Alice that he loved. 'I've seen the river flood three times now.' He sounded pleased. 'They reckon that qualifies me as a local.'

The clipboard was jammed under his arm as Mark lifted the megaphone once more.

'Next up we have the heats of the men's eights, the prestigious Head of the River.'

While the entrants gathered around their boats, Mark called everyone's attention to another event.

'If anyone wants to have a go at climbing the greasy pole, it's over there,' he shouted through his megaphone as he tried to point while still holding his clipboard under his arm. 'There's some great prizes too.'

Tucked away on one side of the arena, a 25-five foot metal pole with a circular plate welded to the top was covered for the first 20 feet in dripping black grease. Swinging from the plate on pieces of string were bottles of rum and bourbon that the climbers tried to reach.

One group of would-be mountaineers had gathered at the bottom of the pole. They formed a pyramid sort of structure with three of them on the base supporting the others, who climbed over them one by one. After five of them had climbed up, the pyramid fell to bits and, covered in the horrible black grease, they went on a recruiting exercise.

Meanwhile, Mark had the Head of the River running smoothly. There were entries, he told me, from all over the country for the Henley-on-Todd. 'Tour buses come here just for this. Then there's others from Woomera and Ayers Rock, Adelaide and Darwin.'

The first of the Head of the River heats was between an entry from Ayers Rock and one from the local casino, while others were scheduled between the American and Australian air forces as well as a youth hostel staff and the local hospital.

At the start, Mark bellowed at the teams to get ready. They stepped inside their brightly coloured boats which were made from light tubing with canvas shrouds bearing the names of their sponsors or companies and lifted them up to their waists.

'Now,' bellowed Mark, 'you've got to have all your hands holding the bottom of the boat.'

When a shout of protest emerged Mark bellowed once again, this time with the megaphone only a couple of feet away from the complainant's ear, 'Cos they're the bloody rules, that's why.'

The point was taken and the heats were under way.

'The two fastest times will be in the final,' Mark explained as we watched the eights struggle through the sand up to the marker buoys, which looked suspiciously like 44-gallon drums painted red, where they turned around and returned. 'You can actually lose a heat and still get in the final.'

Which is what happened. The Ayers Rock Resort team was beaten by the mob in the Lasseter's Casino boat, but as they were the two fastest they would contest the final a couple of hours later.

The finalists appeared to take the event reasonably seriously, as each crew had matching T-shirts and some sort of order in their boats. The others, like the nurses from the local hospital who had dressed in operating gowns complete with masks and hat, were, to be kind, participators rather than competitors.

'But who gives a shit,' one nurse told me philosophically.

After watching Mark concentrate on organising a few of the less distinctive events of the day, like the sand skis, where groups of four strapped their feet onto long planks of wood and walked or ran over the sand, and the waiters' challenge which consisted of bartenders carrying trays of jugs to one end of the course, filling them and returning without spilling or drinking any, I wandered over to see the climbers make another assault on the greasy pole.

As they gathered around the base they thought they had worked out how they could do it. They would use five blokes on the base instead of three and take it from there. The lighter men would be the ones to go up the pyramid while the more solid would be used at the base. I thought they should approach Arnold, who was still sunning himself about 30 metres away and watching, or at least I thought he was watching, through his shades. Every now and again his head would turn slightly as though he were making sure his quads or his biceps were still on view.

The pyramid was formed and the climbers scrambled up the bodies of those on the ground, then reached down for the others who they hoisted up and over their shoulders.

As they clambered, Hillary-like, towards the summit, I wondered what would happen when they reached the part of the pole that wasn't greased. It was, after all, 35 degrees and the first hot day of the approaching summer. The metal at the top of the pole would be like a hotplate, even more so than the black mess with which their bodies were covered.

But they were resolute. Three bottles of Bundy and three bottles of Jack Daniels were not to be sneezed at.

Alongside the greasy pole area was a large marquee set up by one of the major hotels in the Alice. It seemed to be sort of like the Members'.

'Do you think they'll make it?' The question came from a smiling, generously proportioned woman watching from inside the roped-off area.

I wasn't sure that I should answer so she answered herself. 'I don't think they will.' She turned away to pick up a can of beer which she poked at me. 'You look like you could do with this.'

She was right.

Dee Corcoran was the PR consultant with the pub and her

enclosure was just one way of ensuring that the thousands of tourists coming to Alice Springs enjoyed themselves.

'I came here when I was 20,' Dee's eyes, like mine, were still fixed on the battle of the pole. 'I'd borrowed a heap of money from Dad to start my own picture sound and editing company in Adelaide, and lost the lot. But you know it all at that age, don't you.' Dee didn't need, or want, an answer. Her father lived in Alice Springs and she came to repay the debt.

'It's funny, you know, and a bit old fashioned I s'pose.' While Dee was talking, the climbers were struggling to raise one of their number up and over the first two storeys. 'But it is *A Town Like Alice*. It's been 18 years now. It was easy to come here but it's a hard place to leave.'

Watching Dee and me was a tall, angular shadow who flitted past every now and again, his suspicious eyes darting between us. He stood some distance away and pretended not to notice, but I imagined every move of ours was being tucked away in his computer for further reference.

'Oh, that's just Crafty,' Dee said, dismissing my paranoia. 'He's with me.'

They'd met not long after she went up there, I discovered. He with a broken marriage, she with a condition that prevented her from having children. But something had worked.

Dee thought that it could have been The Alice. People seemed to find themselves there.

'I don't know how to explain it.' She sounded puzzled. 'In town it's a town, but you've only got to step a foot outside of it and there's something else. There's some sort of beauty in the dirt and the dust. The space. You get an understanding of the centuries. I suppose it's a bit spiritual. Maybe that's what people feel, I don't know.'

The shadow floated by again, so I left Dee to the entertainment just as the pole climbers collapsed and the megaphone burst into sound once more.

Mark's voice echoed around the emptiness of the Todd River.

'This is the big one coming up. We're going to have the heats of the America's Cup.'

The challenger, to be chosen from two teams representing Australia, would have to face the cocky Americans who had gathered to see who their opposition would be. The team from the Jindalee air force base, that operated the over-the-horizon radar at Mount Everard, were to race against a team from the Woomera rocket range.

The Jindalee crew was led by their base wing commander, whose Lawrence of Arabia hat framed a face which had the traditional air force type clipped moustache.

He was taking part, leading his men from the front as it were, showing them the way into battle as all good leaders should. A 20-year veteran of the RAAF, Darryl Hunter saw this as a way of stimulating the morale among his men. 'This is a special place to us. We don't get to serve in remote areas much and we like to be part of the community.'

Darryl thought his crew were a good thing, and he was right.

From the moment they picked up their craft with its hoisted mainsail, the 10 air force men were for a short while transformed into sailors, using the winds and the tide to advantage. Well, anyway, they ran straight and true for the marker buoys and returned about four boat lengths ahead.

The Americans, however, weren't all that impressed. Chuck, who apart from being the leader was the smallest of the group, spoke to his crew, showing them where the Jindalee boys were vulnerable.

'It's the way they turn round the buoys you guys,' he drawled. 'We'll turn better than that, for sure.'

'So there we have it,' bellowed Mark after the judges had made their decision. 'It's Jindalee versus the Yanks.' Lowering the mega-phone, he licked his lips. 'Shit, I need a drink.'

Mark's voice, I thought, would match his face, red raw and sore.

'That's about it,' he agreed. 'I'll be bloody hoarse for a week after this, but she'll be right.'

Bill had returned to the riverbed to watch the start of his favourite event, the triathlon.

'Vone off the things we needed to do vas to introduce a few new events for the day. And this iss vone vich I started a couple of years ago.'

He had with him a cardboard box of small, gold coloured medals that bore the club logo—a line drawing of a yacht with two sets of feet hanging out of the bottom—dangling from the bottom of a length of yellow and black ribbons. 'For all the winners,' he explained. 'They get vone off these and all participants get a certificate.'

It was a gruelling triathlon course. One of the innumerable differences, quite apart from the obvious, between this and normal triathlons was that it was done in pairs. The swim leg was to lie facedown on a cart and have your partner push you along the rails used for the Oxford Tubs. The run leg was simple, run to the marker buoys and back. But the bicycle leg was perhaps the hardest. Triathletes had to run inside a circular wire cage, the sort you see on the end of large poles at the circus, to the buoys and back.

Bill liked that. 'The biggest problem for them is the steering, not the running.'

Standing in line, waiting for Mark to take his name, was a solidly built, real athlete.

Tony Carter, a teacher on long-service leave from Townsville, was camped out in the bush on his way to the Kimberleys and had come into town for some supplies.

'I saw the crowds here so he thought I'd have a look. Then when they announced the triathlon, I said that's for me.'

Tony had found an Englishman named Deke to partner him, but after only a few minutes he was searching the area. 'Shit, he was here a minute ago,' exclaimed Tony.

I reckoned Deke might have found his senses and gone to a pool or an air-conditioned bar, but no, he turned up.

Sandals, socks, T-shirt and shorts. Anything less like a triathlete I'd yet to see. Still, he pushed Tony on the swim and then ran himself, very slowly, and left Tony to negotiate the wire cage before disappearing into the crowd again.

It doesn't mean much in the grand scheme of things, Tony supposed. 'It's about being able to say I've done it. Nothing more than that.'

The eventual winners of the triathlon were two nurses from the local hospital whose tanned, slim, shapely bodies that had shed the garb of their previous event drew admiring glances, not only for their prowess as triathletes.

Bill smiled bravely as he draped the medals around their slender necks.

After the triathlon there was a lull in proceedings to allow Mark to catch up on a bit of the paperwork on his clipboard, so the judges took the opportunity to climb down from their paddlesteamer and have a spell.

One was Ted Egan, local icon and folk singer, writer, historian and performer. Ted travelled throughout the country, spreading his Gospel of the Inland and of The Alice in particular. He was also the only fully fledged empty-beer-carton, or Fosterphone as he called it, player in Australia. He had lived in The Alice all his life. 'There's a magic about the place. A romance. You tell someone you're from Melbourne or Sydney and it doesn't mean much. But tell them you're from Alice Springs and their eyes light up.'

Ted loved the diversity of The Alice. 'We've got lots of friends here. Some are very black and others very white. Some are very rich and others very poor. But they're all just people.'

According to Ted there is a lot more to Alice Springs than meets the eye. 'There is a delightful irony to the place. Like this thing, for example,' he said, nodding toward the arena, 'and besides that it's home.'

With that he walked the plank back to his judges' seat, and Mark and his megaphone were in action once again.

'We're gonna runa coupla the finals now.' The sound was amplified through the watchers.

Women's sand shovelling was the first. The finalists lined up under the only tree that was out in the middle of the river, throwing shade over the cut down forty-fours they were to fill.

It was a cosmopolitan affair between a young English woman with a tattoo on each shoulder, a well-endowed Irish girl who took the lead twice but was distracted on each occasion as she fell out of her skimpy top and had to readjust herself quickly, an Australian, and an American who came from behind to win.

The Women's Head of the River was won by the team from the Ayers Rock Resort over another team of nurses. There was some confusion as to who won and after the nurses protested, Mark told them he'd listen to their arguments. When they had finished their presentation he told them to 'piss off', but Bill gave them a medal anyway.

'The backpackers are next,' Mark informed the onlookers after the nurses had left the arena happily.

These were teams that had never seen each other before and were made up from backpackers out of the crowd.

One team included a young Scot dressed in big baggy shorts. His pale, highland skin, with lots of zinc cream rubbed on his nose, was hidden under his floppy white hat. With a beer can in hand and strong Scottish brogue, Chris Morrison stood out.

'I've bin travellin' round, y'know, and I heard it was on, so I came down.' Chris' sing-song voice was straight from the lochs. 'I was supposed to go to Henley-on-Thames last year but I missed it. This is better, I reckon, y'know.'

Meanwhile, as Mark was trying to get the two teams organised, I wondered when they'd had the heats.

'We haven't,' Mark replied. 'We've only got two teams so we'll just have a final.' He lined them up just as two other teams appeared from the crowd.

'Stuff it all,' he said. 'This is gonna be the only time we've run heats after the final. Line up over there.' He pointed to the patch of sand the first two teams had vacated.

The backpackers shrugged their shoulders, hitched up their borrowed boats and waited for the starter's signal.

After the starting pistol fired, Mark watched them churn through the sand, some falling over with strain, others with the sun, still others with the effects of their consumption.

'Happy as pigs, aren't they,' he smiled.

As the competitors lined up for the bathtub derby, where four people carry a woman in a bath around the sailing course, and the boogie boards, where two men tow a third who sits on the board, and innumerable other races, I went back to the greasy pole climbers.

This was, I feared, to be their last effort. Two more strong-looking blokes with thighs like legs of beef were eyeing off the pole and the prizes at the top. Then they calculated, together and with the other eight, how they were to do it.

They agreed that they needed six around the base. So that was the first thing to do. Then the next three climbed up, followed by the lighter two and finally a long, skinny lightweight who reached out his hand. His fingers clipped the bottom of the bottle of Bundy, making it move just enough so that he couldn't grasp it.

Screams came from below. 'Get hold of the bastard will ya?' as the basemen's eyes bulged and their shoulders stretched with the strain.

'Have you got it yet?' was another cry. The basemen's stare never left the ground as they steeled themselves, trying to keep the skinny one aloft. He reached out again and once more the bottle was pushed out of reach, swaying tantalisingly back and forward, brushing his fingertips as it swept past.

'Hurry up for Christ's sake,' implored the voices at the base.

But hurry they couldn't, and as legs trembled, the muscles screamed and finally gave way. The skinny one at the top tumbled down over the other greasy, stinking bodies and the lot of them lay disillusioned in the sand staring at the pole.

The Holy Grail was still safe, but in a magnanimous show of belief in the spirit of the event the bottles were cut down after someone produced a ladder. 'Near enough is good enough,' announced Bill. 'Today it is anyway.'

The greasy men clutched their bottles like fathers in a maternity ward, smiling their little smiles of delight as they sat exhausted, black and greasy, at the base of the Everest of Alice Springs.

As Mark and Bill presented a few medals, I went over to one of the more curious stalls that were selling their wares on the riverbank.

The Alice Springs Yacht Club was something that I found a little odd. Where did they sail?

'We don't,' was the answer. 'At least not here,' said Paul Herrick, the commodore of the club which was formed in 1993. 'Six of us were sitting having a beer after a game of golf and we found out that we'd all sailed. One bloke suggested that we form a club—so we did.'

According to Paul, the yacht club is around 1500 kilometres from the nearest water they can sail on. 'That's Adelaide or Darwin,' he told me, 'but we do most of our sailing in Sydney. It's about 3000.'

The reason they do their sailing in Sydney is because it's better for them when they tackle the Sydney to Hobart. 'We went in it the first year we formed,' Paul explained. 'It was the roughest on record and it opened our eyes a bit.'

Paul was born on the Victorian coast at Frankston but had moved to Darwin and become a firefighter, ending up in The Alice. Now he reckoned the yacht club ruled his life.

'I suppose it could seem a bit strange,' he said. 'We're probably the only yacht club in the world where the average club members don't sail.

'The keen ones do when they're on holidays, and we go to Sydney for two weeks before each Sydney to Hobart to prepare.'

Should be plenty of time, I thought. Two weeks to get across Bass Strait. No worries. But it must have worked in 1996 as they won their class that year in a 36-footer they had chartered.

One of the good things is that the club is the cheapest in the world to join and has reciprocal rights with all the prestigious yacht clubs in the world. Not that they go there too often.

But they want to. 'Our next target is to sail the Fastnet in England,' Paul said. 'I reckon we can get there.'

While Paul and I had been discussing how mad they all were, Mark had assembled the finalists for the Oxford Tubs.

Arnold and his buddy were opposed to a team from a real estate agents' conference. I looked into Arnold's shades for a sign of how he was feeling, whether he was right for the task at hand, but all I could see was myself looking back at me.

I knew Arnold would be switched on, though. Anyone built like that was sure to be keen to win. He didn't let me down.

As they sped along the rail leaving the poor real estate blokes in their wake, so to speak, Arnold dug the shovel halfway into the sand as he tossed it behind him. At the end of the line, if someone had not told him to stop, I had visions of him taking off and going the full length of the Todd on the wheels.

When he passed me on his way to collect his medals I looked once more into the shades and congratulated him.

'Yeah man, thanks a lart,' replied Arnold, twitching his arms before retreating to the sanctuary of his shade cover where he sat once more in his bulging seat.

As I watched him pass and sit down, Mark announced the America's Cup would be run in half an hour.

But while he spoke, another megaphone in the crowd barked a message to someone or other. It was the only time for the day that I saw Mark stumble. After all the questions, the heat, the people not turning up and all the other little things that had been sent to test the ringmaster of the Henley-on-Todd, this was the one thing that got to him. Someone else had a megaphone and was using it.

'I think I'll wander across there and belt the thing up his arse,' Mark considered before his smile returned and someone thrust a can into his red hand. 'But why spoil a great day?'

As they waited for the starter to call them into position, the Americans stood in a group and started one of those chants that you see in the movies, where one person leads and they all join the chorus:

I used to date a beauty queen . . . hard work
Now I date my M16 . . . hard work
There's no use in looking down . . . hard work
No solution's on the ground . . . hard work

On and on it went, led by a man whose hair looked like the bottom of a scrubbing brush. The singsong words flowed like honey. The Americans loved it but the flyboys from Jindalee led by their wingco stood there and looked on silently. Then, shaking their heads, walked towards their own boat and stepped inside.

The Americans finally stopped their chant and swaggered forward to start what to them was a mere formality.

Chuck looked across his troops and yelled at them, 'This is ours!'

It was no lightweight matter. This was country against country. Prestige and honour. It didn't matter that it was one of the most ridiculous races in the world; they had to win for the Stars and Stripes.

'We live for this day,' Chuck impressed on me. 'We've trained for months for it. We even talked about it last night in the bar.'

Darryl Hunter and his troops were still silent, waiting. They had no desire to waste their breath.

The America's Cup yachts had two hulls that were joined in the centre. Five men in the front and five in the back. The mainsails fluttered from the masts in the front hull and reached both to the bow and the stern. Instead of seats, pipe ran from gunwale to gunwale so the yachts could be lifted.

Mark called the crews forward. 'It's fairly choppy out there today,' he told them earnestly, 'so take care. Big seas can bring big trouble.'

As the yachts were lifted from the sand the legs that protruded from the bottom walked slowly to the starting line. Hands gripped the pipe handles and a fair breeze filled the sails. All eyes were fixed on the course ahead.

Then they were off.

The Yanks slipped quickly into top gear, leading round the first 44-gallon buoy. Tacking was their speciality and they went round it sidewards.

But hard on their starboard beam were the Australians. I thought I detected a bit of John Bertrand in the boat and a bit of Ben Lexcen in the sand.

At the second buoy the Australians had caught up and in his eagerness to get the lead back, the leader of the chant, who would chant no more that day, tripped and nearly fell overboard.

The Australians charged away and, to the cheers of the landlubbers, crossed the line with all sails filled, all anchors aweighed, mainbraces spliced and all scurvy dogs walking the plank while the scuppers were awash with the salt tears of the Americans . . . Or something like that.

At the presentation of the cup that would grace the halls of Jindalee for the next 12 months, Darryl Hunter thanked his crew and then mentioned that the day was quite special to him. 'After all,' he commented, 'it's not every day that a group of air force personnel can pose as sailors and beat America in a yacht race on a dry riverbed.'

Roger Wilco to that.

CHAPTER TEN

THE WONDERFUL LIZARDS OF OZ

While I was in Alice Springs I met a bloke whose grandfather
had travelled round the country early in the century with a team of Aborigines,
building roads using only picks and shovels.
He'd carried on the tradition, only he worked with contractors.
He laughed when I told him about being in the Alice for the Henley.
He reckoned the best thing he'd ever seen were the lizard races in Eulo.
Who was I to argue?

'Which way to the lizard races?'
My question was directed at the man sitting behind a
fragile wooden desk, his chair tipped onto its back legs, as I sent
liquid gold rushing from his hose into my petrol tank.

I gave him the king's ransom it cost to fill my vehicle and he
waved his hand in some obscure direction. 'Down there.' His chair
thumped back onto four legs as he opened the till. I thanked him and
headed off down the bitumen towards Eulo.

The road was straight and narrow and, away in the distance, the
monument became clearer. The closer I got the larger it appeared
until finally it was in full view. Atop a tall rusting windmill stand, a
huge metal lizard surveyed the surrounding area.

A 20-foot galvanised-tin frill neck, mouth open, frill raised so it
looked like it had two giant ears, and tail hanging halfway down the
tower were the product of a bush artist's powerful imagination.

Underneath its feet a large brown sign declared the patch of red
dirt to be the Paroo Track, named after the local river and home of

the World Lizard Racing Championships. There was no-one around so I jumped the short wire fence and walked around the famous square. Alone, I listened for the sounds of the great racing lizards of the past. I tried to conjure up the history of the races, the sounds of the cheering crowds and the yell of the bookies.

But there was nothing, so I went for a walk down the street, such as it was.

There weren't many buildings in this small western Queensland town. A couple of houses, a couple of churches and a general store whose dusty shelves and wooden floor were awash with everything anyone could possibly want, and lots of other things that no-one would.

The caravan park at the end of the street appeared to be an old cricket ground, the pitch having been converted into a long, thin concrete-floored amenities block. The corrugated-iron walls had rust wounds in the corners, while a large corrugated-iron water tank sat unpredictably on the roof. A donkey boiler, made from a few battered drums, rested in the weeds out the back of the building, surrounded by dead trees that were fed into the furnace by whoever was around.

After the grand tour I crossed the creaking verandah of the pub, where a couple of old codgers sat on rough red-gum seats watching the world go by, and went inside.

Behind the bar that swept grandly around the room a tall young woman of generous proportion with a liking for rings and bangles served beer from taps that protruded from the wall of a large square fridge.

The early drinkers squatted on the few stools, their arms uniformly folded in front of them on the bar. No-one spoke.

'They're filling in time till the lizards get here,' Anna Aspinall explained quietly as she wiped the bar in front of me. 'They should be here soon. Darby's never late.'

Darby was Darby Land, mayor of the local shire and organiser of the World Lizard Racing Championships. I wondered which title he considered to be the more important.

While we all waited for Darby and the lizards, Anna and I had a drink and she told me about her pub.

*

A single-storey building, the Eulo Queen Hotel was named after its first owner, Isobel Richardson, as she was when she arrived in Australia from Mauritius in 1876 aged in her mid-twenties.

She worked as a governess on a station near Bourke and married a man named McIntosh who was the overseer. The couple ended up buying a store in Cunnamulla where the Cobb and Co. coaches stopped and 10 years later, in 1886, bought the pub at Eulo.

'Apparently she got hold of a huge collection of opals.' Anna was a bit suspicious of how. 'You know what legends are like.'

This particular legend had it that miners gave them to her for one reason or another and eventually she had jewels to the value of £4000.

Anna went to fix a couple of empty glasses and a couple of dirty looks. 'That's when she became known as the Opal Queen.'

Isobel was married three times while she was in Eulo. To McIntosh, then to a bloke named Robertson and finally to a Mr Grey.

'She dressed up all the time,' Anna told me as her wrist bangles and neck chains rattled. 'She was short and plump and she wore a necklet, two armlets and a girdle made of opals. Not bad eh?'

I asked Anna if she was the new Queen. 'No, not me,' she laughed, her accessories jingling as her body shook.

Isobel left Eulo in 1924 after the pub had burnt down twice and she had lost all her money. She died in a mental home in Toowoomba in 1929.

'Shit!' exclaimed Anna. 'Gotta go for a minute, there's a few in the garden now.'

Under two enormous peppercorns that spread across the lawn area beside the pub, an array of stalls selling local produce, and tasteful handicrafts like carved wooden lizards, were setting up.

It was late morning when Darby Land arrived. He drove up in his shire council limousine with the lizards, languishing in styrene boxes that bore Moorabooka Broccoli labels, in the boot.

At the end of the racetrack was a stand. Not a grandstand, just a stand that Darby had built a few years earlier. Half a dozen gidgee posts nailed together and rammed into the ground with a few dry hopbush branches for the roof.

A couple of feet off the ground was a wooden deck where the diminutive Darby unloaded the boxes of lizards. 'It's somewhere to stand while I'm commentating on the races, and it's a bit of shade.'

The boxes had a few holes punched in the top for air and scratching sounds came from inside while the 65-year-old Darby plonked them on the planks. 'There's shinglebacks in them.'

Pushing back his hat that protected his balding head, and adjusting his glasses so he could see, Darby pointed to the second stack. 'And bearded dragons in them.'

After he had closed the boot Darby told me the races had been going for some 30 years, but had changed a bit recently. 'It used to be that kids could catch their own lizards and bring 'em along to race. Y'know, the ones that hang around the yard and the chook pen. But now we've got to make sure everything we do is environmentally correct.'

Darby and a couple of mates had to catch the lizards in the bush and were required to tag them all and record their weight and length. I wondered why. After all it was a lizard race not a weigh-in for a world championship fight. They also had to leave a coloured marker at the spot where they came from so the lizards could be returned.

'Look,' said Darby, having a bob each way, 'I reckon we've got to look after the environment and be a bit conservationist otherwise there'll be nothing left.'

I agreed. But I wondered about all the dead and squashed bodies I saw on the roads. Who looked after them? Darby didn't comment.

The political discussion finished as the microphone for the auction was set up and the starting stalls were put into place.

'We'll be ready soon enough.' Darby sounded enthusiastic. 'But there's some other stuff to get through first.'

The lizard races were the main attraction, but the program started with a few woodchop events.

The participants in all three races were the same blokes, one of whom was an Aborigine whose stomach was so large that when he walked he took little gingerly steps as though he expected to fall over at any minute.

One of his opponents was a small, mysterious looking character who wore jeans and a dark shirt as well as dark sunglasses, while the other contestant was the opposite—tall, skinny and fair headed.

The mysterious man won the first woodchop event from the Aborigine, who was out of breath halfway through, and the tall man whose axe kept sticking. The chainsaw event finished in the same order, with the Aborigine's saw not quite as sharp, while the tall man's wouldn't start.

Standing nearby was one of the timekeepers, a middle-aged beauty who paraded the length of the track to where the axemen stood.

Her bright pink slacks were matched with a brighter pink jacket and an even brighter shade of pink lipstick. She wore white high-heeled shoes which buried themselves deep in the dirt with every step and flapped against her soles when she pulled them free. But the crowning glory was her hat—a black baseball cap with Shell Oils emblazoned in gold across the peak. She was a vision splendid.

After the logs were cleared away the ladies' tug-of-war was the next item on the agenda. The pink lady, who obviously carried some sort of title, called the teams onto the track.

Both teams were made up of females who were, well, huge. One, the McKellar's Fencing team, was even huger than the others. Old shirts and tattoos were prevalent. Make-up was not. Work shorts and bare feet were the order of the day, with arms and legs that could kick start jumbo jets sticking out of T-shirts that fell like tents from their shoulders.

The delicate lady in pink was a contrast standing there on the red dirt giving instructions before retreating to the safety of the fence.

When the signal was given, the McKellar's Fencing team, who had won the event for the previous 10 years, nonchalantly pulled their opposition over. It seemed to me they could be champions for the next 20 years. And without training.

The ladies then strolled off, collected their cartons of XXXX that were the prizes, and went looking for some shady trees.

*

The first of the lizard races was the sweepstakes for shinglebacks. Darby took the mike in one hand and reached into a styrene box with the other, emerging with a scaly, sausage-shaped beast held by the neck. He waved it to the crowd.

'Now ladies and gentleman, what am I bid for this great lizard? His name is Rodeo. I reckon he's a fine specimen and anyone who buys him this afternoon is sure to get a good run for their money!'

While Darby spruiked to the crowd, his spotters were around the area checking out the bids in true auctioneering style. The lady in pink was right in the forefront.

Rodeo was soon knocked down for the magnificent sum of $90 and went back in the box to await the start.

It wasn't long before Darby had sold the rights to race the other 10 starters and the crowd watched intently as they made their way to the barriers.

This was done by handing the styrene box over the fence, where the clerk of the course deposited each of the lizards into the starting stalls, a round contraption made of perspex that was divided into sections like the slices of a cake. Attached to the top of the barrier was a rope which wound up through a series of pulleys to a lever which would raise the barrier when the starter said go.

As well as all this technical stuff, there was a red light which flashed when the starter had them ready and a bell which signalled that the race was under way.

'Just like Randwick,' someone in the crowd suggested.

After Rodeo and his mates were placed in the barrier, all neatly tagged with numbers so they could be told apart, the starter set the red light flashing and pulled the lever to lift the barriers, setting the lizards on their journey of 10 feet to a poly pipe layed in a circle around them.

As the barriers went up to the roars of the crowd—well, a couple of cheers anyway—the lizards simply sat there.

Perhaps they were overcome by stage fright, or maybe they just didn't feel like racing. I thought it could be that they were startled to see about 400 people with their eyes set on them, waiting to watch them crawl 10 feet to a black plastic pipe.

Whatever it was, they weren't going to move.

'It's like this sometimes,' said Darby. 'They'll take a while to get mobile and other times they'll be off like shit off a shovel. Like Herbie.'

Herbie was the record holder at the World Championship Lizard Racing. The greatest of them all, he had managed to cross the finish line in 2.7 seconds. An amazing feat!

'Yeah,' remembered Darby, 'he was pretty good and he was a shingleback, so don't get the idea that they're slow.'

No, I thought, I won't.

Meanwhile, inside the ring, the shinglebacks decided to move, or at least a couple of them did.

They looked in terrific nick as they waddled their scaly bodies slowly towards the line. Trained to the minute.

But Rodeo didn't move. He stood in the centre of the ring and looked around, poking his blue tongue at any figure he saw. When he did decide to move he walked around in a complete turn and stopped where he had started.

It took three minutes for the winner, who was listed in the form guide as Joke by Good Management out of Canberra, to cover the journey. As he slid over the pipe the crowd cheered. Joke just kept waddling until Darby grabbed him and put him back in the saddling paddock, heavily disguised as a styrene box.

'Good race that one, eh?' Darby stated.

'Yeah,' I said, astounded.

There was a break between races so the stewards could clear the track and set up the barrier stalls again.

Standing behind me and watching intently was an Aboriginal man who had cut the top out of his stovepipe hat to let his dreadlocks free. They poked up through the empty space and down the back of his hat to rest on his shoulders. His sunglasses matched his black face and he wore a three-quarter length overcoat with rastafarian connotations. I asked if he was enjoying the races.

'Yeah, but I'd rather be eatin' 'em,' he muttered.

Charlie was his name, he told me, from a tribe in Central

Australia, and he'd come over to look for work. I asked how long he'd been in the area.

'Let me think.' He rubbed his chin and then looked at me again. 'Includin' today?'

'Yes, I suppose,' I replied.

'Then it's my second day.' He roared with laughter, slapping his knees and bending in half with mirth. 'Got ya, din I?' He was shaking with the humour of it all.

I waited patiently until he'd settled down again and asked him for the real story.

It turned out his name was Peter and he came from the suburbs of Rockhampton. He was out here working as linesman for Telstra and had seen the crowd as he was driving through the town. 'And I like lamb and pork too,' he grinned.

Peter and I chatted for a while about the difference for him between the cities and the bush. 'Mate, out here, there are real people. We're just people and they're just people. Pity it's not like that everywhere, eh?'

Peter turned to go. 'I've gotta get off now.' He offered his hand. 'Gotta keep the lines free.'

As he walked away his coat which was obviously causing him to sweat came off, revealing a Brisbane Broncos jumper underneath. His dreadlocks bounced proudly on his shoulders.

The auction for the bearded dragons started with Darby reaching into one of his boxes as he was talking into the mike. He wasn't looking what he was doing and his hand came out with a frill-neck attached to it and blood dripping between his fingers. He shook it around but the lizard, beside waving in the air like a handkerchief, had a good hold. Darby dropped the mike and used his other hand to remove the reptile. He wondered aloud if lizards had rabies. No-one seemed to know, or care.

After wrapping his finger in a bit of cloth and then throwing it away because it was too cumbersome, Darby started the auction.

Bidding was fast and furious. The lady in pink stood in front of one bidder and watched her closely. Every time she blinked her eye the lady in pink screamed out, 'Yeess!!'

The lizard under the hammer was number 159, Smooth Run by Full Tank out of Mobil. He was knocked down to the lady in pink's bidder, Simone Tully, a tall, willowy blonde pushing a pram.

Four hundred dollars for a lizard seemed a touch extravagant and I couldn't make out what distinguished one lizard from another.

'Nor can I.' Simone laughed. 'But I owe the Flying Doctor a fair bit with this bloke,' she said, pointing to the pram, 'and if I can help then it's a small price. Besides, anything that bites Darby has to have something going for it.'

The young fellow in the pram had pulled some oxy bottles onto himself while out in the shed on the station and made a mess of his skull.

'Doctor Bob flew in and made him safe before flying us to Brisbane. If he hadn't been around . . .' her voice trailed off, not wanting to think too much about it. 'Some of the money today goes to them. But I'm still well behind. Will be for life.'

Smooth Run was up against some formidable opponents in Mother's Milk, who was by Fourex out of Cunnamulla, and Lock Up by Punched out of Riot to name just two. Likely-looking types they were as well. Fairly similar in appearance to the rest, but to the trained eye they had that something special.

The barrier was put in place and the lizards placed in their holes, all facing the finishing pipe from different directions.

As the red light flashed, Rod, Simone's helicopter pilot who had flown her in for the races from their station ran onto the track and found lizard 159, or Smooth Run, through the perspex.

I couldn't see anything different about Smooth Run, though perhaps Rod could.

'Not really. I just want to know where the money's goin'.'

Bearded dragons are supposed to be flighty and will run away at the slightest provocation but these blokes did the same as the shinglebacks. Stayed there.

The clerk of the course stood in the middle of the track and clapped his hands a couple of times. The lizards took off, scurrying toward the pipe with their backs arched and their heads up, frills raised for protection.

Then halfway to the finish they stopped as if frozen.

'Shit!' exclaimed Darby. 'At this rate they'll never get done.'

Rod was jumping up and down near the fence urging Simone's lizard on.

Smooth Run either couldn't hear him or chose, as lizards are wont to do, to ignore any advice from humans. Then he began to move and after a couple of stammering starts ran across the line to victory.

'Bloody fantastic!' yelled Rod. 'Number 159 to the winner's stall please.'

But the announcement from Darby stopped him in his tracks. 'The winner is number 183. Unbelievable by Speechless out of MP.'

Rod stood there, speechless himself, looking at the winner and then muttering, 'Unbelievable, unbefuckinglievable.'

A couple more exhibition races followed before Darby announced that the Publican's Purse would be run in an hour's time. I went looking for Anna to see if she could give me any tips but, amidst peals of laughter, she told me she was, 'flat out like a lizard drinking'.

Anna had set up a temporary bar in the beer garden so people could sit on the grass and still have a drink if they wanted. They could also listen to Tom Maxwell, country singer, who was entertaining the crowd with songs about ridin', drovin', rustlin', lervin' and leavin'.

In front of him, on a tattered canvas tarpaulin, was a mechanical buckin' bull (another of Tom's songs) being run by two skinny, dark-skinned characters who limped profoundly. No-one, after imagining where their limps came from, would attempt to ride the thing.

Back at the Paroo Track, Darby was having a well-earned break. He looked up from his seat under the hopbush shade and asked if I'd heard about Destructo.

I confessed that I hadn't.

'Well, in 1980 after Wooden Head had won the World Championship here, Destructo challenged him to a race of breeds.'

Destructo, Darby informed me, was a cockroach. Not any old cockroach but a racing one, and fast.

'We set it all up and bugger me if Destructo didn't beat Wooden Head by a fair bit.'

But sadly, after Destructo had won the coveted title, he had met with an unfortunate accident. A drunk in the crowd stood on him.

And now, to his memory, a granite monument stands near the gate at the Paroo Track. On it a plaque is suitably yet simply inscribed

Destructo—champion racing cockroach
accidentally killed at this track 24/8/80
after winning the challange stakes against Wooden Head
champion racing lizard 1980.
Unveiled 23/8/81

Destructo wouldn't have minded the spelling mistake, I thought. After all, he was probably the only cockroach in the world who had raced a lizard, not to mention beaten it.

Leaning on the fence watching me as I read the monument was a hunched-over, wrinkled old snoozer the locals simply called Old Dan.

Dan was a legend in the area. A poet, historian and general old larrikin, he loved the humour of the Outback. He had seen a few hard years, Old Dan. As he spoke to me his voice trembled and his hands shook. We discussed what we found humorous.

'There was a mate of mine in Changi we used to call Cocky,' he recalled. 'Funny bastard he was. And the city types could never understand us you know.'

I started to tell Dan that I did know, but he went on as though he didn't need an answer.

'There was a bit of a show one night and Cocky was raving on, telling all the prisoners how bush blokes were smarter than city blokes. Anyway, he said his name was Cocky and he was from Thargomindah. And a bloke yelled out from down the back, "Where the bloody hell's Thargomindah?"

' "Well," Cocky said, "where are you from?" and the bloke tells him Sydney. "There you go then, that proves it. Everyone in Thargomindah knows where Sydney is." '

Old Dan thought that was wonderful. I couldn't help thinking how good it would have sounded in Changi.

Then he recited a poem. He didn't say as much but I reckoned it might have been about his life. It was the story of a man meeting a woman in a bar out in the Outback and how she is racked with the ravages of time and drink.

'*She had once been someone special,*
   We were lovers, she and I.
Kiss as soft as evening twilight,
   Warmer than a summer sky.

I was born to be a sinner,
   Born to love and lie and leave,
Always taking, never giving
   Never looking back to grieve.

Old Dan was somewhere else as he spoke. His voice softened as he came to the end.

I was looking for a memory.
   I didn't have to look too far,
For my past came back to greet me
   In that little western bar.

Dan was still for a moment, dragging on his smoke. Then he looked up, smiled, and quietly shuffled over to the pub.

Anna came across for the start of the Publican's Purse. As we watched the shinglebacks being prepared for the race she told me that she'd first come here on the way from her home in Warwick to the Innamincka races.

'Friends of mine owned the pub then and I called in to say g'day. They wanted someone to cook for three weeks so I stayed. That was in 1995 and I've been here since.'

She was the permanent cook for two years and then, when her friends moved on, she bought the pub.

Anna had been a nanny, a cook on another Outback station for three years, and a jillaroo before she came here. 'I guess you could say I've been around a bit.'

She also admitted that it was a bit of a challenge being single and being a woman out there.

'Mum reckons I'm wasting my precious years out here in the scrub, but she's from the city. She wants me to go back there. But to what? Anyway, I've got another five years here and hopefully some dashing prince will come along one day and marry me.'

The lizards were now all dressed in their racing colours. Little coloured silks that fitted neatly over their scales between their two sets of feet. Anna's wore red, white and green hoops.

Darby dropped it into the barrier and stood back, declaring the runners to be locked away and under starter's orders.

There were only five lizards in the race. One from each of the neighbouring pubs who contributed to the Flying Doctor: Thargomindah, Hungerford, Cunnamulla, Wyandra and, of course, the Eulo Queen.

The starter raised his hand, turned on the red light and rang the bell. Then he pulled the lever and the lizards were off.

Or as off as standing still can be.

'It must be the weather,' Darby told the crowd. 'They're never usually like this.'

The lizards examined each other for a while and when the clerk of the course stepped amongst them, waving his arms, stamping his feet and whistling, they looked up at him with amazement.

Heads upturned, they flashed their tongues until he stepped back wondering what to do next. The shinglebacks then relaxed until he tried it again, with the same result. Eventually the lizard wearing the red, green and white of the Eulo Queen waddled towards the circle of pipe. Halfway across the dirt he stopped and turned round.

'Stupid bloody lizard,' yelled Anna. Then, turning to me, she exclaimed, 'You'd think they knew how to give a girl the shits wouldn't you?'

Back in the middle of the ring a couple of the others were making slight moves towards the pipe. The yellow and black one from

Hungerford decided it was time for a bit of action and waddled over to where Anna's representative stood.

It must have been the challenge Anna's reptile was waiting for as he scuttled over to the pipe where, at the moment everyone thought he was going to win, he stopped and rested on his scaly stomach.

It looked like he was playing to the crowd because, as soon as the yells and the roars of surprise at his actions had died down, he stood up and took the last few steps to immortality.

Great cheering from the locals greeted his win and he was suitably feted. Then Darby and his helpers picked him and all the other runners up, took off their racing silks and deposited them back into the styrene box.

I was sad for him. That was no way for a champion to spend his moment of glory, but then that's the lot of a racing lizard.

'What do you reckon about that?' asked Anna excitedly.

I thought it was an omen and told her so. I mean who knows who would walk through the bar door now and sweep her off her feet. Not only was she young, a woman, attractive and the owner of a pub, but she had the best racing lizard around. Every man's dream.

Anna laughed. 'Got it all going for me haven't I?'

The presentation of the winner's perpetual trophy, a large wooden carving of a lizard that would grace the bar at the Eulo Queen for the next 12 months, was done by Darby, ably assisted by the lady in pink who handed him the trophy and the accompanying sash that was placed over Anna's shoulders.

'What a great result,' said Darby.

Soon he had the lizards all ready to go back to the bush, but there was one more event to run.

'This is always interesting,' Darby mentioned. 'They have to eat a whole, dry, square Sao biscuit in one go, roll a bale of wool down the street, run back to the pub and skoll a hot stubbie.

'We call it the Iron Man.' Darby looked at me. 'I reckon you should have a go.'

I quickly shook his hand, thanked him and headed for the car.

CHAPTER ELEVEN

WHILE THERE'S RACES THERE'S HOPE

If there is a place that means 'Outback', I found it in Birdsville.
Hot, dusty and in the middle of nowhere, it doesn't have much going for it.
But then again, it does.
It has hope, and belief, and triumph over the odds.
A bit like horseracing, I suppose.
Now that's a sport of belief.
One day, perhaps, a horse will turn up so owners and trainers can live their
dreams.
In Birdsville, it is no different.

The sign behind the bar of the Birdsville Pub wasn't subtle. 'This is Australia. Owners of caps worn backwards will be fined $5.'

Along the rafters behind the sign, and in various stages of degeneration, were rows of large bushman's hats that had gathered a thick layer of dust. Attached to each one was a card with the name of the donor scrawled on it.

The room was devoid of furniture. Drinkers stood on an expanse of concrete and filled the space between the heavy wooden bar and the walls. Empty beer cans, some crushed underfoot and some still round and firm, were piled about five high, like a mouse plague, where the walls joined the floor.

Drinkers waded through the cans as they re-ordered or simply kicked them aside. No-one seemed to care too much about tidiness.

Outside the pub, under the big verandah, drinkers leaned against the white stone walls or sat in the dirt. The table drains that served as the town gutters were awash with cans.

I pushed my way through the masses and stood at the corner of the bar, waiting. After a while an Aborigine beside me, whose sweaty skin shone like patent leather dancing pumps, smiled at me with a grin that flashed white but on closer inspection showed two or three gaps in his yellowing teeth.

'You not from 'round here,' he stated the obvious. 'You bin here for the races before?'

I replied that I hadn't and he smiled again and paused as he looked around the room. 'It different.'

A few minutes passed while I waited for one of the five people behind the bar to notice me. The Aborigine and his five mates stood beside me and studied the drinkers in silence from under their stock-man's hats. Once in a while one would say something to the others that would cause a bit of a laugh, but mainly they just watched.

The young woman who finally handed me a can looked out of place. Her dreadlocks were being constantly flicked away and her left ear was home to about eight earrings of varying size and weight. A silver stud was attached to the side of her nose but her right ear was relatively empty. Leah Fort laughed with exasperation. 'It's madness around here and it's only Thursday night. Wait till tomor-row when the crowd starts to arrive.'

But her grin never faded as she hurriedly thumped can after can on the bar and threw money at the drawer in the till.

I left when the Aborigines did. 'I gotta big day tomorra, helpin' and that,' my new acquaintance told me. 'At the races, y'know.'

On Friday, the first of the two race days at Birdsville, I watched a semi-trailer drive off the Birdsville Track stacked with about 40 pink, portable toilets. They were unloaded by a forklift whose driver raced maniacally round the streets, depositing them in strategic areas in the town.

The police supervised as barricades were placed down the centre of Adelaide Street so the traffic could only drive through one way. 'To protect the people outside the pub,' one cop told me. Later that night the road would be blocked completely.

Across the road from the side of the pub was the airport. Here planes of all shapes and sizes landed with their occupants setting up camps under their wings. Being only 20 metres away, it was probably the closest airport to a pub in the world.

Four-wheel drives rolled into town from off the track or from out of the Simpson Desert. Birdsville was undergoing its yearly transformation for the race weekend.

Inside the pub was quiet as it was still early, but outside, Leah, dreadlocks flapping against her face and grass rake in her hand, was in the gutter raking the previous night's cans into neat piles. Her helper, whose muscles bulged out of his shorts and blue singlet, shovelled them into the back of a ute. 'The school sends them to the recyclers,' she said. 'It raises them a lot of money.' I expected it would.

Leah leaned on her rake when I told her that I was heading out to the track to find the secretary.

'He won't be there yet,' she said, pointing to the other end of the town. 'Go down to his house.'

David Brook's round face looked up from a pile of paperwork. He had been secretary of the Birdsville Race Club for 25 years. 'No-one else has ever put their hand up.' He smiled. 'No coups, nothing like that.'

David's father had arrived in Birdsville in 1918, when he came to work on one of the stations. 'But my mother's grandparents came here in 1870 from Tunbridge Wells in England to open a cordial factory.'

I couldn't understand what would make someone do a thing like that. I mean, there are life changes and then there are life changes.

Through the window David pointed out some ruins of an old hotel that the family had owned at one time, before converting it to an Inland Mission hospital.

'And they also owned the current pub for a while,' he added. 'Actually, the family have lived on every block in the street over the last 120-odd years. I suppose that makes me a local.'

The desk in David's office at the back of his house was strewn with racing club business. Outside the door racebooks, trophies and other paraphernalia spilled out of cardboard boxes that were stacked uncertainly against the wall.

People came and went, either paying entry money, complaining about something or other, or asking questions that only the secretary knew the answer to.

As another person shut the flywire door behind me, David ran a hand over his balding head and adjusted his steel-rimmed spectacles. 'It's a bit of a pain but it's worth it,' he admitted. 'And because it's only once a year, we have to sort of reinvent the wheel each time.'

David's family had a long history with the Birdsville Race Club, winning the centenary cup in 1983 with Brashleigh, and then years later with a horse called Pensami.

'We've always got a few going around on Cup day.'

Just then the door opened behind me and in walked the Aborigine from the pub.

'This is Joey Harris.' David introduced us. 'He works for us.'

Joey grinned and offered his hand, long and bony with one finger missing. He took some instructions from David and left.

'I've got to get going too.' David excused himself.

As I walked out I noticed on the wall a framed picture of David and Joey about 20 years younger sitting on horses in the main street. A much smaller photograph was at the bottom of the frame. It was of the two of them at about six years of age, playing. The small plate at the top of the frame bore one word: 'Mates.'

I nodded to myself and walked out. Joey and David were keen to get out to the track. So was I.

I'd passed the racecourse on the way in from Windorah, about six hours away on a dirt road that had more waves than Bondi. It was the last petrol station before Birdsville and as I filled the Landcruiser the old man behind the counter that was cut into the wall of a corrugated-iron shed asked me if I was going to the races. I replied that I was and noticed that his head didn't move when he spoke. 'Might get down there meself this year.'

Only as I moved from washing the windscreen to the hose at the back did he move. I could see his head following me as I walked around the vehicle. I went to pay him and he asked what was on the bowser. When I told him he turned his head and pointed to a door. 'Better go in there.' The young bloke who took my money told me the old man sat there for most of the day, talking to people on their way through or to the locals who wandered in every now and again.

It wasn't till I had driven off that I realised he was blind.

The Birdsville racecourse consisted of a few iron buildings dotted around part of an inland desert. A large yellow sign, attached to the roof of an iron shed with no front or back, indicated the Birdsville Race Club Entrance. Racegoers walked under the sign, paid their money and looked for some shade, of which there was precious little. There were no beds of roses or trees that changed colour with the seasons. There was just dirt. And then more dirt.

The horse yards were a simple mixture of iron poles with an iron roof, but the jockeys' room had iron roof and walls with a concrete floor. Modern.

The judges' box was perched on top of an iron tower while the secretary's office joined the jockeys' room at the back of what could be loosely called the grandstand. It consisted of a large iron roof supported by iron poles, at the front of which was a three-tiered iron frame with wooden seats. All the buildings seemed to have been designed and built by the same architect.

Two large rails of white iron on white posts indicated the track and around the outside rail were parked a mixture of cars, four-wheel drives, utes and trucks.

Not one square inch of the place was disturbed by a blade of grass, or for that matter, anything else that could call itself a living thing.

A hot northerly kicked up swirls of dust as I approached the stables to study the horses as they stood, heads down, under the iron roof.

In one of the enclosures a small figure was hunched over, sewing bandages onto a horse's leg. One hand steadied the leg on his thigh while the other alternated between stitching and waving at the flies that darted around his face.

As the flies became thicker, his hand waved more vigorously.

'Fuckin' hell!' he cried as the hand with the needle passed perilously close to his eyes. 'Piss off will ya!' The flies took no notice.

Gilbert Baker, 'everyone calls me Potter', had worked as a ringer on the stations around Birdsville until he had fallen from his motorbike and broke his back 11 years before.

'These horses keep me busy now, bit of a hobby,' he told me as he straightened, lifted his hat and scratched his head. After returning the hat to its rightful place and patting the horse on the shoulder, Potter remarked that his old man was a drover. 'I used to go away with him a fair bit. Two or three months. One trip was four and a half. Bin around horses for 50 years.'

Now he lived and trained his horses at Toowoomba, travelling around to country meetings.

I asked Potter about Birdsville and its attraction. 'The money,' he said smiling, 'same as any other horse trainer. I come for the money.'

The gleam in his eye told me that there was more. ''S'pose there is,' he admitted. 'It's the Melbourne Cup of the Outback, innit?'

Potter knew the Melbourne Cup would only ever be a dream. 'But this, well I come here for all the Birdsville Cups with a couple runners. Gunna win it one year, I reckon.'

I stood back as Potter led the bandaged Sir Rastus towards the saddling paddock, a fenced off area of dirt alongside the horse enclosure. Here the jockeys wandered out from their rooms and hopped aboard as the trainers gave last-minute instructions and sent them on their way towards the starting gates.

Potter gave Sir Rastus a chance although the racebook form showed he had been tenth of 12 runners at Roma, fourth of five at Tambo and in his last run had not been quite as successful, as he came last in a field of 12 at Dalby.

I kept my money in my pocket and Sir Rastus ran about as well as his form indicated he might.

Leading the winner back was the smiling clerk of the course, Jim Crombie, a 56-year-old from the Wangkangurru people, who wore an old red waistcoat to signify his standing. Jim's eyes shone like marbles set deep in his face. His voice was high-pitched and excited.

'We nebber go any place or see too many people, so we like these races for the people comin' here.'

One of Jim's ancestors had lived till he was 95 and was famous for being able to bring the rain, a useful talent in this area. Joe the Rainmaker, as he was known, used kopi to call down the thunder and gypsum for the steady rain. Joe was wary of strangers and had two fierce dogs in his camp, but to be on the safe side he kept a large sand goanna under his blankets, just in case.

After the horses had been given safely back to their trainers, Jim balanced himself on the fence rail, holding a rein in one hand and rolling a smoke with the other. He gazed at the distant hills when I asked how long his family had been around here.

'I reckon we bin here forebber.'

The sun was shining like a dollop of butter in a sky the colour of a delft blue plate. The tourists, with the dust tormenting their noses and eyes, crowded under the grandstand while the locals couldn't understand what all the fuss was about.

Leaning nonchalantly against the secretary's office wall was a smiling David Brook whose horse, Spa Hawk, had just won the second race.

'Hot!' he exclaimed mockingly when I complained about the heat and the dust. 'You should have been here in '68.'

In 1968, when they started to put the bitumen down in the main street, the temperature rose to 55 degrees, workmen fainted and thermometers burst.

David shook his head. 'If you reckon this is hot don't ever go to the Betoota races.'

I'd been through Betoota. As I drove the six hours across the vast gibber plain between Windorah and Birdsville, Betoota appeared out of nowhere. It consisted of just one building, a pub. What else?

Opposite the pub was a battered green plywood caravan with a couple of windows hacked from the side. It stood like a sculpture, a dot of green on a vast canvas of varying shades of brown. A badly written sign stood on the side of the track: 'Hot chips, coffee and cold drinks'.

Inside was Ray Rosenlund, 70-year-old entrepreneur. 'I come out here and get the tourists on the way through,' he explained.

I couldn't decide whether Ray was a good businessman or just mad. After tasting his coffee and paying him I decided he was a little of both.

Betoota's population, like its buildings, was also one, a certain 83-year-old Ziegmund Remienko who owned and lived in the pub.

'He's Polish,' Ray told me as I leant against the caravan, hoping I wouldn't damage it. 'Spent five years in a POW camp after the Germans took 'em over.' I thought that a rather interesting description of an invasion.

Ray, who had the mail run out here in the 1940s, was Ziegmund's mate and knew all about him. 'He was put on a train to Russia but he jumped off and walked across Germany to Belgium. He come out here as a refugee.'

According to Ray, in those days refugees had to go to the bush to do a couple of years compulsory work. Ziegmund came to Betoota to work on the roads.

'Anyway,' Ray continued, 'he bought the pub pretty cheap in '56 cos the bloke who owned it, his missus shot through with a drover.'

Ziegmund used to cart all the beer for the pub himself, leaving a staff member in charge while he was away driving the 1320 kilometres to Adelaide and back picking up beer from the brewery. One famous time, Ray told me, he was stuck on the track for 18 weeks with eight tons of beer.

'Closed it last year and won't sell it to no-one,' Ray leaned out of his window. 'Reckons it's his little shack and he'll die there.'

I didn't see Ziegmund, but suddenly it didn't seem to matter that I was standing in the middle of nowhere drinking terrible coffee that cost a fortune.

As I drove off I called out to Ray to see if he was going to the races.

'Nah,' he sneered. 'Last time I was there was '46. Don't like big crowds.'

The betting ring at Birdsville was on a slight sandhill that curved gently from beside the grandstand to the bar. Punters on their way to get a drink could give their money away to either well-dressed bookies who wore matching shirts and slacks and who stood under coloured umbrellas, or to blokes who wore jeans and large hats and who stood out in the sun.

Trade was brisk at the better dressed stands. The scribes were writing furiously and the bagmen stuffed wads of notes away into the darkness of their cavernous white bags. It worried me to see the other bookies with no umbrellas watching jealously. I thought that if you wanted to get rid of some money then you should at least give it to someone who appeared to need it. But then I remembered the saying about broke bookies and felt better.

Everyone wanted to bet on a horse called Likely Lad. One of the bookies said to his penciller in a snide aside, just loud enough for the punters to hear, 'This is the Greyhound bus tip.' He was proved right. Likely Lad ran last by about six lengths.

Half an hour later, the main event of the day was won by a magnificent brown gelding, Dry 'n' Sober.

If ever there was an omen tip it was that one. One part of the name highly likely and the other highly unlikely.

It won by three lengths. Trainer Ken Rogerson had brought Dry 'n' Sober over from Alice Springs specially for the Cup, in which it was top weight. 'I just give him a run today to loosen him up a bit,' he said at the presentation.

While he was accepting the trophy I saw Potter, head down and still waving at the flies, leading his horse Blatonto, who had finished a good last, back to the mounting yard.

Back in the ring the odds about Dry 'n' Sober in the Cup had been slashed. This was no Greyhound bus tip. After all, he'd won a few times in Darwin and Ken Rogerson had won main events in nearly all capital cities.

I wondered why he bothered coming all the way out here. 'It only takes a few of us to stop coming, then a couple of others. Soon you haven't got the Birdsville Races.'

Ken admitted that it would be a big effort for his horse to back up again and that the competition was stiff. 'They're all after the Cup.'

They were indeed. After all, you don't make the effort to get to Birdsville and not want to win.

David Brook had explained the paradox of Birdsville to me. 'The Melbourne Cup is a race that nearly everyone can get to pretty easily but only a few have a horse good enough, or lucky enough, to get a run.

'Yet there are plenty of horses good enough to run in the Birdsville Cup but not many can get here.'

About an hour later after the last race had been run and the cars had left the fence for the short drive back into the town, Potter drove his old truck back to the banks of the Diamantina River where he was camped. 'They settle well out there and it gets 'em used to the area a bit. Bin out there for about a week, me and the horses.'

And what about tomorrow?

'Tomorra?' We'll see what happens tomorra.'

On Friday night the diesel generators that supplied the electricity to Birdsville were flat out keeping the lights on all the stalls working, not to mention the fridges at the pub where around 4000 people stood in the street.

Standing near the pub door was Joey Harris. I hadn't seen him at the races and I wanted to catch up and have a drink. Joey shook his head at me. 'You wanna go talk to them udder fellahs, not me.'

I elbowed my way through the crowd, calling to Joey that I'd see him later, knowing that he'd probably be gone.

In the distance, over the top of a thousand heads, Leah's dreadlocks were bouncing up and down behind the bar. 'Can't talk now,' she had to yell over the noise of the crowd when I reached her, 'but Kym's out the back.'

I'd asked her earlier why she called her father Kym. 'Cos that's his name,' was her entirely reasonable reply.

Kym Fort was drinking coffee at a table behind the Green Lizard bar, which was named after a mob of blokes who got together during the beer shortage of the late '60s and drank only crème de menthe. His tall, slim body leant back in his chair, legs stretched out before him.

Kym was a builder in Adelaide when he bought the pub in 1980 after the front bar had burnt down. 'When I got here I thought: Shit, what have I done?' But they set up a couple of 44-gallon drums with a plank of wood and kept going. 'Took us a while to get it back to square one, but it was worth it.'

Birdsville had changed a lot since Kym had been there, with tourists coming and the roads getting a bit better. 'Most small towns are dying but we're getting bigger.' Kym was philosophical. 'It's funny, really, to keep the meaning of Birdsville and the attraction of it we need to keep the challenge of getting here, but the people who live here would like it easier to get out.'

Kym loved to see the old folk come out on the bus trips. 'Doesn't matter what we think, we can't deny those people their chance to see us. We've had people in the bar that have never had a drink in their lives but have said they've gotta have one in the bar of the Birdsville pub.'

But the Birdsville pub is not the luxurious place that some people stay at. 'We don't make it easy for them when they get here.' Kym was adamant that tourists had to see it for real. 'There's no TV in the pub. There's no point coming here and staying in your room. And there's no Sky Tab or pokies.'

People don't talk in pubs any more, Kym reckoned. 'They play bloody machines or watch their money disappear on horse telly. Here they talk.'

Kym's long, fair frame rose from his chair. 'I'd better get back into it. I've got a heap of grog to sell.'

Ordering was a gamble, he admitted. 'We only get trucks in once every two weeks so I've got to get it right. Got about 80,000 cans in this year, so if it rains I'm left with two year's supply of grog. And the breweries don't want it back.'

It was tough at times in the pub, according to Kym, but it was a lot easier than the old days, before fridges, when beer was poured into big saucers to cool down before it could be drunk. And then there's the five months when no-one comes near the place because of the heat. 'So the fortune everyone thinks I make here on race weekend has to last me a long time.'

Kym opened the door to the bar and a wall of sound rushed through like a tidal wave. I followed him through and a couple of hours later went out into the street where a few hundred well-lubricated people had gathered to watch as a young man passed around the hat for an attractive, well-endowed young woman who was about to respond to yells of 'Show us yer tits'.

After her top went back on I wandered back to my swag past the rows of tourist tents set up like the photos of the lighthorseman's camps in the Middle East, past the pink toilets with queues that stretched for 30 metres, past the old Indian motorbike with a sidecar and past the rusting Citroën with four figures, all sitting up, asleep inside.

Birdsville Cup day dawned hot and windy. Crowds poured in to the racetrack under the yellow sign in larger numbers than the previous day. There were more cars around the fence and the buses ferrying people from town to the course were kept busy.

Potter had turned up with his truck, ready for the big day. 'There's somethin' special about it, int there.'

I suppose there was. Wandering through the crowd were a group of blokes dressed in footy shorts, footy socks, sandshoes and dinner jackets with bow ties. They were on a tour of Australia from Perth and when I asked them why they dressed like they did, the reply was, 'Cos we're a long way from home and no-one knows us here.'

The bar had doubled its size overnight with the addition of a large marquee that had been erected in front of it. Next to it was a trailer that had a woman in a dangly fur-lined coat, with jangling boots and spurs, wailing Patsy Cline songs. After her set she was replaced by a fat bloke on drums and a skinny bloke on guitar who gave even worse renditions of Billy Ray Cyrus than he could give himself.

The noise in the bar was welcome.

I saw Joey Harris standing with David Brook outside the secretary's office and headed over. Joey looked up and saw me coming his way so he took off before I arrived.

'Great day coming up,' promised David, looking resplendent in his official shirt.

With him was Ken Rogerson, who was lamenting the fact that

Dry 'n' Sober had been penalised a kilo for his win the previous day. 'He already had a kilo in the dust that got on him yesterday.'

The racing started with a hot tip for a nag trained by Potter called Grand Affair.

I'm not sure why Potter's nag was held in such regard as the horse had run last at his previous outing, although it had won a couple of times before Potter had started training him. Perhaps it was another Greyhound bus job.

Potter seemed to think Grand Affair was a good thing as well. 'Yeah he's pretty right, he should run okay.'

Unfortunately for the punters and Potter, Grand Affair ran second last. The bookies didn't mind, though.

I caught up with Potter as he unsaddled the horse. 'Didn't run too good, eh? But wait till the third, I've got a good show in that I reckon.' I left Potter talking optimistically to the Ghost of Bengal, who was the good show, and made my way back to the crowds, head down to keep the dust from my eyes.

Just before the second race a horse threw its jockey and bolted. Round and round the Birdsville dust paddock it ran. No-one could catch it.

The crowd loved it. Flemington might have its roses and bands, Champagne and strawberries and well-dressed ladies for entertainment. But nothing beats a good old-fashioned horse chase.

Jim Crombie was after it, red jacket open and flapping around as he chased the runaway through the choking dust. He showed his horsemanship, rounding the sweating horse up against a rail before it bolted again. Eventually, a good 10 minutes later, Jim headed it towards the saddling paddock where a long row of ringers, jockeys, trainers and Joey Harris herded it, arms waving, back into the saddling paddock.

The horse was puffing badly so the vet scratched it. Jim Crombie was puffing badly too, but rolled another smoke as he sat dangling one leg over his piece of fence. 'Bloody thing,' he gasped before lighting up and dragging the smoke deep into his lungs. 'Now I'm right.'

After the frivolity of the chase, Potter lead Ghost of Bengal out for the twelve-hundred metre trip through the outback dirt. He sent it away with instructions to the jockey to keep it pretty handy to the lead and then let it go about 300 out. Pretty sound advice.

At the 500-metre mark it looked as though Ghost of Bengal needed some help from another ghost of the Bengal area, the Ghost Who Walks. As much as the jockey tried, the nag strode home second last. At least he was keeping his record intact, finishing in that spot in his last three starts.

Potter was a bit downhearted by this. 'But there's still the Cup. Y'never know.'

Potter, old mate, I thought, you probably don't. But then again, you probably do.

Ten minutes before the start of the Cup the course announcer, in the beautifully enunciated way that course announcers have, introduced the runners as they were sent for a warm-up down the track. Dry 'n' Sober received the biggest cheer. About six people clapped Potter's horse, Audacious Boy.

As the horses headed for the sixteen-hundred metre mark where the starting stalls were, the crowd in the bar turned around to watch. Some of them actually made their way out of the tent to stand in the sun but most of them just turned around with their backs to the bar instead of their fronts.

The blokes from W.A. had made a small stand of the cans they had drunk so they had a pretty good uninterrupted view and the bookies were frantically taking last-minute bets. 'Get on now before they jump,' was the cry. And the queues of people wanting to donate money to The Lost Bookmakers Home grew longer.

Soon all eyes were on the start. The course announcer called the race, which was just as well, as all you could see was the first two horses, followed by a cloud of dust that looked like a billowing spinnaker.

As the cloud turned into the straight, I'm sure the announcer was making it up. Just making sure that everyone's horse was called by name. About 300 out he was calling names at random, then interrupted himself by yelling, 'And Dry 'n' Sober races away!'

Indeed it had. Dry 'n' Sober charged out of the dust cloud and, as all horses became visible because they were side-on in the straight, the big gelding strode to the front of the pack, accompanied by the roars of the crowd, and won by three lengths.

For the first time during the weekend the bookies weren't cheering the winner.

I couldn't see him, but somewhere in the dust cloud was Audacious Boy.

A couple of races later the racing was all over but the party had just begun. 'It's always a huge night, tonight,' David Brook told me. 'Then we'll get back to normal.'

Birdsville: 100 people to 6000 and back to 100 in a couple of days.

As the cars and trucks pulled away, and the buses ferried their loads back to town, the whole area turned into a brown cloud.

Back in the pub, Leah and Kym were sweating. People were jammed into the bar and the air was thick with the drone of voices.

Kym forced a smile across his exhausted face. 'No worries about being left with any.'

Leah was looking forward to a couple of days' time when she could go out into the great silence of the Simpson Desert and watch the sunset again. 'I'll appreciate the quiet then.'

About midnight I came across Potter, who had loaded his truck and was driving again towards the muddy waters of the Diamantina. 'I'll give 'em a swim and prob'ly have one meself then I'll head off tomorra. There's races at Betoota next week so I'll go and try me luck. Reckon I'll do alright too.'

CHAPTER TWELVE

THEY'LL BE RUNNING 'ROUND THE MOUNTAIN

In my travels I'd seen horses and lizards race, as well as goats and ferrets.
Then I remembered that humans actually race as well.
Professional running has been around for over 100 years.
Stawell, Burnie, Bendigo—all great names.
Then there is Murrindindi.
Not a name that you'll ever see in lights, but to the people who were there, that didn't matter.

It was 12 minutes past eight on Sunday morning and there were three of them trying to raise the pole that connected the electricity lead from the pavilion to where the finishing gates would stand.

'Just hold the bloody thing still,' emphasised Sykesy, the largest of the three. His extravagant stomach rubbed against the pole as he reached around and tied a couple of strange-looking knots in the black, hairy baling twine he was using to attach the pole to an iron picket that had been thumped into the soft earth.

'That should hold it,' he reasoned as they all stood back and admired their work.

'Macca,' Sykesy continued, 'you'd better bang a coupla nails in that side.'

A small figure, hunched over and wearing black leather shoes with toes that curled up like something from the Arabian Nights, placed his smoke firmly in the side of his mouth and held the hammer gingerly.

Macca was an almost retired teacher and the technical knowledge of something like hammering in nails wasn't his strong suit. He proceeded to tap gently at the nails as he tried to get them through the holes in the post and into the pole.

After he stuck a few through at varying angles he took a drag on his smoke and stood back.

'That should be enough, whatdya reckon?' The question came in a voice husky from the drink and the smokes.

Sykesy agreed and Wal, the third of the trio, nodded his head as well. Their mission accomplished, they left the pole swaying gently in the breeze and walked away to find out what was next on the agenda.

As they left the arena they were met by a man with a military bearing and who seemed to be in charge. Don McQueen's greying moustache twitched with anticipation as he issued instructions for them.

'Macca, would you go and get the line marker please?' he asked in his clipped, precise manner, 'and Sykesy, you'll look after the bar. Of course, Wal will help you, won't you Wal?'

Wal would, of course.

As they strolled off Don looked pleased. Everything was coming together nicely. Soon, the lanes for the Murrindindi Gift would be marked, stakes would signify the track around the oval for the distance races and the officials who ran the meeting would arrive. Don was proud. It was, after all, his ground.

For years, Don McQueen, financial adviser and member of the Melbourne Cricket Club, had nurtured a dream. He had travelled a few times to England and had fallen in love with the look of the cricket grounds in the countryside, so he decided to build one himself.

After searching for a while, he drove into a property outside Kilmore in the mountains just north of Melbourne and found what he was looking for.

He could see from the property across a 'valley of a thousand hills' where the clouds and the sun garnished the folds of the mountains in colours no one knew the names of. With the sun filtering through the gum trees, he could see kangaroos grazing where deep mid-off would be while wombats scratched around the fence at backward square leg.

'I knew it was the right place straightaway,' Don admitted.

It also helped that the owners were suspected of being cattle rustlers and the price had dropped significantly because the authorities were hot on their trail and they had to move quickly.

So he built it. And they came. For four years cricketers from all walks of life and from all countries have played on the Hume and Hovell Cricket Ground, named after Don's favourite explorers who camped at the foot of the nearby hills as they trekked towards the south.

The white weatherboard pavilion, full of cricket memorabilia, snuggled into the side of one of the hills while a white picket fence curved gracefully around the boundary. When he's there, Don's in his heaven and all's right with the world.

But cricket is one thing. Holding the Murrindindi Gift there was completely another.

'Well,' Don explained, 'What actually happened was that the Broadford Gift, that was run near here for years and years, collapsed. So the Victorian Athletic League asked me if I had any interest in having a day here because they didn't want to lose an event.'

Don was certainly interested. He was not only a passionate cricket lover but a lover of sport in general. 'Country towns are losing enough things these days,' he mused, 'so if I could help, it was my duty to do so.'

And so it came to pass. The athletes were happy, Don was happy and the Murrindindi Gift, named after the local shire, was born.

There was only one problem. The ground wasn't long enough to hold the traditional gift distance of 120 metres, so they decided to run it over 100 instead. At least it was better than no gift at all and, as the Broadford Gift was the first of the season that culminates at Stawell, the runners were happy that they could get some early competition.

Just to make the event even more interesting, they also decided to hold the only professional cross-country mountain race in Australia.

Don thought that was important. 'The mountains here are so much a part of the area that we had to use them.'

We were sitting under the spreading branches of a tree that had grown despite Macca's attempt at his version of Arbor Day. When he helped Don to plant trees in the then untreed paddock, Macca didn't take them out of their small plastic pots. It took quite a while to unplant and then plant them all properly.

As the sun's rays speared through the branches and the leaves while a couple of butcher birds sat above listening to our conversation, interjecting every now and then, Macca, Wal and Sykesy—the three wise men—wandered past. Or in Sykesy's case, hobbled past.

David Sykes, in his younger days, was a wonderful sportsman. Among other things he played for Fitzroy in the old VFL as well as coaching many good country sides. And he was a hard man. Didn't know when to back down. But his body was now showing the wear and tear. His right leg from just above his ankle stuck out almost at right angles and the only way he could get around was to shuffle. It didn't seem to worry him, or immobilise him too much. 'The bastards told me that they'd have to amputate to fix it, so I told 'em, "Bugger that, I'll hobble".'

'How did you go, fellas?' Don called out as they passed.

'Yeah, good,' croaked Macca. 'We're just goin' up to switch on the power.'

As they looked industrious, I didn't bother asking why it took three of them.

By this time the organisers had arrived. Members of the Runners and Trainers Association and the officials of the Victorian Athletic League (VAL) had set up the finishing gates, the lanes had their ropes along them and a small khaki-coloured tent where the issue of the coloured bibs to the runners took place had been erected in the centre of the oval.

Everything was in order.

'Great job, boys,' Don told his workers as they headed off. 'I know it wasn't easy getting up after last night but I thank you sincerely.'

*

That was true. It hadn't been easy getting up. Saturday had seen a cricket match on the ground, umpired by Wal and Sykesy attired in traditional white coats.

Sykesy had limped in from square leg at the end of each over and stood all day with his leg jutting out. It didn't bother him. 'Yeah, it bloody aches at times, but what do I do, sit down forever?' It was a reasonable question.

Wal Jenkin, a florid-cheeked and sandy, thin-haired early-retired bank manager, had stood at the other end impassively. Shouts for LBW were turned down with monotonous regularity, at least for the team that was fielding at the time. 'Can't have LBs in a social match,' declared Wal. 'It spoils their day, specially in the first coupla balls.'

I thought Wal should umpire in all cricket matches, especially Tests.

At the end of the day which had stretched from ten in the morning until the softness of the evening light at around seven, Wal and Sykesy had been clapped from the ground as Bradman might have been. Mounting the steps of the pavilion they were handed stubbies that during the course of the next few hours never left their hands and never seemed to be empty.

Much later the stubbies had turned to red wine and much much later, after Don had recited 'The Man From Snowy River' to the assembled drunks with all the passion of Henry V speaking to his troops before Agincourt, the trio had tumbled off to their various sleeping positions.

The early morning of Sunday had not been particularly welcome.

After the electricity had surged through the line, the boys went to their various positions for the day. Sykesy and Wal adjourned to the bar and the barbecue, Don roamed around checking that everything was still going well, while Macca, who had pinched one of the umpires' coats, slouched over to amuse himself as a car-park attendant. Resplendent in the white coat which reached below his knees, baggy tracksuit pants that Charlie Chaplin would have been proud of, curly toed black shoes and his smokes, he directed traffic like a pocket-sized, round-shouldered, frustrated copper.

*

The first event of the day was the 70 metres and the runners in the first heat assembled at the start of a track which took them up a slight incline for the first 20 or so metres before it levelled out. Then, at the 60-metre mark it climbed again to the finish. Add to that the fact that the grass was not rolled, or cut very low, and it was a slow, difficult track. But the runners reckoned they needed a hard run this early in the season. And the Murrindindi Gift wasn't about great times, it was about competing.

As they charged up the hill in the heats of the seventy, a small man in a distinctive white hat watched intently. He carried a clipboard and every now and again he would jot something down.

Kevin Seers was the chief steward for the day, representing the VAL, and was looking for inconsistencies, as he called them. Most others who knew anything about pro running called it running dead.

It's one of the great things about pro running in Australia. Since the time of the first Stawell Gift, the world's oldest footrace, in 1878, runners have been protecting their mark, with a view to getting a better handicap in races with more prize money.

The smokie is part of Australian sporting folklore, but there were to be no smokies in the Murrindindi Gift.

'Bit early in the season for them,' thought Kevin. 'And there's no bookies anyway. Still, I've got to keep my eye open.'

And he did. Every so often, after scribbling a name or a time on his clipboard, he would call out to a runner and have a quiet chat about their race.

According to Kevin, injury was the most used excuse for a poor time. 'But the runners are supposed to do their best in every race, not use them as a training exercise.'

Kevin's son Dale had won the Gift at Stawell the previous year and I wondered what sort of mark he had. 'Seven and a half metres,' a grinning Kevin replied. 'Not too bad.'

The quiet chats seemed to be getting the point across. Not that it needed getting across. Anyone who takes the track in pro running plays the cat and mouse game. 'It's all part of what makes this sport great,' said Kevin as he wrote another name down. 'And anyway, that's the bloke who makes the final decisions and who is looking even harder than me.'

Kevin had pointed out one of the legends in the sport. The still extremely fit-looking 50-year-old Ricky Dunbar, 'The Flying Scotsman'.

Ricky was the official handicapper. Not the most popular of positions to hold, especially when runners have their handicaps reduced a couple of metres.

'No-one likes being dragged,' Ricky told me, 'but it's my job. If they run the times, they get the marks. And I look at their history.'

History would look good for him as well. Ricky began running professionally in Scotland when he was just 17 years old. Over the next few years he became the British champion in distances from 100 to 400 metres and won the Powderhall Gift, second only to Stawell in prestige around the world, in 1963. After that he decided to make the break to Australia to try and capture the Stawell Gift as well as other lucrative races that were around in this country.

'I didn't intend to stay when I first came, but this country sort of gets to you, doesn't it?' The question was directed to the air as he watched the runners striding down the track towards the finish gates.

Unfortunately the Stawell Gift didn't come his way. 'It was,' he grinned, 'because the handicapper got me.' It seemed poetic justice that he now ruled the roost.

The heats of the 70 metres had finished with the final looking to be a race between Steve Tilburn, who ran from three and a quarter metres, and Robin Calleja off one and three-quarters.

Steve Tilburn had been around pro running for years and at 35 had just completed the 100- and 200-metre double at the Asia Pacific veterans' meeting in Brisbane. His body was tanned and lumpy, and his shaved head and large gold earrings glistened in the afternoon sun.

He spoke quickly and urgently when I asked how he felt in his heat. 'Yeahmate, prettygoodmateyeahprettygoodyeah.' The words came out like bullets from a Gatling gun but I gathered that he was ready for the heats in the Gift and then, hopefully, the final in both events. 'Yeahmatethat'dbegoodmate, yeahgood.'

Robin Calleja, on the other hand was dark and swarthy— European-looking. He appeared to have done an enormous amount of weights as his upper body was huge and his legs as big as Cathy Freeman's whole body. He was, as they say, bulked up. Robin had been out of training for a few months and had spent the time in the gym. A quiet man, he was just looking to run the best time he could. 'I'm not in the class of the big-time guys but I might do okay here.'

He would need to improve a few metres on his heat though as, on the watch, Steve Tilburn had him covered.

After they had donned tracksuit bottoms and gathered their thoughts, both the runners then went to another closely mown part of the ground that was used as the warm-up track and jogged around to warm down. They both rippled as they moved.

Alongside them were runners of all shapes and sizes. Some were striding through with exaggerated gait, others with short stuttering steps with their knees lifted high to stretch out, while still others practised their starts and the first 25 metres of a race. But there were none of the expensive lairy tracksuits or running suits that you see at top amateur meetings. Not here. Just ordinary singlets with ordinary shorts.

'We're professionals, not amateurs,' Robin Calleja responded when I mentioned it. 'We're not the ones that make the money.'

While the heats of the 400 were being run I headed back to the bar where Sykesy and Wal were doing a roaring trade. Not with the runners of course, but with their support groups. 'Making a quid here,' Sykesy boasted as he lifted another cold bottle of beer from the depths of an old freezer, nearly losing his glasses in the process as his head went in as well. Then, yelling through the gum trees to the barbecue 10 feet or so away, 'How're you goin' with the barby, Wal?'

In front of the bar, which was an eight foot square weatherboard box with a pointed roof, a half-wall that served as the counter, and was named the Boundary Tavern, Wal and Don had the fires lit. As the wonderful, stomach-gripping smell of cooking sausages and chops wafted across the hills, Wal sniffed the air, 'Bloody good, Sykesy, bloody good.'

Macca had shuffled back from the car park by now, leaning forward as though he was heading into a gale. Wal watched him coming, greeting him with, 'Where's our smokes, Macca?' Macca rummaged around in the pockets of his baggy pants and produced a crumpled packet with a couple of bent looking cigarettes in it. 'It's all I've got left,' he said with a hangdog expression.

While Macca and Wal, both fitness and health fanatics, worked out a plan of attack to procure another packet of smokes from somewhere, the rest of us grabbed a snag in bread and, with sauce dripping from the ends like blood from a cut-off finger, we watched a long, angular runner named Kris McCarthy lope around the track to record the fastest heat by far in the 400. I promised myself to keep an eye on him later, in the final.

Four hundreds traditionally are one complete lap of the oval but here, as in the Gift, there wasn't enough room. The circumference of the ground is only 358 metres. We knew that to be the case because the officials had walked around it pushing a little measuring wheel. 'Gotta make sure we run over the proper distance,' Kevin Seers had told me.

Anyway, all they had to do to fix the problem was separate the start and finish lines by 42 metres. Which they did. Although it did cause concern for a few of the runners who, when they arrived at the start line after completing a lap, slowed right down as though it was the end. But luckily, no-one was beaten because of it.

The heats of the Gift had started when I spotted a figure, stopwatch in hand, on one of the small hills alongside the oval.

Graham Goldsworthy was one of the better trainers in pro running ranks, having trained John Evans to a win in the Bendigo 1000, as well as Jim Richardson who won the Stawell Gift in 1993. Added to that, he had a stable of other runners who, according to him, were just as good but either didn't get the mark or had someone better in their races.

'Even though you reckon you're a good thing, there's always someone out there you don't know about or haven't seen.'

Graham didn't have any runners in the Murrindindi Gift but had come to watch, as he did at all meetings, runners or not. 'You've got to be aware of what's going on around the joint,' he admitted, 'and this is such a great place anyway.'

The cross-country course spiralled its way up the mountains behind where we were sitting and Graham told me that he'd walked it earlier. 'It's only 3200 metres but, shit, it was hard enough walking it let alone running it.'

He loved the area and the meeting. 'It's unique, isn't it, here in the middle of nowhere. There's nothing like it that I've ever seen and I've been around a while.'

That he had. As one of the more experienced and senior trainers he reckoned the only thing close to it was an old ground in Ferntree Gully on the outskirts of Melbourne called Brenack Park. 'We used to go there with me dad when he was training in the '40s. He'd train and I'd go down the creek and swim or catch lizards.'

Graham admitted to be only a plodder as a runner, but he was quite obviously a good trainer. And while he was glad he had the good runners, some of the other trainers had their hands full over the years. 'There was these two brothers who stood toe to toe at Sebastapol one year and had an almighty knuckle-on over something or other, and then there was the 400 up at Lavington when there was some pushing and shoving during the race. The bloke who won it stopped on the line and as the other bloke came across he poleaxed him with a ripsnorter of a punch.'

Our attention was diverted to the next heat where Steve Tilburn was stretching his hamstrings at the start.

'He's the class sprinter here today,' Graham conceded. 'He's mid-thirties I know, but he's still got it.'

Graham was right. Steve stormed up the hill, gold earrings and shaved head once again glistening in the sun, and won quite easily.

Soon the heats were all finished. Steve Tilburn was joined in the final by Rob Calleja and a couple of others, Martin Hodgson and

Vaughan Sketcher, who looked impressive in their heats, or at least they did to Graham Goldsworthy.

'They've got to give Tilburn a start but it'll be close' were the words of wisdom from the master trainer.

Over at the Boundary Tavern the three wise men were huddled together intent on something or other. As I got closer I could see it was the racing guide from the paper. The boys had taken a couple of quaddies between them.

'Got the first two legs in,' Macca announced in his husky voice.

Sykesy was pleased with that news, then took four or five movements to turn around before he waddled back behind the bar.

Wal could see the riches coming his way and lit up a celebratory smoke, offering Macca one in the process, which was gratefully accepted. The two nicotine addicts had found someone going to a shop a few kilometres away and had bribed them to bring a packet back.

As they discussed their horses' chances, I wondered why they were studying the form guide after they had made their bets. But not being a racing expert as they obviously were, I kept the thought to myself.

Don came over to see what the boys were up to and the four mates stood under the trees where the sunlight played around their faces, at peace in each other's company.

Don towered over them, tall, square and a leader while Sykesy, with chubby face and immense stomach, leaned on his hockey-stick-shaped leg. Wal's red face had been split with a grin nearly all day while the dark, brooding Macca, whose every thought appeared to be a secret, hadn't taken off his white coat, even though all the cars had been parked for three hours. Still, it was a symbol of authority.

The 70 metres was the first of the finals and Steve Tilburn cruised to victory over Rob Calleja. 'Onlygotthebigonetogonowmate,' he jabbered at me after he caught his breath. He spoke like a doctor writing a prescription.

'Igottabitofasoregroinbutitshouldbeokayireckonmate, yeah.'

Rob Calleja walked slowly away to retrieve his tracksuit. His enormous thighs didn't allow his feet to be as close together as they should have been. 'There's still another one to go but giving him nearly three metres is hard.'

I thought it would be as well. Tilburn looked the goods.

In the final of the 400 the 19-year-old Kris McCarthy ran around the oval as though he were wearing pogo sticks not running spikes. He leapt to the front like a startled Nureyev and won easily.

A big effort, as they say, considering he rolled his car on the way to the meeting. 'I was coming down one of those mountains and I came round a corner a bit too fast and I suppose I panicked.'

At least he was honest. The car had hit the dirt and rolled a couple of times into a safety embankment. Kris had calmly got out of the wreck and walked a few k's until he was picked up.

It was to be a big day for Kris, as half an hour later he turned out for the 1000 metres and the springs in the feet served him well again. He won by about 10 metres after starting from the rear of the field and giving the front marker 200 metres.

The prize money would go towards fixing the car, but with the amount of it, not very far.

The shadows were lengthening as Kris bounced away and the distance runners were given half an hour to assemble for the cross-country, with the Gift final to be run after they had finished.

The cross-country course consisted of a lap of the oval, after which the athletes ran out through a gate in the picket fence and followed the fenceline up the smaller of two large hills overlooking the oval.

Through the paddocks they ran, their legs whipping through the tall grasses that grew wild and strong almost up to their knees. They passed cows who lazed around, occasionally rising from where they lay to nibble at the grass or to turn their heads and follow the passing humans.

The runners straggled their way up the hills. Small, lithe figures with skinny yet muscular legs attached to skinny yet muscular torsos. A special breed were the distance runners. Not stocky with big upper bodies, but strong nevertheless.

All the other runners had stopped to watch this event. Graham

Goldsworthy had spoken earlier about what is needed from an athlete. 'Commitment is the main thing,' he'd told me, 'From them and from me. As long as they want to do it I'll get the best from them if they give me the time they need to.'

Now Graham stood beside me. 'That's what I mean.' He pointed to the figures who emerged from the gully between the smaller and larger hill. 'You have to drive yourself, not to win necessarily, because only a few are ever winners, but to do what you can.'

The runners dropped from sight into one of the gullies before struggling out and labouring up the hill again. Two laps of the hills seemed cruel to me. 'Think of their quads,' Graham muttered as the runners leant forward in an effort to make it easier for themselves as they forced their legs to do what their mind wanted. 'They'll be screaming now. Not to mention their brains.'

The runners headed down the mountain at a furious pace, or it seemed like that to me, and passed us going at a rate that was about twice as fast as I could run for my first 10 metres, let alone after three and a bit k's up and down mountains.

The applause was long and loud as a stick figure named Matthew MacDonald crossed the line in what I thought was a great time: 11.11.11.

If the three wise men, Don and I had attempted the route it would really have been remembrance day.

The barbecue had a few uneaten, burnt snags left on it when the runners assembled for the start of the Murrindindi Gift.

Don and Wal had run out of customers. Sykesy's business had slowed to a trickle as well, but he and the others were working on reducing the contents of the freezer by themselves. Macca's quaddie had fallen over at the third race.

As Steve Tilburn and the others gathered at the bottom of the ground and hammered their starting blocks into the grass the hills behind them changed colour as the clouds passed over them and then, after they had rolled away, the sun lit them up once more.

Ricky Dunbar and Kevin Seers had met the runners as they made their way down the track from the finish line in the traditional manner of all Gift finals. They wished them good luck, then told them they expected everyone to do their best.

A hush fell over the Hume and Hovell Cricket Ground as the starter sent them to their marks. His cry of 'set' was followed a second later by the sound of his starting pistol. As they sped up the incline, Rob Calleja hit the front while Steve Tilburn hung on grimly. The back markers Martin Hodgson and Vaughan Sketcher gathered the front men in at about the halfway mark and looked like charging past them. But they reckoned without the resilience of the old man of the field, Steve Tilburn. He stuck to his rhythm, his groin held on and in a blanket finish he won the Murrindindi Gift by a whisker.

'Bloodyfantasticmateyeah,' he gasped afterwards. 'Bloodygreatmateyeah.'

After the sash was draped around his shoulders and he stood on the small, unsound wooden dais that almost crumbled under the collective weight of three hulking athletes, a satisfied smile flickered around his mouth as he wiped the sweat from his sparkling head.

Watching from under the trees stood Don and his cohorts, all looking as though they had almost reached the bottom of Sykesy's freezer. Don's face beamed like a beacon as he gazed proudly across his kingdom.

'Bloody great life, isn't it?' he muttered to the mountains.

CHAPTER THIRTEEN

MORE THAN ONE WAY TO SKIN A RABBIT

Thousands of people travel to Melbourne for one of the great days on
Australia's sporting calendar—the Boxing Day Test match at the
Melbourne Cricket Ground.
But not me.
I travelled to another MCG, and another great Boxing Day sporting event,
admittedly with a slightly smaller crowd.

The car park was in a gully down off the road. Someone had
slashed the grass for the big day and the cars had flattened it
even more. Along the three-strand wire fence, however, it was still
long and bent in deference to the breeze.

At the end of the fence was a small tin shack. So small in fact that
the individual accepting the entrance money—whose head, with
spectacular long grey hair, rose above the roof of the structure—
couldn't fit inside.

Through the space where a gate had once been was more long
grass, and beyond that was the football oval. Goalposts stretched
towards the sky at one end and a scoreboard painted in a colour
vaguely resembling khaki green, that had MOYS written in large
white letters with VIS underneath, stood impassively halfway around
the fence. I wondered where the other goalposts were. Perhaps they
only scored at one end.

Opposite the scoreboard the Moyston Cricket Ground's wooden

grandstand was frayed around the edges and history creaked out of it as feet traipsed up the bowed steps.

In front of the stand was a stage. A metal square on legs with old bits of wood on top of it for the platform. A barrier like a ship's guardrail ran around the square which could be reached by climbing three crudely manufactured steps.

In a small tent, open to the weather that swapped between skiffy showers, freezing wind and sunshine, and sitting at a table which had been borrowed from someone's kitchen, sat Veeda Pearce, president of the Moyston World Rabbit Skinning Championships.

'Merry Christmas,' was her greeting. 'Welcome to the MCG.'

Veeda was in the festive spirit, and why shouldn't she be? After all, it's not every woman who gets to be in charge of the Christmas roast one day and of the World Rabbit Skinning Championships the next. Veeda was a lucky lady.

She had been president for three years. 'I was on the committee for years and one night there was this phone call to say that I was missing a meeting.' So Veeda had run down to the oval, where the meeting was being held in the changing rooms under the stand. When she walked in all positions were declared vacant, she was nominated for president and was voted in unanimously.

'I didn't really mind. I didn't think it would be too hard. Not too stressful.' Veeda's look was one of not really believing what she was saying. 'Anyway, here I am,' she muttered as she turned to take another $5 entry fee from a skinner.

The World Rabbit Skinning Championships program was a full one, including an under-16s and a women's event as well as the novices. Then the heats of the open would be contested, with the grand final— the winner of which would be the world champion—to be conducted between the successful skinners of the heats, plus the winners of the novice and the women's event—if they wanted to compete, that was.

I felt sure that whoever won the women's title would love to be pitted against the men skinners. Anything to break the drudgery of the Christmas demands.

On the rail around the stage hung lengths of wire, bent in half, that were used to peg the skin on after the rabbits had been divested of them. The wires hung next to metal rabbit motifs that were welded on the railing posts—small cartoon rabbits with erect ears that were waving and smiling and dressed in red tails. I assumed they didn't get any local rabbits for models.

Back in the tent, Veeda was busy with a steady influx of entries but said there would be more later, after people had watched for a while before deciding they'd like to try.

Within a few minutes the judges had gathered at the back of the stage, the crowd had assembled and the knives were sharpened. Only one thing was missing. Rabbits!

'Someone's gone over to Killer's place,' Veeda reassured the judges. 'Shouldn't be a minute.'

And she was right. About a minute later a small ute pulled up, the driver emerged and lifted out a sack that was tied at the top by a length of red baling twine that was wound around about six times and heavily knotted. Inside were the rabbits, dead of course.

I wondered why the bag needed to be tied up so tightly if the rabbits were dead. Wasn't Easter the season for resurrection, not Christmas? And Killer—what a name! I hoped it didn't mean what I thought it might.

Veeda smiled at me when I mentioned the name to her. She looked over towards the road that ran past the ground, partially raising herself off the seat in an effort to see what was coming. 'He'll be here soon,' she assured me. 'He's Mr Rabbit Skinning, he's lovely.'

Meanwhile the judges undid the sack, tipped the contents onto the grass, and while the under-16 skinners mounted the stage and stood in front of their allotted places I watched and waited for Killer.

I didn't have long to wait. Veeda pointed him out as he weaved his way through the crowd, smiling and waving to the many greetings coming his way.

Tall, slender and erect despite his advancing years, Killer Crawford looked nothing like his name suggested. His grey checked trousers were complemented by a grey shirt buttoned to the neck. Over his shirt he wore a grey cardigan and grey jacket, both of which had all buttons done up. On his greying head was a grey trilby hat, the sort men of his generation always wore. On his feet were brown desert boots.

Killer had lived in Moyston all his life. 'Since 1914,' he told me proudly. He reckoned he'd seen rabbits come and go over the years, but 'it was the mixo that really fixed 'em up years ago. And now they've got that virus.'

He'd been a shearer for most of his life and trapped rabbits when there were no sheep to shear. 'Shore for 57 consecutive seasons,' Killer boasted. 'Started when I was 16 and a half.'

During the Depression, Killer lamented, there was no market for rabbit carcases, but there was for skins. So he worked on the poison trails, where the government would lay out poison and he and his two mates would follow, collecting the dead rabbits for skinning.

'We'd pile 'em all under a tree and skin till it got too hot and their guts blew up. Then we'd knock off.'

He calculated that he and his mates would do around 2000 a day.

'We'd get one and thruppence a pound for 'em.' Killer's eyes sparkled at the memory of money during the Depression. 'There'd be about seven or eight to the pound, worked out at about tuppence each. We'd send 'em away in wool bales.'

I thought that would have been a fair day's work, skinning 2000 rabbits.

'I could do about five a minute.' Killer told me. 'I'd give 'em a nick behind the ears, hold 'em into me crutch and rip their clobber off. Easy.' Then he added, 'And we'd peg 'em out after that so the skins'd dry. Hard work, but it wasn't so bad, we were the lucky ones.'

Killer was lost in his memories as he stood watching the under-16s undress their rabbits, his hands clasped behind his back, one finger tapping gently on the others, his eyes never leaving the youngsters' hands.

He turned to me when I asked how it all started, although his eyes kept darting back to watch the kids.

'We was up at Whirly Wilson's pub one night and Old Mac Maclean and Dasher Douglas was arguing the toss about who could skin the quickest. They went on and on so I told 'em to present 'emselves at the footy grounds the next day. It went from there. That was 31 years ago.'

I wondered what Whirly Wilson had to do with it all. 'He was president for a while,' Killer reckoned, 'and he had a good car.'

Whirly acquired his name from the old Dodge car, nicknamed the Southern Cloud, that he used to drive around the district. Somehow he had put an engine in the back and fixed a big blade like a helicopter's that protruded through the roof.

'Never did anything except whirl 'round,' Killer sounded almost disappointed, 'but it looked good, and everyone liked it.'

And now Killer was pleased that the event had grown and that there were kids still around who wanted to skin rabbits. 'It's good to see 'em interested and havin' a go.'

As the skun rabbits lay naked at the feet of the youngsters, Killer showed me what it meant to be a good skinner. 'Well, that one's bin slit up the guts, so he's out.'

The idea in championship rabbit skinning was to make sure the skin comes off with no cuts to the carcass. The one that Killer pointed to was lying on the stage with its entrails spilling from the front of it in varying shades of red.

'No good,' Killer stated.

He then examined the others and concluded that they were okay except for a small incision into the leg of one of them. 'Y'see, you lose points if you cut 'em and you're disqualified if you let out the guts, or you rip the head or a leg off.

'Not too bad, though, for young 'uns,' said Killer as he finished his examination.

The judges agreed and gave the event to Chris Carey, a lumpy Ginger Meggs type who had come down from Sebastapol, near Ballarat, for the day. When I asked Chris why he did it he replied casually, 'I go shootin' wiv me dad, he taught me. It's fun I suppose. I just like doin' it.'

Killer stood behind him, smiling.

While the bodies of the skun bunnies were removed Killer was joined by the chief rabbit catcher for the championships. A retired teacher,

Ray Whittaker was probably the only man in Moyston without a nickname. Or at least if he had one I never heard it.

Killer used to be the main catcher, but over the last few years Ray had assumed the mantle and had it down to a fine art. 'I like to get 'em early but I've just had me golden wedding anniversary and it slowed me down a bit,' Ray confessed.

After Ray caught the rabbits he left them in an old well on his property so they wouldn't escape on him, and fed them on oats. On Christmas Eve or Christmas Day they would then be transferred to Killer's backyard shed before being taken to the ground as required.

However, this year was a bit different to most. They needed about 80 rabbits but, due to his matrimonial commitments, Ray couldn't get enough, so Veeda put a call out to all the kids in the area to help out. The going rate was a dollar per rabbit.

'That was alright,' Veeda had explained to me, 'only after a while the ringleader reckoned that a dollar wasn't enough and that we should be paying two.'

I could see the union movement was alive and well in Moyston.

'Anyway,' continued Veeda, 'I told the little buggers that'd be right. Thing is I haven't told the committee yet, s'pose we'll have to pass it next meeting.'

So the rabbits began to accumulate in Ray's well. 'I had an old plastic trough in the bottom so they could have a drink and an old door to keep it from gettin' muddy.' Ray was determined to look after the rabbits. 'One night I've knocked off and come back the next day and I've forgotten to turn the bloody hose off and all the bloody rabbits were floating around on the bloody door.'

Ray reckoned it was lucky some of them didn't drown. I didn't think it would have mattered much in the whole scheme of their lives.

Eventually all the surviving rabbits had been transferred to Killer's shed where they waited until that knock on the door. Which is what had just happened to a bagful as the ute pulled up again and the judges threw the rabbits onto the stage where they flopped down, lifeless, waiting for the novice event to start.

*

The announcer on the stage was Mister Martin, known as that because if anyone was to be quoted in the local paper it was usually him, and the paper always used the formal title. He was dressed formally too, houndstooth coat, woollen tie, hat and trousers all making him look like the definitive rabbit-skinning announcer.

The novices, who qualified as such because they hadn't won anything before, took their positions on Mister's command. One was a youngster with a crop of pimples and dimples, another a middle-aged bloke whose pink baseball cap rested on his grey head, the third was more nondescript, while the last wore a permanent droop to his head and shoulders as though there was a hook attached from his chin to his feet that pulled everything down.

Mister then told the skinners to get ready. 'It'll be on the count of three,' he announced, then promptly called, 'One, two, GO.' The droopy looking bloke waited for the three but the others decided that GO was close enough.

The drooper was still completing his first rabbit when the pimply one and the pink hat finished their second fairly close together.

After the judges had examined the two carcasses they announced a dead heat and a 'skin-off' for first place.

More rabbits were produced and the two lined up again. This time there was no contest as Murray Wilson, the pink hat and no relation to Whirly, won comfortably. Murray was pleased with his effort and looked forward to the final although his opinion was that, 'It's goin' to be hard when I'm up against a bloke who can skin like Ray Kelly.'

When they build a Rabbit Skinning Hall Of Fame—if they ever do, that is—Ray Kelly will be the first inductee, after Killer. He is a legend of rabbit skinning, having won the event 15 times, 13 of them in a row. 'S'pose I've got a knack for it,' he confessed when I asked him what made him a champion skinner. 'And I've got a bit of a different technique to the rest of 'em.'

Kell rolled the skin off down the legs, he told me, and then that left the skin a bit longer so it was easier to tie when he pegged them out. Of course I understood all this perfectly and I nodded every now and again as he spoke and demonstrated what he meant with his hands.

Kell was a decade younger than Killer but the two had been friends for years. Where Killer was long and lanky, Kell was short and stockier, although he too wore brown desert boots. His eyes danced behind his tinted glasses and a small tea-cosy-like woollen beanie sat on the back of his head.

Kell had given skinning away a couple of years ago but had returned this year when he heard that there was prize money on offer. I wondered if he'd also come back for the prestige.

'Prestige is okay but they've got $500 for a prize this year. That'd be nice, I reckon, and I've gotta have a show, havent I?'

I supposed he would, but then I realised that halfway through that sentence Kell had stopped talking to me and was now addressing Killer, who had wandered up, hands still behind his back.

'You've got a show alright.' Killer laughed in my direction. 'This bloke's put my name down too. That right, Kell?'

It was right. Kell had entered Killer. 'Well, you gotta have a go, mate.'

How many times had Killer won it I wondered.

'Well, I won it that first year, y'know.'

But wasn't that between Old Mac and Dasher?

'Yeah that's true, but what happened was that after they said they'd have a skin-off, I told 'em I'd supply the rabbits. So I got a couple for 'em on Christmas Eve and put 'em in me freezer with a bit of mint and that, ready for Boxing Day.'

That should have done the trick—frozen in their fur with a bit of mint and that.

Boxing Day came and Killer was away at his son's place but he'd left instructions.

'I told 'em to take the rabbits out about eight o'clock and let 'em thaw out slowly. But no, they took 'em out about midday and it was a stinking hot day and they blew up and stank the joint out.'

So the skinning was like the rabbits—off. Even the mint didn't work. Killer remembered the complaints about the rabbits being presented badly so he got a few more and said that he'd take 'em both on, which he did. And for the first three years Killer was the champion. 'Won it six times in all, but then me hands got a bit tight and me times got worse.'

He hadn't participated for a couple of years but was willing to have a go now that Kell had put his name down.

I left the two talking about rabbits and guts and sharp knives and, as Mister had announced a half-hour break and told me to have a look around, I wandered over to a large marquee to see what other treats were around.

The Rabbit Skinning Championships were the main part of the Moyston Boxing Day Sports. Along with the championships, there were a few running races, a sheep show, a couple of sideshows and the ubiquitous highland dancers. And there were art and craft displays in the marquee.

On the way over I passed the bar where the owner was doing a brisk trade. Opposite the bar near the fence that circled the ground, and under the shade of his big umbrella, was a bookie. Frank Minahan adjusted the odds on his board for the third in Melbourne as he told me he was continuing a tradition handed down through his family of fielding at country sports meetings.

'We don't make much money now, but in the old days it was quite big,' he told me. 'The old man and me grandad used to go to all the small towns around the place. Now there's not that many small towns, is there?'

In the marquee was a display of local paintings that a couple of people were studying. A bigger crowd was next to them, a few of the skinners and spectators standing in front of two large square pieces of wood that had rabbit traps hanging off them. They were studying them the same way.

These jaws of death were ancient but had been restored to working condition and were greased and oiled as though they were ready to go out to the paddocks and try again. The owner of the display was one Darol Walsgott, who informed me proudly as he flicked through the pages of his book on rabbit traps that it was the 'most authoritative book on rabbit traps anywhere'. I was suitably impressed until he told me that it was the only book on rabbit traps.

On his boards were traps called Grip and Imperial Box, as well as others that had slightly less grand but more gruesome titles. They were all different; some vastly so, others with more subtle differences such as a few more teeth or a bit less chain.

'The earliest I've come across was a trap from 1858,' Darol enthused. 'Most of 'em came from England in those days, of course, but we did start making them out here in about 1919.'

I was pleased about that. After all, we didn't want our balance of trade figures to be upset. Apparently, at that time there was a rabbit-trap company in England called H. Lane, that had four generations of H. Lanes—all of them being named Henry.

Darol was warming up now, his eyes alight with his knowledge of the history of rabbit traps. 'The second generation Henry eventually came out here and set up his own business in Newcastle. They made a trap every nine seconds in their heyday.'

The old men, and some women, who stood around the display listened in wonder. The old men fingered the traps gently and shook their heads at the enormity of it all.

I looked through Darol's book before I left and marvelled at the drawings of the hundreds of traps he had painstakingly researched. 'Five hundred and thirty, in fact,' I was informed. 'And I've got about another 150 for the second edition.'

Darol was keen to discuss traps further and asked if I wanted to buy a copy of his work, but I made an excuse about having to hurry away as the women skinners were lining up at the foot of the stage's steps.

'She'll win it for sure.' Killer had surveyed the local ladies who all had their knives out, waiting. 'She's won it a coupla times before.'

He pointed to the tallest of the woman, Pauline Graham, a statuesque lady who towered over the other three. Her long hair had been tied back so it wouldn't flop around when she was cutting and the blade of her knife glistened in the pale streaks of sun.

Pauline was also six months pregnant. 'She'll be right,' was her cheery answer to my question. 'I can skin around the bump.'

I was sure she could and anyway, what else does a six-month pregnant mum want to be do after spending Christmas Day with her hands in plum duff or a turkey's behind. It all seemed so natural.

And she was right. She could skin around the bump. She did it in the grand time of one minute and 50 seconds, and as she came off the stage her three-year-old was there to proudly greet his sporting hero mum.

I thought Killer was a good judge. He thought so too. 'My word,' he agreed as he unclasped his hands from behind his back and transferred them into the pockets of his jacket. 'Gotta keep 'em warm. They don't work as well when they're cold.'

Half an hour later, Killer and I watched the ute of death quietly slip away once more, a bit like a cart in Paris during the French Revolution, although here the victims had met their fate long before being transported to a stage.

This time it returned with a couple of bags of rabbits that had not enjoyed the festive season. It pulled up near where we were standing.

'How'd you get your name?' I asked Killer as the bags were dropped near the stage.

He laughed, but then, as his name was called, walked over to the desk in the tent where Veeda and Kell were chatting. I walked over behind him. The three of them discussed how the rabbits were really good this year and were skinning well.

'It's the oats, don't you think?' asked Kell, 'If you give 'em too much green stuff then they get a bit harder to skin.'

'True', answered Killer, nodding his head.

This was a bit much. Were they taking the mickey out of me or what?

Apparently not. According to the experts—Killer and Kell, that is—it is a scientific fact that when rabbits eat seeds, as against leaves, they form a little layer of fat between their skin and their meat which makes it easier to get the skin off.

I was sure the rabbits would have been impressed with that news. But it hadn't answered my question, and as Killer had found a couple of old snoozers to chat to I went back to the stage to await the start of the first of three heats of the open.

The World Title was about to begin.

Kell was in the first heat. The judges stood in the middle of the stage as they drew for stands. Not that it was important, or at least not to me. It didn't seem to make any difference where you skun. There was no wind advantage or wet track or anything. But the judges ripped a bit of paper from the bottom of their sheet and wrote the five names on it and then ripped those off individually and chucked 'em in a hat that one of them had taken off for the job.

As they announced who would start from where, Killer's voice came from behind me.

'It was from a sheep.'

'What was?'

'My name. I was goin' up the neck of an old ewe and it must've had a heart attack cos it died in me arms. At smoko, an old codger, a bit of a hard doer he was, reckoned he'd seen me kill it. Wasn't true of course, but the name stuck.'

I was relieved. I was glad his name came from something like that.

Kell took his knife from his pocket, opened the blade and wiped it furiously across one of his desert boots. I had no idea why, but then I had no idea about much that had gone on during the day. But I assumed it was either to get some gunk off it or to make the edge a bit keener.

As the rabbits were thrown unceremoniously at the feet of the contestants, who picked them up and rearranged them so as to get a good start, I asked Killer if he'd played any other sports in his day.

'Cricket,' he remembered. 'Loved cricket. And footy. But it's all different nowadays, of course.' Killer removed his hands from behind his back and shook a finger gently in the air. 'Everything's about money. Bloody money.'

It wasn't that Killer was against money but he was against it being the answer to everything.

'When we played footy we used to throw a shillin' in for the ball and the barrel. Now everyone wants to be paid. Times change, I know, and that's good, but is it still a sport?'

Good question, Killer, I thought.

They'd got under way in the first heat as we spoke and Kell had finished his rabbits at about the same time as Killer and I had finished our conversation. Killer could talk as he watched but I had been looking at his face and missed out on the battle between Kell and the others. Kell had won decisively on the watch but he was a bit concerned at the state of his rabbits as he had nicked one on the back leg.

He came across to the rail. 'Whatd'ya reckon Killer, I'll be alright won't I?' He seemed anxious.

'Yeah,' scoffed Killer. 'You got no worries.'

Killer was right, as he usually was. Ray was the first into the final.

'Geez that's good,' Ray confessed. 'I was a bit worried that I'd miss out on the 500.'

Next heat was Killer's. He mounted the stage to great applause when he was introduced by Mister. After examining his rabbits and placing them just as he wanted, Killer stood up and smiled at all the spectators. I expected him to remove his jacket at least, but no, all he did was doff his hat and hand it to me. Then out came his knife. On the blade was the brand—Old Timer.

Still dressed in jacket and cardigan, Killer skun his rabbits in good time but was beaten into second place by Tom Howlett, the reigning champion.

But he didn't care. As he placed his handkerchief around an index finger he'd cut while 'goin' up one of the legs', I handed him his hat. His check trousers were flecked with blood but it wasn't a real worry to him. 'I nearly had it, but these fingers won't work like they used to. Anyway, it's good to see the youngies winnin' it.'

That was good. Tom Howlett was about 60.

A short time later, a real young bloke, Michael Heenan, about 25, won the third heat and joined the other two in the final. They would be contesting against Pauline, the women's winner, and Murray Wilson, the novice.

*

Ten minutes before the final started, the ute once more travelled over to Killer's place and removed the rabbits from his shed, and once more they were tipped out on the ground when they returned. The crowd had built up a bit by now and they applauded as the finalists were introduced by Mister.

The five finalists stood around as Mister took off his hat for the draw. I asked Killer if it really mattered where you stood. 'Nah, not really, but some people like bein' on the ends so they can't see the others.'

Just in case there was any sledging or loose elbows I presumed.

Pauline drew the middle stand while Kell drew the spot at the same end he had in the heat, which pleased him. 'I feel a bit more comfortable here,' he assured me as he leant against the rail.

The rabbits flopped in front of them and all the skinners picked them up and felt them, touching them all over. Sort of like a doctor when he doesn't know what's wrong with you and just presses every-where until you yell. They weren't confirming that the animals were dead, merely testing the carcass to try and feel whether they were tight or loose skinned. Whether it would come off easily or not.

I was beginning to appreciate the technique required in this most difficult of sports.

'Too right, there's a skill,' agreed Killer. 'You need a sharp knife, but not too sharp, and you must make sure you leave some length on the legs so as you can peg 'em out properly.'

That was the trick, of course. It might be easy to get the skin off the rabbit, but putting it on the bent wire was harder if you didn't leave any length on the legs.

After they had poked and prodded the rabbits the contestants all grabbed their pegging wires and felt them as well. These U-shaped bits of 12-gauge wire had to be just the right width so the skinners could slip the skin over easily and not have to worry about it spring-ing too far out. Bending it again while trying to put the skin on cost valuable seconds.

Soon all the skinners were standing by their allotted two rabbits and, after Mister had counted his numbers again, they were on their way.

The knives were slipped across the legs and down the stomach, then held away as the rabbit's feet were stood on. Then the ears were grabbed with one hand while the other pulled the skin up over the head, where it was gently slit once more, and the whole skin came off in one piece. Sort of like pulling a woollen jumper over your head.

Kell was slower than Tom Howlett at the skinning but made up his time in the pegging. His length was what helped him, Killer told me, as I watched these creatures being changed into skinless wonders. After they had been finished with, they lay on the stage with just their feet and head covered with fur. They looked like they had gone to bed with a balaclava and socks on.

Tom finished a few seconds ahead of Kell but the result was still up to the judges, who had to examine the carcases and the pegging.

Pegging is important. Not only does it have to be done with speed but you have to make sure the legs are in the right spot, balanced as they would be on either side of the body when they were alive. All very important in the world of rabbit skinning.

I asked Killer whether the rules were universal.

'Whatd'ya mean?' He seemed surprised. 'There's no-one else does this is there?'

Pauline had finished last, the bump slowing her down, although she wasn't that far away from Michael Heenan and Murray Wilson.

While the judges were inspecting the skun beasts, Kell was chatting to Killer.

'Should be right, d'ya think?' He appeared anxious. He could see the 500 threatened.

'Yeah,' Killer assured him. 'Yeah, yours are better pegged and anyway, he's got a nick on that second one.'

Killer was right again, as Killer usually was.

The judges announced Ray 'Kell' Kelly in a time of one minute and eight seconds, to be the World Champion Rabbit Skinner for the sixteenth time.

Veeda presented him with his cheque, a sash and a trophy which, instead of a little man doing something or other, had a little golden rabbit sitting hunched up on the top.

Kell was a happy man. In his victory speech to the crowd he spoke about coming for the money but then added, 'I'da probably come anyway.'

Killer was talking to Veeda as I left, saying he was heading home. 'Bin out a bit long,' he supposed.

I wondered what he'd do with the rest of the day.

'Well I'll watch a bit of the cricket on the telly for a while. Have a rest. Then I might let the other rabbits go. I dunno, but after all it is Christmas, isn't it.'

CHAPTER FOURTEEN

THE NOT SO SWEET SCIENCE

If there is one thing that has typified sport in the bush over the years, it is the boxing tent.
Years ago, crowds flocked to them throughout the country.
The spruikers would be up on the platforms goading the crowd, mainly local youngsters who thought they were tough.
Everyone was trying to make a name for themselves.
Every old codger I met remembered them fondly.
All had a tale to tell about the tents.
Now, sadly, there is only one tent left.

The boxing tent rose from the Birdsville dirt like a canvas colosseum. The orange banners stretched along its front bore faded pictures vaguely resembling past champions: Ali, Fenech, Mundine, Leonard, Ellis. All instantly recognisable, although I wondered who amongst the crowds over the next few days would remember Ezzard Charles and Joe Walcott. The freshest painting was of Mike Tyson spitting out an ear.

Two ladders of welded steel tube leant against the boards where the fighters and their challengers would stand, their six rungs leading to rough wooden planks lashed to rusting poles with knots no seaman ever used.

Five Australian flags fluttered proudly above a picture of the smiling owner, and painted in scrolls around the portrait were the words 'Fred Brophy's Famous Boxing Troupe'.

A row of lights were strung beneath the flags. Two of the globes had blown.

There was no-one inside, but behind a sheet of canvas that fell from a rope strung between the side of the tent and an old battered caravan, I met the Cowboy.

'G'day mate.' His smooth suntanned face broke into a grin. 'Fred's not here at the moment, he's over in the pub.'

In front of a couple of old mattresses that lay in the dust, two knucklemen sat on dilapidated kitchen chairs surrounded by empty beer cans. At their feet a blackened camp oven wallowed in the coals of a fire fed by two slowly burning logs. A dark, swarthy man sporting a half-closed black left eye, the legacy of a fight outside the tent a week before, held the lid while he poked the meat cooking inside with a long fork.

'Meet the Duke of Earl,' said Cowboy.

The cook stood up. 'The bastards got me when I wasn't lookin'. But I fixed 'em later.'

'And this here's the Spider.' Cowboy pointed to his other companion, whose arms and legs lent credence to his name but who was having trouble staying on the seat.

Duke moved the oven slightly as he replaced the lid, sending sparks from the fire darting towards the stars that sat above like jewels laid out on a black drape.

It had been a slow day so Spider had enjoyed the time with a few more than a 'couple of shandies'. He argued with the Cowboy about which of them was the toughest. Cowboy had the brashness of his 25 years against the Spider's 40-odd of experience. Both were around the middleweight class, but I could tell that nothing would come of it.

'Nothin' serious.' Cowboy was dismissive as Fred Brophy appeared from the night. 'Anyway, he'd get rid off us pretty quick if we were, wouldn't you Fred?'

Fred's intense eyes were set deep in his leathery face. I felt myself being examined as he looked right into me. The eyes were those of a man who made a living out of judging people by their faces.

'These are,' Fred pointed with fingers shaped by their years in gloves, 'the toughest and best fuckin' blokes in Australia. They'll fight anyone I tell 'em to.'

Fred had been over at the pub to renew a few old acquaintances and find out what was happening in the town. It was Wednesday evening and the tent would have its first show the next night when the crowd that came to Birdsville for the races started arriving, but there was always some information in the pub as to who the local tough men were.

'You can play cricket and rugby and Aussie rules and all the rest.' Fred was warming up. 'But this,' he pointed towards the tent, 'is the toughest of the lot. They get in there and none of 'em know who they're goin' to get. But they'll fuckin' fight 'em. And there is nowhere to fuckin' hide.'

The fighters listened intently as Fred sang their praises, although they were fidgeting, scratching at the ground or sitting with their heads down. Cowboy stared straight ahead, his back ramrod straight as he became more proud with each word from Fred.

'These blokes,' Fred was firm, 'are true Australians. And when the bitumen comes through places like this, we're all gone, every fuckin' one of us.

'This is it. This is the last little bit of somethin' that belongs to everyone in Australia. We're the last of this frontier, so have a fuckin' good look.'

Fred was looking forward to a big week. 'All I really want is for everyone that comes into the tent to leave with a smile on their face.'

With that, Fred wandered off into the night to wait for his wife, Sandie, who was towing a hot-dog van out that would supplement their income for the week.

Cowboy and the Duke sported tattoos of a pair of red boxing gloves with 'Brophy's Boxing Troupe' written around them.

'All he tells us is don't lie, don't steal and don't be racist,' Cowboy said quietly of Fred. 'We love him.'

Spider agreed, then promptly fell off the chair and wrestled with himself in the dust trying to stand up again. When he finally managed it, he declared, 'I've had it. I'm goin' to fuckin' bed.'

After he left, Cowboy turned to me. 'Fred's right, it is a big week for us this. Me, I want to win every fight and not hook a snag.'

He knew I didn't understand.

'It's like when you hook a snag fishin'. You don't know it's there. A tough bloke.'

Cowboy reckoned it was the last thing he thought about before he went to bed the night before a show. 'Everybody wants to fight the Cowboy,' he remarked, 'and there's always someone, somewhere.'

The food in the camp oven was ready so, as the others started to eat, I too wandered off into the night and headed for the camping ground.

The tent was all quiet when I returned, my 12-year-old son asleep in his swag. Zac and I had come to experience, as Fred put it, 'a last little bit of Australia'. But the long, monotonous drive across the Queensland Outback had tired him. And his father.

Midday on Thursday and the tent looked somehow different. At night, the lights cast shadows that hid the cracks in the paint and made the orange hoardings glitter. The daylight could hide nothing, but there was something about the way it stood there, battered yet elegant.

'The Boys from the Bush are back, Challenging All Comers', declared the message across the bottom of the banners, while all the time Fred Brophy's grinning face looked down on the other message, 'Where Champions are Discovered'.

Inside I walked around, touching the canvas walls that were secured to the support rope by frayed pieces of string scrounged during the day and threaded through holes cut in the edge.

An ex-army truck showing signs of the Outback miles was parked on one side of the tent, providing additional support as well as being the grandstand for some spectators who could sit in the back.

Cement blocks that sat in the dirt a couple of metres apart, with planks of wood laid on them for makeshift seats, were arranged in an oval shape around the centre of the tent. The two main support poles had faded coloured pads tied to them to signify the corners and in front of each pole were the kitchen chairs from around the fire.

The ring, a square of canvas on a bed of sand, lay imposingly in the centre of the tent.

I thought if I listened closely enough I might hear the spirits of fighters long gone, but Zac brought me back to reality with a poke in the ribs. 'Fred's here, Dad.'

A fourth-generation showman, Fred was the great-grandson of circus people. His mother was a trapeze artist and his uncle, Selby Moore, owned a boxing tent.

Fred reckoned he could remember fighting for a few bob outside Selby's tent. 'That's when I decided I was goin' to own one. It's all I've really wanted to do.'

While he waited he ran shows in the sideshow alleys throughout the country. Shows like the Psychedelic Mouse Circus and the Tattooed Pig with the Gold Tooth. He eventually got his chance when he bought a tent from a bloke named Bill Leech who had stopped touring.

'Nobody reckoned I'd last, but I showed 'em.' Fred laughed. 'I'm not rich, but shit I'm lucky.'

The first show was scheduled for around 7.30 that evening, so Zac and I lounged around the tent with the fighters. I asked Cowboy if he ever got bored.

'Nah,' he replied dismissively. 'There's always somethin' to do. We talk a fair bit or go for a walk around, or sleep.'

Cowboy was a warm friendly larrikin, an entertainer. 'We're not here to belt blokes up. Everyone that comes in this tent is looking to be entertained. They don't want blood and guts all over the joint.'

I wasn't so sure. I reckoned they wanted to see good fights.

'Yeah, that's right,' said Cowboy. 'But it's how we do it. It's gotta be fun when it can be.'

He was a light-middleweight who spent most of his time on the Gold Coast, but whenever Fred went on tour, Cowboy went with him. His tanned body had been hardened by training and his black silk boxing shorts bore his name, embroidered in sparkling white lettering on the front and back. They looked as though they would be more at home fighting in a casino than a boxing tent. Which they had been.

Cowboy was, in fact, the South Pacific champion in his weight and had fought some of the best professional boxers in Australia. When I asked how on earth he'd got into the tent, he laughed.

He had joined Fred's troupe after challenging at one of the shows.

'Fred reckons he knew I could fight when he seen me jump up on the boards but I told him I'd never fought in me life before.'

Fred matched him with his best fighter but Cowboy dropped him three times in the third round. Afterwards Cowboy went to Fred and collected his $45 for the win and asked if he could come back to have another go.

In his definite way, Fred told him, 'You can come whenever you like, but you'll never, ever fight one of my blokes again. If you want to fight in my tent, you can fight for me.' Fred's fighters got paid $120, win, lose or draw, as well as their keep.

Cowboy hadn't been able to get it out of his system since. 'The people and the fun we have, I can't leave it.' He grinned. 'The accommodation is mostly swags on the side of the road, but shit, mate, what a life!'

Spider had surfaced by this time and was apologising to all and sundry if he offended anyone the previous night. No-one took any notice of him. 'Nothin' happened, Spider,' Cowboy told him.

Soon all the fighters were around the ring. There was the Meatman, the Caveman, the Masked Mauler and the Duke of Earl, as well as the tent trainer, Barry Russell.

Barry was trying to get the fighters to do a bit of loosening up before the evening came.

'Come on youse blokes,' he yelled. 'Let's go.'

Cowboy started shadow boxing. He moved barefoot across the canvas, the swoosh, swoosh of his sliding feet in a steady rhythm. His hands moved quickly and precisely.

Spider did the same, only more slowly, and the others didn't bother. 'It's too fuckin' early for this shit,' the Meatman said quietly as he lay down on one of the planks.

Barry gave up and went for a walk. 'It'll be alright till some snag belts the crap out of youse all' was his parting comment.

I sat down next to Meatman, whose blue and yellow footy shorts matched the socks that crumpled out of his sandshoes. The tattoos on the front of his thighs were of two giant roosters. Or at least that's what I thought they were.

'They're cocks.' He rubbed his hand across them almost tenderly. 'Me pop used to fight 'em, you know, in the backblocks. I had a lot of time for me pop, it's a bit of a tribute I suppose.'

Meatman was the sort of bloke I imagined tent fighters to be. Cowboy and Spider were tent boxers, but Meatman was a fighter. Tough and uncompromising. He had the look. 'Mate, I'll go however they want to go,' he said of his challengers. 'If they want to be silly then I'll belt 'em. If they want to be reasonable then I'll be that too.'

About seven o'clock Fred grabbed the microphone that played out the front of the tent through a portable stereo system.

'It's not long to go now,' he barked. 'We'll have the boys out soon. They're in here warming up at the moment, getting ready for all youse tough blokes out there who want to make a name for yourselves. It won't be long and youse can have a go.'

As Fred switched off the mike, he called out to the Masked Marvel, a short wrestler whose body was covered by shag-pile hair, to get out the front and do some warm-ups.

'There's always someone who likes a wrestle instead of a fight,' Fred explained as the Marvel came over.

Trouble was, the Masked Marvel had lost his mask. After a quick and fruitless search, and with the experience of years of making do, a calico bank change bag was produced from the caravan, thrust on the Marvel's head and slits cut in the front for his eyes.

Out he went and Fred was back on the mike. 'This bloke is so ugly that we've been told we'll get arrested if he ever takes off his mask. He comes from Yugoslavia and can't speak a word of English.'

While Fred was talking, the Marvel, in real life a cattle-yard builder from north Queensland who had never wrestled until he joined the tent in Longreach, started swinging from the boards like a three-toed sloth.

Fred started again. 'I'll try to get him back inside, ladies and gents. Moosha, Moosha.' That presumably was Yugoslavian for 'go back inside the tent'. The Marvel disappeared and the gathering crowd roared. Even Fred started to chuckle just before he turned off the mike.

'Shit it's hot in this fuckin' thing,' the Marvel complained as he passed Zac and me. We grinned at each other in excitement. This was it. It was a bit like waiting for the start of a grand final.

We watched the fighters warm up for 10 minutes or so. Cowboy and Spider did it well. Meatman wandered around throwing his well-muscled arms in every direction while the Caveman—a tall, skinny Aborigine with a beard that looked like a handful of steel wool—stood at attention and shook his body.

His started with his head, then his torso and arms, followed by his legs. He rotated his neck in a couple of circles and then sat down, declaring himself ready. Caveman reckoned he was about 39 but the other blokes reckoned maths wasn't his strong point.

At the back of the tent Fred had changed into a blood-red shirt and had a whistle dangling around his neck. He paced up and down like an Outback Olivier readying himself for the rise of the curtain. He carried a can of beer and swigged on it as he concentrated.

At the entrance to the tent was Sandie, tattered bookie's bag around her shoulders ready to take the money as the people flocked in. The fighters sauntered around, waiting, thinking.

Barry Russell sat in the red corner sorting out the plastic drink bottles while in the challengers' corner sat a hulking, slope-shouldered brute of a man who used to be the Birdsville Mauler when he fought for Fred, and who would look after the fighters who wanted to have a go.

Each person prepared themselves for the evening.

Then, suddenly, Fred bounded over to the entrance, and with shouts of good luck to everyone he leapt onto the boards to the cheers of the assembled crowd.

Outside, a thousand people were gathered in front of the tent.

'Wait till Saturday.' Cowboy had snuck up behind me to look out through the gaps in the canvas. 'There'll be four times as many.'

Up on the boards, Fred had grabbed his drum. BOOM, BOOM, BOOM, he belted out a slow rhythm. After quite a few BOOMS, he yelled, 'Let's bring out the bell man.'

The crowd roared. Old blokes being taken back to their youth, younger ones experiencing a lost art for the first time.

Out came the Duke of Earl. He bounded up the ladder, made his way down to the end of the boards and grabbed the bell rope. Fred told me later the Duke was the only one who could keep time.

Then Fred was off again. A performer at his best. 'My name's Fred Brophy and I'm the fairest referee in the Outback.' And then the words that have been uttered by boxing-tent spruikers throughout the ages, 'Give us a rally on the bells and drums.'

The crowd watched intently while Fred and the Duke, slowly at first, then faster and faster, boomed out the tradition of the tents.

'Ladies and Gentlemen, I'd like to welcome each and every one of youse all here to Birdsville. Last year out here a few of me blokes got a good hidin' and it's been hard t'get good tough fighters, so I've brought out a few blokes that can't fight to give youse all a chance. It's $20 a minute for local challengers here tonight.'

Fred's voice went up a couple of decibels, 'Twenty dollars a minute—tax free. If you win you get $20 a minute, you draw you get nothin', you lose you get the experience.

'The boys are inside now gettin' ready. The Duke of Earl's here, the Meatman, the Caveman's here, Kojak's here, and the Cowboy.'

Fred took a couple of breaths and continued. 'This is the last boxing tent in the world. We travel the length and breadth of Australia but the only states we work in are here in Queensland, the Territory and South Australia. When we get to the border of New South Wales, I put me foot down.'

Great jeering erupted at this statement.

'And when we get to Victoria, same thing.'

Even louder jeering.

'And I'm goin' to tell you why.' Fred knew the crowd was waiting for it. 'It's because of the politicians and the bureaucrats.'

The booing and jeering reached a crescendo.

'But the best place we've worked, without a doubt, is here in Birdsville. And let me tell you somethin', if you've never bin to Birdsville you've never bin to Australia. Give us a rally on the bells and drums.'

As Fred and the Duke struck up their steady rhythm again, I noticed the gleam in Fred's eye and the smile on his lips. He was born for this.

'Now I'm goin' to introduce my fighters. First of all the fella down there on the bell. This bloke used to be the Queen's gardener at Buckingham Palace but the head gardener tried him on so this bloke knocked him out and he had to leave the country. From London, England, the Duke of Earl. Give us a rally on the bells and drums.'

As soon as the cheers started to die down Fred started again.

'Now this bloke down the other end would put the elephant man to shame. He accidentally pulled four arms out of their sockets at the last show. The Masked Marvel. Give us a rally on the bells and drums.'

The rallies were only short in between introductions but the crowd loved it. The fighters stood impervious to the yelling, searching through the crowd for the challengers. Cowboy had told me earlier that they could nearly always pick them out.

Fred was at his best now. 'I've got a man here that used to work in the meatworks at Kununurra. He had a blue with his boss and cut his arm off with a meat cleaver. Now he's on the run. The Meatman. Give us a rally there, Duke.'

The crowd started to clap in time with the bells and drums.

'And now, ladies and gentleman, I found this bloke up in the Territory livin' in a cave. If you've ever wondered why there aren't any dinosaurs left, it's because he ate the last one. The Caveman. Give us a rally.'

Everyone laughed at Caveman.

'And last we have the only bloke who's come out of New Zealand that would prefer to ride a horse than a sheep, The Cowboy.'

The crowd was delirious by this stage. Fred had them in the palm of his hand. Zac was rolling in the dust laughing.

Then came the challengers. It didn't take long to fill the boards. Fred was right when he said there would always be someone out there. 'There's the blokes who get brave after a couple of beers and there's them that come specially to fight. And there's the smartarses.'

Fred picked a couple of those out straight away. 'You blokes over there singing out, come up here, you're just the blokes I need.'

Not one of them moved. 'They don't very often,' remarked Fred.

When the crowd was invited to move into the tent they surged forward like a tidal wave, money in hand and trying to get the best spots.

The fighters and the challengers muscled their way through the spectators and sat down in the dirt behind their corners. Soon there were around 400 people jammed into the tent and when Fred jumped into the ring the din was dangerous to the ears.

He welcomed them again and then pointed to the corner with the challengers. 'That's the locals' corner, where the champions that are waiting to be discovered sit.'

Loud cheering from the crowd.

'And over there,' he continued when the noise had died down, 'is my corner, reserved for the toughest men in Australia.' Loud booing followed.

A buzz went round the tent as Fred stood in centre ring and called out the first fighters. He had matched Kojak with a strapping young council worker named Roodog.

Kojak had left home to work as a ringer in North Queensland and had joined Fred's troupe for something to do. His shaved head, bulbous nose and tattoos made him look older than I suspected he was. Roodog on the other hand was skinny but tough, hardened by the days of working on the local roads.

In the ring Fred introduced them again, and with his stopwatch in his hand blew the whistle for the first round.

Roodog, who had taken off his shoes and shirt and rolled up his jeans, leapt straight from the corner and threw punches like a threshing machine. They came from above and below Kojak, who was taken by surprise but managed to stave off anything dangerous and held on for the first round.

The second round was much the same, with the crowd yelling for the Roodog to belt him and Kojak bravely coming forward each time into a flurry of punches.

The crowd liked Roodog. He gave them what they wanted and in the last round his punches flew just as fast. Poor Kojak wasn't up to it and when Fred raised the Roodog's arm as the winner the crowd roared their approval.

Next was the Masked Marvel, who had been matched with a small rotund public servant from Sydney. When he was asked his name on the boards he answered, 'Wal'. Fred then asked what his second name was and once again the reply was 'Wal'.

'That's bloody amazing,' Fred looked over the crowd, who were in stitches, 'a bloke from Sydney called Wal Wal.'

'Take off your jumper,' someone called out as the Marvel prowled in the corner. That amused the crowd as well as Zac, who looked around at me from where he was sitting with the fighters in their corner. 'His hair's thick isn't it, Dad.'

Thick wasn't the word for it. It joined the hair on his head around his neck and chin at the shaving mark. It flowed down his chest, back and legs and only stopped because his feet did.

Wal and the Marvel were evenly matched—apart from the hair, that is. Wal was almost bald which prompted the obvious remarks from the crowd, 'Don't pin him, get a hair transplant instead.'

Wal went straight for the mask and when he ripped it off to the amusement of the crowd, the fighters and Fred, there were yells of, 'He's not a human at all. Put it back on.'

Over the three rounds neither wrestler could make a proper pin so Fred called it a draw. The Marvel went back to the caravan and Wal Wal went back to the obscurity of the public service in Sydney with memories that would last him a lifetime.

In between rounds Fred's 14-year-old daughter Emerald swept the ring of the dirt that had been kicked on during the fights. She and her young brother, Fred Junior, had driven out with their mother for the week to spend some time with Fred, who had been on the road for a couple of months.

While Emerald tidied up, Fred Junior fiddled with the boxers' gear. He was a bit of a lair. A street-smart 12-year-old who was older than his years. Likeable young kid but couldn't sit still, he was into everything.

Fred waited for Emerald to finish before he announced the next fight. He'd explained to me that matching the fighters had come with the years. 'I can usually tell if a bloke is a fighter or has been one.' Fred smiled with the knowledge that no-one could put anything over him.

I knew he was right. He couldn't afford to be wrong very often. 'But there's always a hard boy. Someone you don't know, a snag. It's my job to match 'em up right. We don't want anyone gettin' hurt. That's why it's only three one-minute rounds.'

But the fights are always serious. 'If they don't want to have a go or they're just dancing around, I'll call it off. My tent's fair dinkum.'

Fred called out for the Spider, who stood in the ring without a movement. He knew it wasn't long before he had to give it away. 'I'm 41 so I can't keep matching it for much longer without gettin' belted up.'

To Spider, this was business. He said that to Cowboy it's fun but to him it was serious. 'Cowboy's got the ability to make it fun. To muck around with 'em and entertain. Me, I come to do business.'

His opponent was a tall, flabby Victorian who must have weighed about the same as a freezer of lard. The crowd were evenly split, half wanting him to cop a hiding because he was a Victorian and the others wanting him to beat the favourite.

While Fred was going through the rituals in centre ring about a good clean fight, which was a touch out of place, the Victorian was staring at Spider, trying to psych him out. When Fred stepped away and waved them to start the fight, he began to mouth off.

'I'm goin' to belt the shit out of ya,' he screamed at Spider. 'Come over here and get it.' He beckoned with his hands.

Spider slowly circled the ring with his hands held high. The Victorian could contain himself no longer. He'd worked himself into a rage of confidence. He rushed across the ring, flailing his arms at Spider, who took a step sideways and stopped him in his tracks with a short straight left that thwacked into the side of his head. Serve you bloody right, I thought. It's not a smart move to mouth off to these blokes.

Again he rushed at Spider, telling him it didn't hurt and that he wasn't much of a fighter. Again, not smart. And not true. In his youth Spider had held the Australian amateur light-heavyweight crown, so he knew what he was doing.

The Victorian came again, although not as quickly. He towered over Spider, who thumped two short rights into his kidneys. Large red welts appeared on the flab. Then another right to the side of the head. The Victorian hadn't hit Spider yet and all his talk was getting him nowhere. He grimaced as another punch, this time a sweet left buried into his midriff just as Fred whistled to end the round.

During the break the Victorian puffed and panted while Spider stood in the red corner, watching him. At the start of the second Spider jammed another couple of punches deep into the paunch of the Victorian, who raised his hand in surrender. He'd had enough.

The crowd booed wildly. Not at Spider or at Fred, but at the Victorian. It seemed that you don't bounce into this tent and mouth off and then not be able, or prepared, to back it up.

'You bloody dogged it,' yelled a bloke beside me. 'Weak as piss.'

The Victorian slinked off, pride, head and body all hurt badly.

At the back of the tent Spider swigged on a can. 'They're the sort of bastard we love,' he said. 'They get what they come for. They can have it easy or hard. Whatever. That prick deserved it.'

I retreated to my spot behind Zac, who was showing distinct signs of bloodlust. He informed me that the Cowboy was next.

Cowboy's opponent had been christened Beanbag by the crowd, a description that fitted perfectly. Fred had matched these two for a bit of fun. Cowboy dodged and weaved, tapped the Beanbag on the head, kissed him, pulled his pants down and generally kept the crowd in fits of laughter. At one stage he stood with one hand on Beanbag's head while the other circled around him like a windmill.

'Where do you want it, sweetheart?' asked Cowboy.

It was a bit of light relief after Spider's fight. Cowboy loved it, the crowd loved it and even the Beanbag didn't mind. As he left the ring with Cowboy's arm draped over his shoulder, his face beamed. He was still alive.

'What didya think about that?' Cowboy asked as he ruffled Zac's hair.

Zac didn't answer. The look on his face was enough.

The Duke's opponent was short and curly headed with two buck teeth protruding from under his thick top lip. He had been a fighter in the tent but Fred asked him to leave. 'A bit of a trouble-maker,' was how Cowboy described him. But he was game and could fight. Duke had some six inches on him so kept him at bay, but needed his wits about him. Afterwards, Wolfgang told Fred he'd be back the next night.

All the boys wanted to be matched with him.

There were two challengers left so Fred reckoned that Meatman could fight 'em both, tag-team style. There were no complaints from Meatman.

The tag team were two ringers from a station the other side of the state and both thought they were a bit tougher than was the case. The first in the ring shaped up pretty well but made the mistake of rushing at Meatman, who didn't like getting hit too much. His reaction punch was a short left that landed with a dull thud to the side of the ringer's head and laid him out cold. As they carted him off the canvas Fred called out to see if there was someone who wanted to take his place. To my surprise a stockily built man made his way through the crowd.

'Give him a big hand ladies and gentlemen,' Fred urged the crowd. I thought they should be giving him sympathy.

Meatman just flexed the muscles in his jaw as he watched all this going on. When the fight resumed the new bloke circled warily. Then, after throwing a few quick jabs and seeing Meatman's stare become colder, he went for the tag. The original member had seen his first mate's fate but rushed out bravely towards Meatman. Trouble was he ran straight into a right hand that spun him round and he too hit the deck not knowing what day it was.

This was the best action of the night as far as the crowd was concerned and as they left the tent Fred knew that the next couple of nights would be full houses. I didn't think the tag-team fighters would be amongst them.

A few minutes later the tent was empty except for the fighters, Fred, us and all the empty cans and smoke packets scattered around in the dirt. The air was still heavy with the smell of sweat that mingled with the dust and smoke.

But there was a poetry about the junk. No-one could have painted a picture of Australia with more effect.

'Fuck it,' Fred declared in a gravelly voice as he wiped his sweaty forehead. 'We'll clean it up tomorrow. Let's have a drink.'

On Friday morning the tent was quiet. Fighters lay around on scruffy mattresses and in swags dozing or sleeping, recovering from the previous night. Not the fights necessarily, but the afterwards. 'Yeah it was a good night,' grinned Cowboy as he watched the enticing figure of his night's companion quietly slip away. 'That's another of the good things about this sorta life.'

Every now and again during the day people would wander in and ask where they could book seats and how much it cost to get in. One, obviously not a boxing historian, asked if 'that man Ellis on the front is fighting tonight?'.

Meatman, who was lying on a seat close to the entrance, didn't bother looking up but was at his sarcastic best. 'No, he couldn't fuckin' make it.'

The man walked off none the wiser.

'Jeeesus,' sighed Meatman.

A little while passed with the fighters doing nothing and Zac and I watching them when Sandie and Emerald appeared.

Emerald and Zac took off for a walk around the town while Sandie, blonde hair pinned up ready for work, opened the door of the hot-dog van. 'Anything extra we can get is welcome,' she explained as she started to mix up a drum of batter to dip the dogs in.

Sandie was a gentle person but tough at the same time. She had met Fred at a show in Brisbane. 'I didn't find it difficult to go on the road,' she remembered. 'I'd spent three years travelling the world and a couple around Australia so it wasn't new to me.'

She laughed as she dipped another dog. 'My friends said that I'd run away to join the circus.'

Both Fred and Sandie wanted a good education for the kids and, although it was difficult when Fred was away from their home in Bundaberg, she didn't think about it too much. 'We just look forward to him coming home and then we can all go out on the road together. That makes it worthwhile.'

As we talked the haunting sound of a didgeridoo floated through the air. I looked around to see Caveman instructing the Duke of Earl on the finer points of getting a six-foot long piece of black polythene pipe to sound like a didg. He wasn't doing too badly.

Sandie, her hands white with batter, nodded at them. 'That's what makes this special.' She grinned. 'We're a big family, so diverse but we all fit in.'

When she first met the tent fighters she thought they were all idiots. She laughed out loud at the protest from the Duke, who was eavesdropping,

'Still bloody do. I reckon we need a resident psychiatrist here.

'But,' she continued, 'I wouldn't change anything. It's one long adventure.'

By now the fighters had Barry to worry about. He was prowling around trying to get them up and going. He'd told Duke that he'd help him with his footwork and jabbing, so he was his first stop. To Cowboy and Spider this was old stuff that they'd learned early in their careers, but to tent fighters such as the Duke it was different.

Duke followed Barry around the ring throwing punches into a couple of mitts he wore. The 56-year-old trainer carried a huge gut in front of his medium frame but was still light on his feet. 'Been doin' this for about 40 years so I musta picked up somethin'.'

Barry enjoyed the humour of the tent. When he was 18 he had gone to New Zealand as a clown with Wirth's Circus. 'I've always liked humour, that's what I like in here mostly, it's non-stop fun.'

Except when the fighters pulled a snag.

'There's fighters around who train specially to fight one of these boys. Bookies turn up with 'em. They come in with mouthguards and their hands already bandaged. That's why I tell these boys to be prepared.'

The fighters had finished their 10-minute training session. Some went to the pub for a drink to complement the training, while others lay down again. None seemed overly concerned. The evening show would bring what it may.

The show started like all the others. Fred wound himself up, so did the fighters, and when the drum and the bell started the crowd was packed in front of the tent like lemmings at a cliff. Holding the drumstick and the microphone in the same hand, Fred started again, 'Tonight we're going to make the shirt on your back go up and down like a venetian blind.'

And he had more introductions. Two more of his fighters had turned up, the Friendly Mauler and the Baby Mauler, who were father and son.

Friendly was, according to Fred, 'the most friendliest fighter you'd ever meet. He just gets friendlier the more he hits ya.'

Baby Mauler wasn't like his father, who was well over six feet and a real heavyweight build. Small and slight but with every inch muscle, he was 15 years old.

Kojak was missing because he was injured. He'd been to the Flying Doctor base and they cleared out the passage in his nose but told him it was broken in a couple of places. When he came back with the news, the others weren't sure that it was just his nose that was keeping him out. They thought it might be 'a bit of a ticker problem'.

I thought that was a bit harsh. I had a ticker problem just watching.

Among the challengers, Wolfgang had turned up again and so had Roodog, who must have liked the money and the applause.

The crowd loved it once more and pressed forward when Fred gave the okay. I looked around for Zac but he had already grabbed his spot behind the corner. Tonight he had progressed to handing out drink bottles.

If there is one thing these people liked as much as a fight it was a new member of the family. 'You're one of us while you're with us,' Cowboy told Zac.

The Masked Marvel started proceedings against a walking postbox who called himself Slugger. Before the start, Duke rushed into the ring armed with a hairbrush and, amid howls of laughter from the crowd, proceeded to brush Marvel's body hair into shape.

Slugger was all over the Marvel, at one stage lifting him high above his head and twirling him around a couple of times. The Marvel was pinned early in the second round and he and the Slugger left the ring to wild applause.

Cowboy thought he had drawn a snag. Fred had said as much when the bloke jumped up on the boards.

'Ever fought before?' he asked.

'Never,' was the reply

'I dunno about that.' Fred's eyes were firmly on the challenger's nose. 'You didn't get that from pickin' tomatoes.' Then he added quietly, 'I reckon we've got our first snag.'

With his shirt off, The Fly, as he called himself, looked superb. His body was a V shape from shoulders to waist and the rumour sweeping the tent was that he had been Golden Gloves champion in Western Australia. Cowboy was nervous. He needn't have been. The Fly was nowhere near the fighter he looked. He had little rhythm and the Cowboy picked him off easily.

'He's no fuckin' Golden Gloves,' sneered Barry in the corner.

Spider had an easy night against a ringer who'd had a few too many and was embarrassed into it by his mates, while Meatman had to sit the night out as there weren't enough challengers for him. Or at least none that were foolhardy enough to get in the ring with him. He patrolled the back of the tent, jaw clenched, punching one fist into his other palm. 'I just want to fuckin' hit someone.'

Fred had matched the Baby Mauler with Wolfgang. They were about the same height and weight but Wolfgang was a street fighter, whereas Baby Mauler was a proper boxer. Wolfgang threw so many punches it was hard to keep up with them. The Baby Mauler stepped back so far he was in the crowd, who pushed him back into the ring. Wolfgang followed him everywhere, there was nothing he wouldn't do. I thought I could see a touch of revenge in his eyes, as if he wanted to prove a point to Fred and the rest of them.

But Fred wasn't one to hold a grudge. He gave him the points victory which the crowd acknowledged with raucous cheering.

Roodog had been put in against Caveman, who looked like a cartoon character with his long skinny arms poked into two big boxing gloves. He came from Lake Nash just over the border into the Northern Territory and he'd been with Fred for about 15 years, 'learnin' fightin on the way'.

He had copped more beltings than most but he was the one fighter who could make the crowd laugh by being uncoordinated and by getting flogged each time he fought.

I asked Caveman if he ever got picked out by the challengers because of his colour.

'Sometimes,' he said softly.

'Does it worry you at all?' I asked.

'Sometimes.'

Roodog was fearsome. He belted Caveman to all points of the ring. Into the crowd and back again. On the dirt and on the canvas he pursued him. The crowd bellowed their appreciation. Caveman should have been knocked out, but then it occurred to me that this was all part of it. Caveman could protect himself pretty well, although a lot of the punches got through.

After it was over and Caveman had lost again, he sat at the back of the tent and smiled at everyone who said it was a great fight.

The most popular contest of the evening was between the Friendly Mauler and a local by the name of Smithy, who didn't rate the dignity of a nickname.

He was a bit smaller than Friendly but then so was everyone. He was full of himself but when Friendly connected with a couple of body punches at the start of the third round, he went to water and gave up, much to the annoyance of the spectators, who wanted a bit of blood before they left.

Afterwards Fred told me that Smithy was one of the biggest louts he'd come across. 'You know the sort,' he snapped. 'Beltin' up drunks in pubs, but this shows him he's not so tough.'

They were the sort of challengers they liked. 'Heroes,' Cowboy reckoned. 'As we said before, we'll look after the blokes who jump up. What's the point in beltin' 'em. If we do that there'll soon be no-one left that'll have a go. But the smartarses are the ones that we can give a flogging to.'

It was true, I thought, bullies deserved what they got. And Cowboy, being the entertainer that he was, had his own way of sourcing challengers like that.

'I go and find out who they are. Someone always knows.'

He told me how he once found out—from a barmaid, typically—about a couple of locals in Winton who were pretty brave when they'd had a few.

'So, the pub's full.' Cowboy liked telling the story. 'And I walked through the crowd and told them as loud as I could that I'd heard they were the toughest blokes in town and did they want a fight.'

According to Cowboy they looked at each other and spluttered for a minute before he went on. 'Well I don't reckon you're tough at all. My reputation has been proved round Australia, yours is only here, beltin' up drunks. I'll fight you both at the same time and if you don't, then I reckon you're cowards.'

Of course by this time the crowd in the bar had parted like the Red Sea and the tough men were left on their own. 'What could they say?' grinned Cowboy. 'They had to jump up.'

That night Cowboy, true to his word, took them both on at the same time and gave them a thumping. 'Funny thing is,' Cowboy added, 'they didn't muck around in the pub anymore.'

After the tent was cleared the cans came out, somebody put on some country music, the Masked Marvel played the spoons as he listened, and the stories of life on the road began.

Cowboy remembered the time they got bogged in the bulldust after a storm, 150 k's out of Urandangi. 'We pushed the truck and the trailer about 10 k on this sticky, shitty track. We'd push for a while then have a blow and get back into it again. The five of us could just get the truck's wheels moving. Took us hours but we got there. Good feeling, doin' that together.'

In the silence, everyone nodded.

*

On Saturday morning, Zac sat listening to Cowboy rave on while I talked to the Friendly Mauler, who was lying nonchalantly on a mattress.

Friendly was 45 and the son of Bronco Johnson, a famous Australian boxer of the early '50s who toured North Queensland with his own boxing tent for a while. 'Well, it wasn't so much a tent,' Friendly remembered. 'It was just some hessian that he'd peg down in a square. I had my first fight in it when I was four.'

Bronco's first wife was an Aboriginal lady who bore him four children and Friendly, born on the side of the road between Hughendon and Prairie, was the first of seven from his second wife who was white. 'Me older brothers were all dark so Dad used to get us to have a stoush in the tent every now and again. We used to fight all the time anyway so it didn't matter.'

Friendly's large frame stretched as he told me why he kept fighting. 'It's in the blood, naturally enough, but it's more than that. It's the culture.'

He loved the sounds and the feel of the tent. 'They're all yellin' and screaming for your blood one night and the next they're all laughing their heads off. It's all their emotions at the same time. And then they go home and talk about it, about the feeling.

'You hear about Australia having problems with identity. Some reckon they don't have one.' Friendly wasn't lecturing, that wasn't his style. He just spoke quietly. 'All those city people who reckon that should come and spend a night in here.'

I had a feeling he was right.

As I spoke to Friendly I hadn't noticed Cowboy and Zac, who were squaring off in centre ring.

'I'm goin' to teach him a few moves,' Cowboy called to me.

This was a revelation. My son was tall for his age but was a kid who liked movies, books and pursuits a touch more gentle than fighting. But as Cowboy said, it wouldn't do him any harm to know how to shape up. After all, there were a few years ahead of him.

Zac followed Cowboy around the ring as he was told, chin tucked in, guard up and jabbing his left out into Cowboy's hands.

I watched, not knowing what to think. Fred watched too and when the lesson had ended he asked Zac if he'd like a spar with Fred Junior that night. Zac sat close to me and looked fearful. Mucking around with his mate Cowboy was one thing but a real fight was another.

'He won't get hurt,' Fred assured me. 'It'll be a bit of fun.'

Zac wasn't sure and his look when I asked him what he thought was half of terror and half of, I suspect, wanting to please his father.

'No Dad, I can't.' He seemed out of his depth as his eyes filled.

I assured him that it didn't matter, that I'd be happy whatever he chose to do.

Half an hour passed while we watched Barry and the boys spend their 10 minutes training. Then Zac turned to me. 'I think I'll do it.'

Fred assured him again that nothing bad would happen and Zac told me that he trusted Fred. So did I.

An hour or so later Fred was on the boards and Zac was in the crowd. Halfway through the usual rallies and the usual spiel came the announcement. 'Here we have the fourth generation of Brophy's to fight in the tent. Fred Junior. Give us a rally on the bells and drums.'

After Fred and the Duke had ceased their musical interlude he called for a challenger. Up to the ladder strode Zac. A born bloody entertainer, I thought.

In front of a crowd of about 5000 people, some of whom were sober, my son was being interviewed by the last of the tent men. Great boos erupted from the crowd when he said he was a Victorian and great cheers when Fred had organised the fight.

As the crowd battled their way in, the fighters and the challengers made their way to the corners. Fred Junior was in a dressing-gown made of the same material as his father's shirt while Zac sat in his corner wearing a T-shirt with Mambo written on the back.

Young Fred had a small stockwhip with him and he walked around the ring cracking it to entertain the crowd, who were generous with their applause when he sat down again.

Zac then casually wandered out into the middle of the ring and, with boxing gloves stuck on the ends of his arms like balloons on sticks, proceeded to do five push-ups.

The crowd went wild. Zac just grinned.

'Hey Mambo,' came the cry from behind me, 'stick the whip up his fuckin' arse.'

Nothing like a quick English lesson I thought.

The canvas walls of the tent stretched as the crowd packed in and Fred had to fight his way through. He didn't seem to mind. After all, everyone was happy.

As he introduced the two kids, true to form, the crowd booed Fred Junior and chanted 'Mambo, Mambo, Mambo' for Zac.

The first round was a low-key affair. Fred Junior not wanting to hit Zac too much and Zac not really knowing what to do. There was generous applause at the break, during which the English teacher behind me had some more words for Zac. 'Hey Mambo, I've got 20 fuckin' bucks on ya. Give it to 'im.'

The second round was more interesting. Fred Junior bounced around the ring flicking out his left hand. Backwards and forwards he went, light on his feet and loving the limelight. Zac followed, copping a couple but answering with a few of his own. The crowd laughed and cheered and roared. It was deafening. A flurry of punches ended the second with both kids flushed.

Zac was now intense. He had been stung. Then I realised that he had no mouthguard and no headgear. But so what, none of them did, this was a boxing tent!

Anyway, I had to make the best of it as I was going to be a dead man when his mother found out.

The third round was a classic. Well, perhaps not. But there were quite a few punches landed from both fighters, with Fred Junior still dancing and weaving and Zac still following relentlessly around the ring. It reminded me of Joe Louis. 'He can run but he can't hide.' Well, again, perhaps not.

What had started out as a spar had turned into a treat for the crowd. At the end Fred held both hands up and declared it a draw.

That was the signal for the crowd. Coins flew into the ring in the traditional shower. They came from all points of the tent. Silver coins and gold. The two kids spent five minutes crawling in the dirt gathering up their booty on two ragged, dirty towels. When they left to go and divide it up, they left to the biggest roar of the weekend.

Zac returned a few minutes later and took up his by now customary position in Fred's corner. He looked, somehow, different to me. As he sat there he smiled and held up his plastic bag full of money. His face was flushed with pride. Mine too.

Not because he fought but rather because he took an opportunity that he would never get again. Because he made the hardest decision of his life. He overcame his fear.

By now the crowd was well and truly warmed up. Fred was as well. They would have been swinging from the rafters if there had been any. As it was they were packed in, hanging off the truck with the ones at the back of the tent craning their necks to try and get a glimpse of the action through the smoky haze and the kicked-up, swirling dust.

The Masked Marvel again copped a huge opponent. Floppy guts and large head, he was the closest thing to a sumo wrestler that Birdsville had ever seen.

Once more the Duke came out and combed the Marvel's hair and once more the crowd loved it. And, once more, the Marvel was twirled around in the air before being crunched to the ground and pinned. The huge bloke leapt around the ring scratching under his arms like a gorilla. I wondered if the Marvel cared.

Mick, who came up from Tumbarumba, was next. He got the Baby Mauler. Mick shaped up like a southpaw and then changed his mind after Baby Mauler had hit him with two good jabs. However, he got hit with a couple more standing the normal way, so he changed back. He spent the three rounds doing that. Occasionally he caught Baby with a couple, but more often than not it was him changing his stance and Baby hitting him.

During the break between fights a voice called out from the back of the tent, 'You're fuckin' weak, Fred. This is shit.'

The crowd stepped back and the voice was left on his own. A very silly boy. Fred just looked at him, his stare dropping the bloke's head.

A couple of the fighters stared as well. There was one wise move the voice could make and, sensibly, he made it. Out of the tent, alive.

'Anyway, on with the show,' bellowed Fred, just as the lights went out.

Fred wasn't happy, although the way the leads for the lights wound around everything else in the tent, I thought it was a wonder they stayed on as long as they did.

But I reckoned without Fred. 'Shit!' he snapped. 'We've bin doing it this way for 20 fuckin' years. Why shouldn't it work now?'

After 10 minutes of every comedian in Birdsville doing lights-out jokes, and one of them trying to get a Mexican wave going in the dark, the lights flickered and came back on, much to the delight of the well-lubricated crowd and the relief of Fred.

'Next up . . .' Fred called into the microphone but it didn't work. 'Fuck it,' he continued as he tapped it on his hands. 'Fuck it, I'll just have to yell.'

Which he did and introduced the Meatman and Bluey, a young, modern-looking type who might have been a member of a private-school boxing team.

He was a good head taller than Meatman and had a longer reach. He made all the right moves and Meatman grinned with surprise when he was caught with a solid punch to the midriff. But he was a boxer, not a fighter, so Meatman looked after him. The crowd wanted him to be knocked out and I sensed Meatman did too, but he was charitable. 'What can ya do?' Meatman confided to me as he left the ring. 'The kid's got guts.'

The next two fights were what the crowd had come to see. Spider took on the Butcher from Camooweal, who fought like his trade but was effective, even against the height and reach of Spider.

They stood toe to toe in each round and with each punch the noise became louder. Fred, happy that the crowd was happy, declared a draw.

Caveman's opponent wore long city sideburns, long hair and, of all things, a scarf wound around his neck. They also went at it toe to toe, with the scarf wearer winning the first two rounds easily. In the last Caveman started to get a few in and eventually, to the appreciation of the crowd, drew blood from the scarf man. Fred stopped the fight, partly because of the blood and partly because of the glazed look in the scarf man's eyes.

Caveman looked startled. He had actually won.

Jimmy and the Duke were next. Jimmy was a snag. He'd walked around the previous night sizing up all the fighters. He wanted to choose who he went in against.

Fred didn't seem to mind, and nor did the boys. But they sniggered a bit when Jimmy thought that Meatman was too tough and Friendly was too big.

'There's a couple of fuckin' dwarfs down the road, we'll fuckin' get them up here for you,' Meatman mocked.

After Jimmy had been promised the Duke, Meatman remarked that he just wanted an easy mark. 'You've gotta fuckin' give it to him, Duke, you gotta.'

And he did. Jimmy was a pretty fighter but couldn't hit very hard. He was all muscle and stripped like an exhibitionist at a gym. Duke just shuffled around, thumping him as he went. All the boys were pleased at that.

'Fuckin' smartarse,' growled Meatman.

Fred had saved the best till last. The last fight of the weekend was to be a tag-team match between Cowboy and Friendly against three of the rodeo boys who had just arrived in town. Fred introduced them all and then told the crowd that the rounds had been lengthened to give everyone some action. He knew what was coming.

The rodeo boys were as tough as the bulls they rode. They threw everything at Cowboy and Friendly. It was mayhem. Crowd bellowing, arms swinging like propellers, Cowboy and Friendly trying to get shots in anywhere and all the while the three roughriders were rotating quickly.

It was three rounds of unremitting action. To the fore were blood, dirt and roughhouse tactics, culminating in an all-in blue in the third.

Cowboy had been pushed off the canvas by the biggest of the roughriders and had slipped over trying to get back on. He was set upon by his opponent, who thumped him, not only when he wasn't looking and on the ground, but from behind as well.

You just don't do that.

The rest of the fighters flew into it. The front few rows of the crowd were into it as well until Fred restored order by blowing on his whistle until everyone stopped.

The noise in the stadium couldn't have been bettered by the Thriller in Manila.

It was half an hour before everyone had come back to earth and left the tent, the buzz only fading with the last few to leave. As they filed out, Fred's smile split his face. 'That's what I wanted, everybody happy.'

Much later, after Zac and I had sat in the dust drinking and listening to more stories, Cowboy was reflective. 'Wherever Fred and the tent goes, I'll go.'

Spider took me outside when I asked him what being out there meant to him. He pointed towards the sparkling sky and said simply, 'Have a fuckin' look above you.'

Fred said the tent was to come down in the morning. I wanted to leave before that happened.

We walked back to our tent in the moonlight, Zac with $64 of coins in his plastic bag and a million dollars worth of memories.

Me—I had the sound of leather on flesh and the roar of the crowd echoing in my ears. The memory of the bloodlust and the laughter. Of an Australia that was disappearing.